ENDING SLAVERY

Ending Slavery

How We Free Today's Slaves

KEVIN BALES

UNIVERSITY OF CALIFORNIA PRESS BERKELEY LOS ANGELES LONDON

University of California Press, one of the most
distinguished university presses in the United States,
enriches lives around the world by advancing
scholarship in the humanities, social sciences,
and natural sciences. Its activities are supported
by the UC Press Foundation and by philanthropic
contributions from individuals and institutions.
For more information, visit www.ucpress.edu.

University of California Press
Berkeley and Los Angeles, California

University of California Press, Ltd.
London, England

Library of Congress Cataloging-in-Publication Data
Bales, Kevin.
    Ending slavery : how we free today's slaves /
Kevin Bales.
        p.   cm.
    Includes bibliographical references and index.
    ISBN 978-0-520-25470-1 (cloth : alk. paper)
    1. Slavery—History—21st century.   2. Anti-
slavery movements.   3. Poor—Employment.
I. Title.
    HT867.B356   2007
    306.3'620905—dc22   2007008235

Manufactured in the United States of America

16 15 14 13 12 11 10 09 08 07
10 9 8 7 6 5 4 3 2 1

This book is printed on New Leaf EcoBook 50, a 100%
recycled fiber of which 50% is de-inked post-consumer
waste, processed chlorine-free. EcoBook 50 is acid-free
and meets the minimum requirements of ANSI/ASTM
D5634-01 (Permanence of Paper).

Contents

Photographs follow page 60.

Introduction

Imagine a world where slavery is normal, where slavery is considered good business, offering solid returns. In this world "excess" people—the very poor, for example—can be put to productive uses that benefit everyone. In this world every dirty, dangerous, and demeaning job has someone to do it. In this world every war produces a rich harvest of new slaves. Once oil is burned, it's gone, but slaves are the product that keeps on producing (and reproducing, for that matter). With a little food and shelter, you can squeeze work out of your slaves for years and years. They are livestock with the brains and motor skills to do factory work or be your sex toy, care for your children or run your shop. In this world the profits of slavery build universities and concert halls and hospitals. The slave trade finances mansions and art shows and political careers. People who don't have a slave want one, and people who have slaves want more. Slaves are such flexible investments—you can put them up as collateral, lend them out, or rent them to a neighbor. You can make it your business to insure slaves, deal in slaves, or sell the tools and chains needed to control slaves. You can wholesale or retail slaves, ship them, or run a stable for slaves. You can leave them to your children, or sell a few to fund your retirement. And when you go to church, you will be reassured from the pulpit that this world is not just normal but good, and that God is smiling down on you and your happy slaves.

Sound crazy? It shouldn't. This has been our world for most of human history. From the dim moment when the first scribe started to scratch symbols in the first mud tablet, recording the life of our species, there were slaves. Greece, Rome, Renaissance Europe—great empires that created the beauty, art, and literature of our past—were powered by slavery, stoked up to creative heat with the burning muscles of slaves.

After five thousand years of slavery, some people began to question this fixture of human life. At first a few people, then more and more, began to think of slaves not as livestock but as human beings. When enough people thought that way, religion changed its view as well, and slavery became first distasteful, then wrong, then deeply morally repugnant—for most people. Some leaders had a true change of heart, other politicians found that even though the donations were fatter from the slave traders, the abolitionists had the votes, and a change of heart came over them as well. In a wonderful sleight of hand, they delivered a world where slavery was "abolished." With a stroke of the pen, slavery was gone, and everyone felt much better.

But making something illegal doesn't make it cease to exist; making it illegal only causes it to vanish from view. The abolition of slavery was immensely significant when laws were effectively enforced, but it also blinded people to ongoing slavery. Subsequent generations have been unaware that legal abolition didn't make slavery go away, that it only masked the problem. Behind closed doors, in remote places and right under our noses, slavery has continued, making people rich, feeding our lifestyles, and burning up lives.

THE MIRROR WORLD

Now imagine a world with no slaves, where every person is equal, not in wealth or brains or opportunity, but in dignity. Imagine a world where everyone faces the same sort of problems we all face—earning a living, taking care of children, making a marriage work. This is a world where women aren't for sale or rent so men can get drunk on the cocktail of sex and power. This is a world where children don't work sixteen-hour days so we can have a pretty rug in the living room. This is a world where parents don't have to choose between food and freedom for their children. This is a world without slavery, and now, more than at any time since the first laws to abolish slavery were passed in 1807, it is within our reach.

A world without slaves is also a richer world. Every slave is a creative intelligence in shackles. Yes, slaves make things, but slowly and often poorly. They feed into the production side of the economic equation, but they consume almost nothing. They may eat, but they cannot build, except when ordered to and never for themselves or their loved ones. Freed slaves stretch out and dream, then work hard to turn those dreams into reality. Slaves know how to work, and in freedom they work furiously to make their lives stronger, richer, more secure. Without the parasite of slavery, poor countries begin to grow. When workers don't have to compete with slaves, wages go up.

Without the wasting moral disease of slavery, our ethical dilemmas diminish as well. Today many of us are troubled by the ugly fact of slavery in our lives. But imagine never having that pang of doubt when you buy something you like, never having to wonder "whose freedom was stolen to make this?" Imagine never having to spoil the enjoyment of that delicious truffle in your mouth with the thought of the slave child who harvested cocoa for your treat. Ending slavery won't end crime, but it will mean things will be stolen, not lives. Billions of dollars that flow to vicious, violent criminals and fund everything from crack houses to child pornography will dry up when there is no slavery. Imagine the twenty-seven million people who are in slavery around the world, and the tens of thousands of people in slavery in America today, waking up tomorrow in a flood of joy. Their lives won't be perfect, their lives won't have any more of a guarantee of happiness than yours or mine, but they will have a chance, which is all that any of us asks for.

THE WATERSHED

It can happen. Five thousand years of slavery can end forever. Two hundred years of pretending we don't have slavery anymore can end forever. The ugly crime that stains and divides our species can end forever. The use of violence to turn other people into livestock can end forever. It can happen, and it can happen starting now.

If there was ever a tipping point when slavery could be brought to a full stop, it is now. The positive trends in our economies and cultures, the growing acceptance of human rights, and the relatively small part slavery plays in our world economy mean slavery is ripe for extinction. Slavery is a big problem, but it is not as big or as intractable as global warming or global poverty. Yes, twenty-seven million in slavery is a lot of people, but it is just .0043 percent of the world's population. Yes, $13 billion a year in slave-made products and services is a lot of money, but it is exactly what Americans spent on Valentine's Day in 2005. If human trafficking generates $32 billion in profits annually, that is still a tiny drop in the ocean of the world economy.

No industry or corporation, no political party, no state or country or culture is dependent on slavery. No government or business would collapse if slavery ended today. The cost of ending slavery is just a fraction of the amount that freed slaves will pump into the global economy. For those of us in the world's wealthy countries, the cost of ending slavery would be so small we'd never notice it—small coins here and there, pennies from our pockets.

Never has the world been so rich, never have travel and communication been so easy, never have so many countries been ready to work together, never has the world had the end of slavery so easily within its grasp. Of course, all of us have opportunities every day, and that doesn't mean we reach out and take them. But what if, with a vote here, a few dollars there, and the occasional conversation or e-mail, we could all help bring slavery to an end?

Ending slavery may not be terribly expensive, but wiping out this crime won't happen overnight. The things we have to do to end slavery in the United States are somewhat different from the things we have to do in India or Ghana or Thailand. Like a lot of crimes, slavery takes on the coloration and culture of its surroundings. Slavery is tangled up in both local and global economies. Ending slavery means attacking it at all levels. Local police, the United Nations. businesses, churches, and governments—all will have to play a part.

And we need a plan.

Here is where this book comes in. We need a place to start. We need some concrete steps that will get us moving in the right direction. Slavery can end, but it means pulling together and that means getting organized. With luck, people who read this book will come up with even better ways to end slavery, refining the preliminary ideas I've assembled. I have collected the stories and experiences of people from all over the world who help slaves to freedom, who are ending slavery today in ways big and small. Their stories show that freedom is not just possible, it is inevitable, for the seed of freedom planted grows and grows. Our job is to nourish those seeds.

1

The Challenge
Understanding the World of New Slavery

It is just like a fisherman going to fish. . . . If he don't put out the bait, he can't get a fish. So they tell the parents a lovely story, you know, what [their children] will encounter when they come to the United States. But behold, when they get into the United States the picture is completely different.

LOUIS

Louis works for the phone company near Washington, D.C. He also frees slaves. When he got together with family and friends for the Thanksgiving holiday a few years ago, Louis did what everyone does—he got out his video camera. As he recorded the holiday gathering, he noticed something strange: in the large group of family and friends, one teenage girl always tried to hide when he turned on the camera.

And I asked myself, you know, what's wrong with the young lady? At first I asked her, where do you come from? She told me she was visiting from Indiana. That is, she was staying with my cousin there. But something stuck in my mind.

Louis had visited his cousin in Indiana several times and didn't remember ever meeting this young woman. Driving home from the party, he asked his wife what she knew about the girl. His wife had heard that the girl had eloped and was now hiding with their cousin. Yet this seemed a little odd as well, because normally a girl seeking refuge would look first to her own family.

Louis had come to the United States from Cameroon, West Africa, in 1985 and eventually became a U.S. citizen. With a degree in management from an American university, he had a good job and served as an elder in his Presbyterian church. Living in the suburbs in Virginia, Louis and his family were pursuing the middle-class dream of stability and security. By his late forties, Louis had achieved much of his dream. But he found himself deeply unsettled by this strange and troubled girl in the middle of his family's Thanksgiving holiday. Things just weren't adding up, so a few days later he drove over to visit a relative, where the young woman was staying.

And then she began to tell me the story. And I felt so bad about it. . . . I mean everyone has a human feeling, if you hear a story which is so terrible, you are moved, being human. I began to put down in writing the stories she told me, and probably if you read the whole report that I wrote, you would come to the conclusion that something was really, really wrong.

The more Louis heard, the more sickened he became. There was no elopement in this girl's past. He listened as, confused, isolated, and still in shock, she painfully recounted years of slavery in the suburbs of Washington, D.C.

Her name was Rose. Back in Cameroon, at the age of fourteen, she had just begun her school's summer vacation when a friend of her aunt stopped by her house. This woman explained that a Cameroonian family in the United States needed someone to help around the house. In exchange, the family would help Rose go to school in America. It sounded like a great opportunity to Rose and to her parents. They talked it over carefully and agreed that she could go right away. Since the summer vacation had just begun, she would have time to settle in before starting school in the United States. Away from her parents, Rose was introduced to the family she would be working for. They bought her air ticket and escorted her through customs and immigration, passing her off as one of their family when they reached the United States. Everything seemed normal until they reached Rose's new home in America. Then the trap closed.

The husband and wife showed Rose the jobs they wanted her to do. Soon the jobs filled her day completely, rapidly taking control of her life. Up at six in the morning, Rose had to work until long past midnight. When she began to question her treatment, the beatings began. "They used to hit me," Rose said. "I couldn't go for three days without them beating me up." The smallest accident would lead to violence. "Sometimes I might spill a drink on the floor by mistake. They would hit me for that," she said.[1] In a strange country, locked up in a strange house far from home, Rose was cut off from help. If she tried to use the phone, she was beaten; if she tried to write a letter, it was taken away from her. "It was just like she was lost in the middle of a forest," said Louis; "she was completely isolated."

Under the complete control of others, subject to physical abuse, paid nothing, working all hours, this fourteen-year-old schoolgirl had become a slave. The promise that she could go to school in America was just the bait used to hook her. In Cameroon her parents received no word from her, only occasional reassuring messages from the family who had enslaved their daughter. The beatings and constant verbal attacks broke Rose's will, and her life dissolved into a blur of pain, exhaustion, work, abuse, and fear. Rose lived in slavery for two and a half years.

Someday we may know the details of what happened in these years, but probably not. Until recently Rose was often nervous and withdrawn, still suffering from the trauma of her enslavement. Demonstrating remarkable resilience, she has moved on to a new life, and it would be understandable if she never wants to revisit that period of unspeakable pain. Her mind has deeply buried her memories. What we do know is that not long after she had turned eighteen, Rose was found trying to talk to a neighbor by the woman who controlled her. Dragging her away, "the woman started yelling at me, started cursing me," Rose explains, "and I couldn't take it anymore. I just had to run away." Later that day she ran to the home of a friend of her "employer." She pleaded for help, but this woman called the family who had enslaved her. When Rose realized the betrayal, she ran again, this time to the parking lot of a nearby K-Mart. Her only hope was a Cameroonian man she had met in her employers' home. He had seemed nice, and she had learned his phone number. Begging change from a stranger to make a phone call, she managed to leave a message for the man, asking him to pick her up. Without a coat, with no other place to go in the cold November night, she waited in the parking lot outside a store. Four hours later, at nearly 11:00 P.M., she was picked up and taken home to the man's family. This man was Louis's cousin.

Although in safety, Rose was still in limbo. The family she was staying with simply did not know what to do with her, and she feared that in time her "employers" would try to take her back. Then came Thanksgiving and the meeting with Louis. As Louis gently drew out Rose's story, he was shocked and saddened:

I felt terrible, I mean, I felt really terrible, because I couldn't imagine, not even in my slightest imagination, that in this day and age someone would treat somebody's child the way she was treated. It made me sick in my stomach.

Soon Louis took Rose to stay with his own family, and as she opened up to him, more shocking facts came tumbling out. It occurred to Louis to ask Rose if she knew any more girls in the same situation. "Oh, yes," she replied. Following up on what Rose could remember, he found two more young women in slavery, and by himself, with real daring, he liberated them. One of them, Christy, had been brought to the United States at seventeen and had spent five years as a domestic slave. Sally had been brought at age fifteen and had spent three years in bondage.[2] Now Louis had three young women staying with his family, with their care and support coming from his own pocket. His first job, he decided, was to reassure the women's families, so he took videos of all three relaying messages to their families and then traveled to Cameroon. He showed the video footage to the girls' families, who were shocked but overjoyed, as Louis explains:

They were very happy to see me, and especially the fact that I took the video of their children, they were extremely happy, because even if they now saw what their daughters had gone through, at least they had firsthand information from their children. I felt good about it because it was like a conclusion to me that I had done the right thing. I could see their faces, and I could see that they realized at least that someone was concerned about the lives of their children.

More than a year before, Sally's family had been told that their daughter had died in America, and their emotions at seeing her alive are hard to imagine. Meanwhile Louis was investigating the connections that had smuggled the girls into the United States. He found a network that recruited girls from poor families by promising education and jobs. One woman provided a house where the girls were taken after leaving their families and were prepared for the trip to America. Some respected members of the Cameroonian community in the United States were involved, and Louis began to understand that he was up against something big.

With the help of lawyers from an organization called CASA Maryland, the girls' "employers" have now been prosecuted in both criminal and civil courts. Rose bravely went through the ordeal of being cross-examined and having her slavery and abuse exposed in open court. The trial resulted in a conviction, and the couple who enslaved her were sentenced to nine years in prison and ordered to pay her $100,000 in restitution. Of course, being awarded restitution and actually getting it are two different things, and Rose will probably never see the money. She'll also never see her parents again; they both died in 2002.

Christy's "employers" got five years in prison and were ordered to pay $180,000 in back wages. So far, Christy has received about $2,000. She and Rose live together now, sharing an apartment in the Washington, D.C., area. Both are working as nursing assistants and dream of being nurses. For the moment they can't afford to go to college, because much of what they earn is sent back to Cameroon to support their families. Christy's remittances are building a house for her parents and are paying the school fees of her younger brothers and sisters.[3] Louis supported the three girls as long as they needed help. Although he slowly used up his savings, he is convinced that he did the right thing. "People treat dogs better than these girls were treated," he told me. "Anyone who cares about other people would do what I did."

If the story of these young women were unique, it would be shocking enough. That there are slaves in the suburbs of Washington, D.C., the capital of the land of the free, might cause us to question our assumptions about this country. Our questions become more troubling when we face the fact that Rose's story is one of many such tales in the Washington, D.C., area, and one of thousands in the United States. The U.S. Department of State estimates that as many as 17,500 people are brought into the country *each year* and forced into agricultural work, prostitution, domestic service, or sweatshop labor. These are not poorly paid migrant workers; these people are slaves. According to conservative estimates, there are tens of thousands of slaves in America today.[4] And the thousands in the United States and other developed countries are just a fraction of the total across the globe. The estimated twenty-seven million slaves in the world today equals more than twice the number of people taken from Africa during the 350 years of the Atlantic slave trade.[5] But given that legal slavery no longer exists, how can we call these people *slaves*?

WHAT MAKES A SLAVE?

Slavery has been with us since the beginning of human history. When people began to congregate in Mesopotamia and make the first towns around 6800 B.C., they built strong external walls around their towns, suggesting the occurrence of raiding and war. We find the first depiction of slavery in clay drawings that survive from 4000 B.C.; the drawings show captives of battle being tied, whipped, and forced to work by the Sumerians. Papyrus scrolls from 2100 B.C. record the ownership of slaves by private citizens in Egypt and list the first documented price of a slave: eleven silver shekels. When money began to be used, slave trading became a way of making a living, and we see records showing slave-raiding expeditions from Egypt capturing 1,554 slaves in Syria in one season. Around 1790 B.C., the first written laws introduced the legal status and worth of slaves. These Babylonian law codes clearly stated that slaves are worth less than "real people," a principle that is repeated for the next four thousand years. The ancient code is gruesomely clear: a physician making a fatal mistake on a patient, for example, is ordered to have his hands cut off, unless the patient is a slave, in which case he only has to replace the slave.

In past centuries, people had no problem understanding who was a slave and who wasn't, even given the existence of temporary enslavement. Slaves then and now share one central condition: violence is freely used to control them or punish them. The Babylonian code again: "If a slave strike a free man, his ear shall be cut off"; and the Louisiana Slave Code of 1724: "The slave who will have struck his master, his mistress, the husband of his mistress, or their children, either in the face or resulting in a bruise or the outpouring of blood, will be punished by death." For nearly four thousand years the right to inflict violence on a slave was enshrined in law. When the legal ownership of humans ended, as it did in the United States in 1865, many people thought that slavery had ended as well.

But even when people in the United States no longer owned slaves legally, they often continued to control them—by restricting their housing and food supply, refusing them education, limiting their movements, and threatening them with violence. This fact does not diminish the great achievements of the abolitionists and the slaves who fought for their freedom; if there are tens of thousands of slaves in the United States today, it is worth remembering that there were once four million. Still, no matter how many laws were passed against it, de facto slavery never stopped. Throughout history, slavery has meant taking total control of a person and exploiting that person's labor. The essence of slavery is neither legal ownership nor the business of selling people; the essence of slavery is controlling people through violence and using them to make money. Before laws gave one person the right to own another person, even before the invention of money as a means of exchange, slavery was part of human life. Today the laws allowing slavery have been repealed, but people around the world are still brutalized and broken and reduced to slavery through violence. Their free will is taken away. Their labor, their minds, and their lives are consumed by someone else's greed. Slavery, at its most fundamental, has just three elements: control through violence, economic exploitation, and the loss of free will. Slavery is not about race, color, or ownership. Any one or all of these may be used to justify slavery, but they are not essential for its existence.

If people are not legally recorded as being slaves, how can we really call them slaves? The answer is relatively simple, though as with most human conditions, there are always cases that defy clear definition. We can start by asking, Can this person walk away from the situation without fear of violence? If the answer is no, if the person is beaten when trying to leave, then you have one indication of slavery. Another question we can ask: is this person paid nothing, or at a level that barely keeps the person alive from one day to the next? Look again at Rose. She couldn't leave because of the threat of violence, she was paid nothing, she was given only enough food to keep her alive, and she was economically exploited. Her ability to exercise free will was taken from her. Rose was a slave. The newspapers might have called her condition "virtual slavery," or said she lived in "slavelike" conditions, but make no mistake: like women in bondage in ancient Babylonia or the antebellum American South, Rose was a slave.

Slavery is also not a matter of duration. The fact that Rose spent "only" two and a half years in bondage does not make her any less a slave. Slavery isn't necessarily a permanent condition. That was never the case, even when slavery was legal. The ancient Babylonian law and the Louisiana Slave Code both allowed for temporary enslavement. For thousands of years people have been captured, snared, coerced, tricked, sold, kidnapped, drugged, arrested, swindled, seduced, assaulted, or brutalized into slavery. A fortunate few have then managed to make their way out again through any number of exits. Some were released when their health and strength broke down and they were no longer useful. Some managed to escape after decades, and others after just weeks. For some families of slaves, it took generations. On rare occasions a master would free a slave as a gift, but that did not change the fact that the person had been a slave. The same is true today.

We have to put behind us the picture of slavery most of us hold in our minds, that of slavery in the antebellum South. Contemporary slavery shares with the slavery of the past the essentials of violence and exploitation, but today it is not a legal institution, a key part of any country's economy, or a relationship crucially dependent on race or ethnicity. Today, as in the past, slavery exists in many different forms around the world. But modern slavery has two key characteristics that make it very different from slavery of the past: slaves today are cheap, and they are disposable.

A CATASTROPHIC FALL IN PRICE

This new variant of slavery arrived with the twenty-first century. Today slaves are cheaper than they have ever been. The enslaved fieldworker who cost the equivalent of $40,000 in 1850 costs less than $100 today. This dramatic fall in price has forever altered the basic economic equation of slavery. When the price of any commodity drops radically, the balance of supply and demand is fundamentally changed. Today there is a glut of potential slaves on the market. That means they cost very little but can generate high returns, since their ability to work has not fallen with their price. The return to be made on slaves in 1850 Alabama averaged around 5 percent. Today returns from slavery start in the double figures and range as high as 800 percent. Even when they are used in the most basic kinds of work, slaves can make back their purchase price (however that acquisition occurred) very quickly.

Slaves were far more costly in the past. Although finding a clear equivalent between modern dollars and the currency used in ancient Babylonia or Rome is impossible, we can look at how much slaves cost in terms of things that don't change very much over time. An understanding of slave prices from the past is based on three measures: the value of land, the annual wages paid to a free agricultural worker, and the price of oxen. For all of human history (and still today), people have maintained records of the price of land and the cost of keeping a worker in the fields. And for thousands of years, until the Industrial Revolution, oxen were used as a power source to get food out of the ground and onto the table. (When you read *oxen,* think *tractor.* Today an American farmer may pay upward of $100,000 for a tractor; in the past oxen were expensive.) For the price of three or four oxen, a farmer could buy a productive field big enough to support a family and then some, or pay the annual salaries of two or three agricultural workers. Three or four oxen were a big capital investment. Yet, on average, they were worth the price of only one healthy slave. Or consider that for the price of one slave in the Deep South in the 1850s, a person could buy 120 acres of good farmland. It should not be any surprise that slaves were expensive; after all, slaveholders were buying the complete productive capacity of a human being, all the work they could squeeze out for as long as they could keep the slave alive.

In India today you can still buy slaves as well as farmland and oxen, which remain the essential "tractors" that keep farms going. But when we compare the price of a slave to the modern prices of land, labor, or oxen in India, the slave costs, on average, 95 percent less than in the past. This precipitous collapse, unprecedented in all of human history, has dire consequences for slaves.[6] If you could buy a fully equipped, brand new car for $40, do you think your relationship to your car would change? If your car were that cheap, you would begin to treat it as something to be used and then discarded. Why even fix a flat tire if the whole car costs less than the repair? Most slaveholders feel that way about slaves today.

The inexpensiveness of slaves is good for the slaveholder and great for the bottom line but disastrous for slaves. A low purchase price means that a slave does not represent a large investment requiring special care; the slave is easily replaced. Slaves today are treated like cheap plastic ballpoint pens, the kind we all have in our desk drawers or pockets. No one worries about the care and maintenance of these pens or about keeping a careful record of their whereabouts. No one files a deed of ownership for these pens or sends out a search party if one goes missing. No one takes out insurance on these pens. These pens are disposable, and, because they are so cheap, so are slaves.

If slaves get ill, are injured, outlive their usefulness, or become troublesome to the slaveholder, they are dumped—or worse. The young woman enslaved as a prostitute in Thailand is thrown out on the street when she tests positive for HIV. The Brazilian man tricked and trapped into slavery making charcoal is tossed out when the forest is razed and no trees are left to cut. The boy in India who spends all day rolling bidi cigarettes is dumped or sent back to his family if he is injured or ill, and the slaveholder will try to take another child in his place. The young woman in "ritual slavery" in Ghana, who has been exploited, sexually abused, and impregnated again and again by a *trokosi* priest, will be sent back to her parents when the priest tires of her or her health breaks down. Enslaved domestic workers around the world will be discarded when their "family" moves to another city or country. Like plastic pens or paper cups, slaves and potential slaves are so numerous that they can simply be used up and thrown away. Rose, for example, was fairly expensive as slaves go today, yet her slaveholders paid nothing for her. Her acquisition cost involved only the time needed to spin a web of lies to her and her parents and the expense of bringing her to America.

WHERE DO ALL THESE SLAVES COME FROM?

How do we explain a world in which twenty-seven million people are in slavery? Where did all these slaves come from? And how did these people become enslaved? Basically, three factors that converged after World War II gave birth to the resurgence of slavery. The first factor is the world population explosion. After 1945 the world population grew like never before in human history. This growth was the product of many positive developments: the control of infectious diseases, better health care for children, and a prosperity that provided sustenance for the coming billions. World population exploded from two billion to over six billion in about fifty years, with most of this growth occurring in the developing world. Figure 1 plots world population growth along with the fall in the prices of slaves. What becomes clear is that the population explosion helped create a glut of potential slaves flooding the market and leading to a crash in prices.

Population growth helps to explain the drop in prices, but it doesn't necessarily explain the growth in numbers of slaves. Simply having a lot of people doesn't make them into slaves; other things had to happen to lead them or force them into slavery.

The second factor pushing these growing millions toward slavery is a collection of dramatic social and economic changes, many of which were supposed to make those people's lives better. Like the world population, the global economy boomed after 1945. As colonies in the developing world gained their independence, many of the new countries opened up to Western businesses. In the 1950s people remarked on the spread of Ford cars and Coca-Cola all over the world; by the 1960s the rapid economic changes in the developing world were seen as commonplace; by the 1990s no one thought it surprising that teenagers in India, Malaysia, or the Ukraine were eating the same McDonald's hamburgers and humming the same tunes from MTV as teenagers in Chicago, Tokyo, or London. As the economy became global and grew exponentially, its benefits were shared in many parts of the world. But other parts of the world did not take part in that growth. Whole pop-

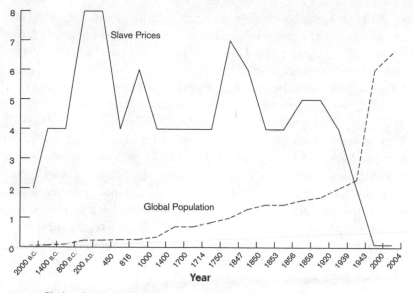

(Numbers along the left side are both human population in billions and the slave price index.)

Figure 1. World population and the price of slaves, 2000 B.C. to A.D. 2004. The Y-axis represents both the global population in billions and the Slave Price Index, which is composed of equivalency measures for oxen, land, or agricultural wages and which varies from 0 to 8. The irregularity of the years along the X-axis is due to the lack of any regular data on slave prices; the years given reflect those years in which slave price information can be obtained.

ulations were left behind, stuck in the subsistence poverty of the past, or worse.

Poverty is often thought of as having two levels, though this is just a rough guideline. At the bottom level are more than one billion people who live on $1 a day or less. All these people are living in the developing world, and for the most part, they are living outside towns and cities living out the same hand-to-mouth existence that was the rule for most of human history. What does it mean to be this poor? It means you are always hungry and that access to medical care and education for your children is pretty much out of the question. It means you are unlikely to have the basic needs of life: clean water, a roof to keep out the rain, adequate clothing, or even a pair of shoes.

This is life without options. Every action must be aimed at day-to-day survival, and even that survival is not assured. Desperation is the norm, and families are ready to do anything to survive. These families are found especially in rural South Asia and rural Africa, areas where slavery thrives. Later in this book you will meet families in India who are trying to live on forty cents a day. These are families whose children are regularly harvested into slavery.

One step up from this extreme poverty, again as a guideline, are families living on approximately $1 to $2 a day, a level that is sometimes called "moderate poverty."[7] Many of these families are living in the vast shantytowns that surround the major cities of the developing world. For example, Mexico City has a population of twenty million, and about half of the residents live in shacks and lean-tos of cardboard and scrap wood that lack basic amenities. Many of these families are economic refugees from rural areas where family farms have been converted into plantations growing cash crops for export. Their lives as subsistence farmers, based around the village and church, were shattered when they were dispossessed of the land they had worked, often for generations. Searching for jobs, they migrated to the city, only to find themselves competing with millions of other campesinos. In the shantytown they have lost the neighbors, the church, and the customs of the rural village. Criminal gangs control much of the shantytown areas. The government has little time or attention to give these poor and disenfranchised people, relegating them to second-class status. This pattern is repeated across the developing world, and the result, whether in Rio, New Delhi, Manila, or Bangkok, is extreme vulnerability. The police do not protect you, the law is not your shield, you can't buy your way out of problems, and any weapon you have is no match for those of the gangs and the police.

In fact, if we compare the level of poverty and the amount of slavery for 193 of the world's countries, the pattern is obvious.[8] The poorest countries have the highest levels of slavery. The relationship would be exact except for the effects of global human trafficking in which the vulnerable are enslaved and transported from poor countries to rich ones, with the result that the richest countries have significant pockets of slavery.

This link between poverty and slavery holds almost any way you measure it. For example, the United Nations has classified thirty-eight countries of the world as being "high-debt countries," which means that these countries are carrying a crippling load of debt owed to international lenders. A high-debt country has to use what little income or taxes it can gather to service debt rather than to invest in its own people. This is often called a *debt overhang*. Debt from the past bears down on a country, paralyzing it and preventing any growth in the future.[9] The types of investments a high-debt country is *not* able to make—schools, law enforcement, economic growth, and so on—are exactly the ones that are most likely to reduce the amount of slavery. If you look across all the countries in the world, those with the largest amount of debt overhang also have some of the highest levels of slavery.[10]

One of these poor countries is Cameroon, where Rose came from. Cameroon has all the usual markers for serious poverty: half the population is poor, the economy carries a high debt load, infant mortality is high, HIV/AIDS is rampant, and life expectancy is around fifty years and falling. This level of poverty creates many hardships, but just having a very large number of poor people still doesn't make those people slaves. Rapid population growth and the impoverishing impact of globalization, epidemics, natural disasters, war and civil conflict, kleptocratic governments, and the international arms trade all support the emergence of slavery but do not cause it. To turn the poor into slaves requires violence, and violence needs the right conditions to grow unchecked.

ON THE TAKE

Corruption, especially police corruption, is the third force that drives the growth of slavery. For slavery to exist, the slaveholder must be able to keep the slave where the law can't protect them. Rose, enslaved in the United States, had to be isolated and locked up. But in many parts of the world, a simple payment to the local police allows a slaveholder to use violence without fear of arrest. Sometimes the police themselves will provide violence for an extra fee. When governments fail to protect their citizens and to maintain the rule of law, those citizens can become slaves. And because slavery is now illegal everywhere, the complicity of crooked police is a fundamental requirement for slavery to take root. In Western Europe, Canada, and the United States, slavery happens *in spite of* the efforts of the police, but in many countries slavery flourishes *because of* the work of the police. Almost everywhere you find slavery in the developing world, you find police or government officials on the take, turning a blind eye.

It is not difficult to understand the pressure on police to join forces with the slaveholders. If a police officer's salary is $10 or $20 a month, the opportunity to bring in an extra $100 a month is the difference between poverty and being able to feed a family, send the children to school, and have electricity. Taking the bribe is even easier when the police officer is urged to do so by the boss. Landlords, moneylenders, and businesspeople, the solid citizens of the town or village, are likely to use slavery in their businesses. Does a policeman really want to jeopardize his job, put his family at risk, and alienate the most powerful members of his local community just to protect people no one seems to care about? Since the enslaved are often migrants from somewhere else, or members of a lower caste, lower class, or different ethnic or religious group, serving their interests will offer few rewards and carry many penalties. Again, if you examine most of the world's countries in a systematic way, you find a strong relationship between slavery and corruption.[11]

The pattern is strong and clear: more corruption means more slavery. This is a special challenge when corruption becomes institutionalized. The bribes pass up the chain of command and into the hands of politicians and government officials. Soon law enforcement is dedicated to protecting systematic law violation. In Thailand, for example, lucrative police commands are sold to the highest bidder, and the regular payments from slaveholders join the flow of money from other criminals into the pockets of police and government officials. Russia is now a major exporter of trafficked women; in Moscow a single monthly payment providing protection from government taxes, police investigation, fire, theft, vandalism, safety inspections, and parking tickets is deposited directly into a U.S. bank account.[12] The size of the payment depends on the size of the business and whether or not it is legal. The bribes required for smuggling drugs or people are high, but then these crimes make huge profits.

If this sort of corruption is widespread, the national government faces an enormous task. Pakistan, for example, enacted a strong law against debt bondage slavery in 1988 and revised it in 1992, but in spite of a large number of cases coming to light, not a single offender has been convicted. The enslaved may be freed, usually through the actions of human rights organizations, but because of corruption the slaveholders are never punished. Instead, the ex-slaves and their liberators are at great risk of violent retaliation and persecution.[13] More than twenty-five years ago India enacted an excellent law against debt bondage slavery, setting a three-year prison sentence and a fine for anyone convicted of forcing someone into, or keeping them in, bondage. To my knowledge, of the hundreds of cases prosecuted, no convicted slaveholder has ever served prison time. Today fines of just 100 rupees (less than $2) are common for those convicted, making a mockery of the law. The linchpin of slavery in many countries is government indifference or, worse, complicity. When corruption is widespread, governments must do more than just pass tough laws; they must also root out corruption and give protection to those who have come out of slavery. At international meetings, many countries make statements of heartfelt concern for the enslaved, only to forget about them as soon as their representatives return home. In any event, slaves are voiceless, and unless they have powerful friends, their cause is forgotten.

WELL, THAT SHOULD BE EASY

When we look at all the elements that support slavery around the world, things seem a little discouraging. Apparently all we have to do is end world poverty, eradicate corruption, keep people from being greedy, slow the population explosion, halt environmental destruction and armed conflicts that impoverish countries, convince the big lenders to cancel international debts, and get governments to keep the promises they make every time they pass a law. How tough is that?

The good news is that we don't have to do all these things at once, and we don't have to solve all of these problems before we can end slavery. There are millions of slaves who can be freed *today*; we just have to change the situation in their lives and communities. Some slaves are ready to come to freedom now; others need big systemic changes to occur, if not completely then enough to open the door to their freedom. There are practical solutions to nearly all of these problems (though I'm not so clear about how to keep people from being greedy). Some are tougher than others. Seemingly intractable problems like corruption can take time to fix, but they too have remedies. Remember that a hundred years ago the United States would have scored high on any corruption scale. When was the last time you had to bribe a police officer to be able to park your car or get your trash picked up? United Nations programs have shown that with the right resources and leadership a culture of corruption can be cracked, and citizens can stop assuming that every interaction with an official requires a payoff.

International debts are being cancelled. The population explosion is slowing down. The struggle against environmental destruction has never been so fierce. The number of people living in extreme poverty has actually fallen from 1.5 billion in 1981 to 1.1 billion in 2001, even as the world's population continued to increase. There are clear plans to significantly reduce extreme poverty by 2015 and then end it by 2025.[14] Governments can be encouraged to enforce their own laws in a number of ways, some involving carrots and some involving sticks. Stopping armed conflict is going to be tough, but if poverty and corruption are reduced and good governance is increased, the likelihood of conflict also falls.

Many changes in the world are heading in the right direction for the eradication of slavery, but we must provide the brainpower and the economic muscle to make it happen. We also need a plan. The pages ahead offer a preliminary plan for moving the world from slavery to freedom. It is not a foolproof or complete plan—there are still unclear areas we will need to fill in as we go along. If we want to end global slavery, we have to improve our understanding of it and locate its weak points. No all-encompassing plan will stop slavery in every country or village, and we must find the right combination of solutions for each situation. But we know that in the United States, Ghana, India, Pakistan, Italy, Brazil, Japan, and a host of other countries, slaves are being liberated. Every time a slave comes to freedom, we learn another lesson about how slavery can end.

2

Building the Plan

How we end slavery once and for all is the twenty-seven-million-person question. Sometimes it seems as if slavery has outdistanced our ability to think about and understand it. This is not surprising. The same often happens with crime; the media regularly introduce a new wrinkle in crime that has been "discovered." Crimes like child abuse hide in the shadows until they are "discovered." Like slavery, they had been there all along; people just weren't aware, or pretended not to be. Usually, when a new outrage is discovered, the media announce a "crisis." But slavery hasn't even had the advantage of being declared a crisis, and if it were, that would be a mere first step toward solving the problem.

At the moment, the crime of slavery has moved ahead of us. The response to slavery tends to be unplanned and disorganized. This is not because of a lack of will or commitment on the part of those who are working against it. These new abolitionists are so committed that they often put themselves into danger, and some are even killed in the struggle. But everyone working against slavery today has to face a pervasive lack of public awareness and indifference.

American abolitionists of the 1830s confronted the same indifference, and their anger and frustration would sometimes boil over. William

Lloyd Garrison was one of the most outspoken of the early abolitionists, and his colleagues urged him not to upset so many people. One said to him, "Do try to moderate your indignation, and keep more cool; why, you are all on fire!" Garrison replied, "I have need to be *all on fire*, for I have mountains of ice about me to melt."[1] Within twenty-five years Garrison and others had melted those mountains and made slavery the key political issue of the day. But when legal slavery was abolished, the ice began to slowly build up again. Today, in terms of public awareness, we're just coming out of an Arctic winter.

A few years ago I was just as frozen in ignorance as most people. I was walking around enjoying a kind of general self-satisfaction: "We may still have problems, but at least we got rid of slavery!" Then I had the opportunity to meet some of the new abolitionists, and I woke up to the reality of slavery. I wanted to understand the nature of slavery, and my first step was to do research. But what I learned about the nature of slavery quickly led me to many other questions. A little boy named Raj will help me to explain these questions.[2]

Located a few miles outside of New Delhi, India, is a rehabilitation center called the Mukti Ashram. When I drove up to the big steel gates set in the walls around the ashram for the first time, I worried that they seemed a little too threatening to be the entrance of a children's home. But inside I found a garden overflowing with flowers, and children happily rebuilding their lives. I also found the reason for the strong gates: the ashram is a place where child slaves are brought when they have been freed, and the gates protect them from slaveholders who sometimes try to drag them back to slavery. Raj is typical of the children who live there.

Kidnapped at the age of eight, Raj was taken hundreds of miles from his village and forced to work at making carpets. Locked into the hut that housed the carpet loom, he was fed little, slept next to his loom, was sometimes beaten, and was never paid. He and a number of other children were under the complete and violent control of the man who ran the looms. Raj was forced to work from very early until very late; he was given no schooling and no play. He was beaten if his work slacked off. As he bent over the loom, his spine began to curve. As he constantly breathed fine wool dust, his skin and throat itched and his lungs clogged. His eyesight began to fail as, shut inside the dark shed, he strained to see the tiny knots he was expected to tie over and over again. Cuts, injuries, and illnesses were ignored. After five long years of bondage, antislavery workers carried out a raid on the loom. They found a stunted, confused, sick, and intellectually underdeveloped child. Raj was withdrawn, in shock, and frightened as a result of the trauma of beatings and enslavement. His total being, his body, mind, and spirit, needed immediate help. Raj's story is not unique; he is one of thousands of children in the same situation. The crucial difference is that Raj is one of the lucky few who have been rescued.

The children at Mukti Ashram make up just a small part of the millions of slaves around the world. Antislavery organizations do their best with limited resources, but their work is often reactive and piecemeal and is accomplished in the face of official resistance. And once Raj has been freed, what then? How to treat his injured body may be clear, but how do you reach into his injured mind? In the United States or Europe, a child who has been kidnapped and held in captivity for five years would automatically be given therapy and counseling. It would be assumed that the child would need help for years to come. The trauma of slavery is just as bad, and recovery takes time. Freedom is not the end; it is only the beginning.

Raj is scarred. The scars on his body will fade with time, and proper nutrition will strengthen him. The scars on his mind and on his spirit are harder to see but no less deep. The obvious course of action would be to consult the body of knowledge and expertise built up by doctors and psychologists about how to help freed slaves—except that this body of knowledge does not exist. What knowledge we have gained is in the process of being assembled and tested; preliminary studies of different rehabilitation techniques are just now being published. And surely government agencies will fulfill their responsibility to help children, including Raj, recover their place in the world—not in India, they won't. The state does have a responsibility to free him and punish the slaveholders, but in fact Raj was freed by antislavery activists, and through government indifference, the slaveholders were allowed to walk away. Along with many others like it, the ashram that is helping him runs on donations, not government funding. The workers there may be the most experienced in the world, but they have learned almost everything they know by trial and error. Even the emerging body of knowledge on slave rehabilitation is not reaching the people who need it most.

LIKE MOSQUITOES BITING ...

Raj's case raises a swarm of questions. They touch on Raj but also on the lives of slaves the world over; to end slavery we must answer these questions. The questions start with Raj himself: How do we help him recover from slavery? What skills does he need to learn first? Where should his education begin, and how far should it go? What diet, medical care, and physical rehabilitation will return his health and youth? How do we reach his mind? Can his spirit recover? Will he be able to trust and love other people? How will the trauma of slavery affect him as he grows? Will Raj grow angry? And if he does, how will he direct that anger? Can we find his parents? And how will they deal with the reunion if we do? What if we can't find them—who will be responsible for Raj then? What about the other children still in slavery? How do we find them? How do we get them out? There are answers to all of these questions, and many of those answers are clear and unequivocal. Other answers are specific to a particular child or slave or place. There are two things that must be done with these answers: the first is that they need to be tested and refined, and the second is that they need to be universally known and made so clear that no slaves anywhere will lack the help they need to reclaim their lives.

More questions expand beyond Raj and the ashram: Why do we have to rely on antislavery groups to free enslaved children? How many children can the groups reach, and how many are beyond their ability to save? Are they using their resources effectively? Should they be spending more time lobbying governments or freeing children? How can they be trained to best help these children, who have been so terribly abused? What happens if they run out of money? Why isn't government helping them? Why aren't we?

Still more questions are raised by what the government did or did not do. The Indian government has passed laws to ban slavery and to provide for rehabilitation. Why won't it enforce those laws? Why won't the police do their jobs? Why aren't the politicians pushing them? Why do the legally mandated rehabilitation funds rarely arrive when and where they are needed? The local slaveholders may be powerful, but they are not as powerful as the government. Why hasn't the state intervened? What new laws are needed? What training is required for the police and the local officials so that they know what to do and how to do it?

Then, disturbingly, some of the questions relate back to us. Raj was enslaved to make rugs. Who buys them? What about the wholesalers and retailers in the United States and Europe that profit from these rugs: do they know they are profiting from slavery? How do we differentiate a slave-made rug from one that is made by a free worker? Was the rug on your floor made by Raj or some other slave? If we all stopped buying rugs, would that make the lives of child slaves better or worse? What about the other things that slaves around the world make? Are they in our homes as well? Children aren't enslaved because someone wants to be mean to them; they are enslaved to make a profit. Can the business of slavery be wiped out, and if so, how do we do it?

Ending slavery in the world means solving a lot of puzzles. Some concern a single child, and some relate to fitting the pieces of government policy together: What should governments be doing about slavery? Should our own laws keep slave-made goods out of our country or take advantage of their cheapness? Do they arrest the slaveholders in our own country or punish freed slaves as "illegal aliens"? Did the countries of Europe and North America really end slavery? Or did they just transfer it out of sight and now reap the economic benefits without suffering moral discomfort? Can our politicians do anything about slavery in other countries? Will we always have to rely on overstretched volunteers and underfunded charities to do the work? Shouldn't the United Nations be dealing with this? And if not—why? They send out weapons inspectors, why not slavery inspectors? How do we break the link between international debt and slavery? What is the role of the World Trade Organization? Does opening the global market have to lead to the impoverishment and enslavement of some people?

Then some of the questions hit us right in the heart: Are we willing to live in a world with slavery? Are we willing to share in the profits it generates? Is there some difference between our own children and children forced into slavery that makes their enslavement acceptable? Do all humans have a right to freedom, or is freedom just for the fortunate? Are we willing to pay more for goods made by free people? What would we be willing to give up if it meant slaves were freed? What if our government had to intervene in other countries? Are we willing to pay more taxes to pay for the rescue and rehabilitation of slaves? What can you and I do to stop slavery, and what should we do first?

QUESTIONS AND ANSWERS

This book is about answering those questions. For years I have been traveling around the world investigating slavery. I have met slaveholders; antislavery workers; politicians; slaves; and the children, wives, husbands, mothers, and fathers of slaves. From what I have witnessed, I have built a picture of the enormity of slavery in the world. I have been able to answer some of my questions, but every answer has generated more questions. And while those questions sound objective and cool headed, my motives are not as dispassionate as that. Meeting slaves, getting to know about their lives, has torn at my heart. Meeting children who have never known childhood has given me bad dreams and a feeling of sick hopelessness. Up close, slavery is ugly. I've found it hard to stay clear, to be objective, to stay cool and collected, but behind all those reasonable questions are the ones that churn out of my gut: How can people do this to one another? How can we be so blind as to let it happen? And sometimes confronting inaction I have lost my cool. At the United Nations I went into a slow burn. I saw an organization that I thought was leading the fight against slavery but seemed to be doing a lot of talking and little delivering. (Later I found pockets of real commitment in the United Nations, but I had to dig to find them.)

As I traveled in the United States and Europe, I talked to people about slavery, and they asked me simple questions: What can be done? What can we do? My job is to look for answers to these questions, especially the last one. In this book I try to find the most effective ways to end slavery and help slaves. To write the book, I took off around the world again, visiting people and organizations trying to stop slavery. The contrasts were striking: chatting with the prime minister of Nepal as servants hovered with drinks, then a few days later sitting in a stinking hovel with an enslaved stonebreaker who was dying of silicosis and coughing up blood. I found people with money and power doing nothing and people with nothing doing more than anyone could expect them to. Some of these people are simply heroes.

FOLLOW THE HEROES

These heroes are leading the liberation and rehabilitation of slaves and can show us the way ahead. We need to understand their successes and failures, and I will discuss these liberators in chapter 3. But before we start analyzing the different approaches to slavery, we need to review what we already know about how to confront slavery. We know that public awareness, education, honest law enforcement, government action, economic support, support for antislavery workers, and rehabilitation are all key ingredients.

THE FIGHT FOR PUBLIC AWARENESS

In many ways, public awareness drives the other approaches. In Britain in the eighteenth and nineteenth centuries, slavery was supported by the idea that it was crucial to the national economy. Too many jobs depended on slavery to meddle with it. But as public awareness of the realities of slavery grew, public outrage buried that argument. In the United States slaves as property was held to be an inviolate right guaranteed by the U.S. Constitution, but public concern and commitment overruled that interpretation of the Constitution, though it took a civil war to do it. Unlike the abolitionist movements of the past, the fight for public awareness and public opinion today has three great advantages. The first is that the moral argument is already won; no government or organized interest group is pressing the case that slavery is desirable or even acceptable. No minister is standing in the pulpit and giving Biblical justifications for slavery. The second advantage is that the monetary value of slavery in the world economy is very small, so the end of slavery threatens no country's livelihood. No country can say, "We would *like* to end slavery, but we just can't afford it." The third advantage is that, for the most part, the laws needed to end slavery are already on the books. Given these advantages, bringing an end to slavery requires the political will to enforce law, not campaigns to make new laws. But political will (in most countries) is directly proportional to public awareness and concern. Until slavery reaches the public agenda, slaves will continue to suffer.

READING, WRITING, AND FREEDOM

One of the best defenses against slavery is education. Many people who are enslaved are tricked into it. Violence comes only after trickery has given the slaveholder control. This is an ancient method for enslaving people. Four hundred years ago slavers on the West African coast offered free food and a free trip to a fabulous paradise to the local people. The reality, once on board the slave ship, was brutality and enslavement. Around the world today, "recruiters" hold out the chance of a good job to the economically desperate—the hoax revealed once they have taken control of the people's lives. Women in the Ukraine, men in the slums of Brazil, girls in the villages of northern Thailand, and boys in Nepal—all repeat the story of deception and tragedy. The con men of slavery know exactly how to lure the vulnerable into bondage. But against this deception a little education goes a long way. In Nepal one organization frees young women who were sold into prostitution in India, then sends them around to the villages to talk about their experiences. The parents who were once ready to believe the lies of the recruiter, the girls who once yearned for jobs in the big city, and the local elders who were flattered and bribed by the con men are all less likely to be tricked once they have heard the truth. For the young village women especially, meeting someone much like themselves who is facing the death sentence of AIDS is a shocking but needed awakening.

Although education is one key to the fight against slavery, we are hardly taking advantage of its power. Yes, the group in Nepal sends out its workers, and, yes, the International Organization for Migration carries out public awareness campaigns for young women in Eastern Europe, but literally millions of people at risk are not getting the word. When programs are started, they tend to close the barn door long after the horse has bolted. The response to this need for public education is slow and fragmented. In the United States and Europe, for example, we have well-trained teachers and specialists employed in our education systems, and many of these teachers volunteer to work in the developing world. But how many are trained to teach the skills needed to help someone keep their freedom? We spend large sums to develop educational campaigns against teen pregnancy or drug use, but how much do we spend to educate people against slavery? Most important, how can we help teachers spread the word in the areas most at risk of slavery?

Training is also needed in law enforcement. The United States spends more on law enforcement than any other country, but it set up a task force on human trafficking only in 1998. The task force has begun to train police, but even those programs have been criticized for being haphazard and of low priority. A report by the Central Intelligence Agency (CIA) in 1999 found serious shortcomings in information sharing and coordination and, worse, a lack of a comprehensive law and few resources to fight against human trafficking in the United States.[3] Compare that to the billions of dollars spent in the War on Drugs.

WHEN POLICE ARE FOR SALE, SLAVES ARE CHEAP

In the developing world, police need more than just training; police departments often need a radical shakeup to get rid of deep-seated corruption. This corruption grows in several ways. If police are poorly paid, they face a strong temptation to use their position to earn more cash. If their superiors are already abusing their positions, the alternative to going along is unemployment or worse. Over time, corruption becomes institutionalized as a family business. Once it has penetrated deeply into a police force, it is extremely difficult to root out. Corruption is supported by vast sums of money (think of the economic power of the Colombian drug cartels), and the brute force controlled by the police, and rented or sold to slaveholders, is a powerful deterrent to reformers. Yet every country in the world has corruption; the question is the extent to which it is tolerated. The level of corruption in the developing world today is similar to that of the United States in the nineteenth century, when this country was undergoing rapid economic and demographic change. Bringing corruption in the United States down to its current levels took a long time, but everyone agrees that it was worth it. Police corruption enables the violence that is the key support for slavery. For many countries stopping slavery means stopping corruption too.

Corruption plays its odious part in another way. There are laws prohibiting slavery in virtually every country in the world, but these laws often languish on the books without enforcement. There are several reasons for this. In some countries a lack of resources means that many basic rights and services are neglected. The countryside of Pakistan is dotted with schools for the local children—but these schools have no desks, no books, and no teachers. The government of Pakistan has recently invested heavily in atomic weapons. With such priorities, the pie of government spending is much too small to meet fundamental needs, and since the "squeaky wheel gets the grease" in government funding everywhere, the voiceless often get nothing. Unless they have champions, the bonded laborers of Pakistan and the rest of South Asia have no voice and get little attention. Those who control government positions, or can influence policy, address their own agendas, gaining support for their own industry, town, party, or personal Swiss bank account. In the struggle for attention, slaves aren't even a blip on the screen. So even though the laws stay on the books, only the activists and the nongovernmental agencies work to enforce them.

GOVERNMENT (IN)ACTION

With an average income of just a few hundred dollars a year, Mauritania is one of the poorest countries on the planet. The foreign investment the country has attracted has not enriched the country but tended to strip it of the few assets it holds, and humanitarian foreign aid makes up a significant part of the national budget. Mauritania can't even maintain its two paved highways, built as gifts by other countries. Although we might expect that a lack of resources would make it difficult for the government in Mauritania to enforce its law against slavery, a lack of money isn't what keeps Mauritanians enslaved. In 1980 Mauritania abolished slavery for the third time, but no one told the slaves. In an attempt to appease donor governments, Mauritania tackled its slavery problem—through public relations, subterfuge, and oppression. The abolition of slavery in 1980 was widely publicized by the government, but the provision in the law that called for compensation to be paid to the slaveholders usually wasn't mentioned. That any government would recompense slaveholders is morally repugnant, akin to making cash grants to buy off cooperative armed robbers. This compensation, however, has never been paid, so the "freed" slaves are still held under violent control while their masters wait for their money. When groups like the Mauritanian Human Rights Committee tried to expose the subterfuge, their members were placed under arrest. Someone who talks to a foreign journalists can wind up in prison in Mauritania. This is not a shortage of funds; it is sheer self-serving mendacity by the government. Throughout the world, slaveholders are men of property and power. The rule of the powerful in their own interest is the most ancient form of government on earth, a form that people have been trying to overthrow for centuries. In many countries laws against slavery are just tattered window dressing, barely concealing systematic support for bondage and exploitation.[4]

It doesn't have to be this way. Ghana is also a poor country, and one that was a staging ground for the transatlantic slave trade. Ghana got a new constitution making it a democratic republic in 1992, and in the same decade slavery again became an issue. The trafficking of children into domestic service, as well as ritual slavery known as *trokosi* and agricultural slavery in the countryside, all emerged into view. Unlike Mauritania, however, Ghana admitted that slavery was a problem and set out to do something about it. In 1996 a law was passed against the *trokosi* ritual slavery, and by 2000 the most active antislavery group in Ghana had freed around two thousand women and girls from 132 shrines. In 2001, Ghana hosted a meeting of cabinet ministers from all fourteen countries of the Economic Community of West African States. In that meeting the ministers hammered out a plan to bring all their anti-trafficking laws into harmony and cooperate in stopping the exploitation of child slaves. In 2005 Ghana passed a new and comprehensive law on human trafficking and built a shelter for freed slave children with international help. Of course, Ghana still has problems, mainly because the country is poor and cannot afford to do all the antislavery work that is needed. Antislavery groups have to pay to send children to the government rehabilitation center, for example, and the minister of the interior admitted in 2007 that the new law was not being fully enforced. Some of the slavery in Ghana happens on remote farms or the rural areas near Lake Volta where it is simply hard to uncover. But workers from the International Cocoa Initiative are successfully freeing abused workers in agriculture, and other antislavery groups are freeing the child slaves from the fishing industry.

In Mauritania and Ghana we can see that slavery is not just an odd vestige of ancient practice but is inextricably tied to larger political and economic questions. The eradication of slavery requires ripping away its foundations: economic and social vulnerability, corruption, lack of education, and government indifference or lack of resources. Although corruption or education might respond to local or national initiatives, the economic context and the political system are often beyond the control of an individual country. The economies of the developing world are at the mercy of Wall Street and the London and Tokyo markets. In the developing world, dramatic shifts in production, the exploitation of natural resources for export, the influx of jobs from developed countries, the forced addiction to international lending, the austerity programs (including the decimation of education, health care, and social services) required by the World Bank when debt addiction becomes severe — all of these can create a context conducive to slavery. So while slaves wait for freedom in the workshop or field, their chains may be forged or broken in New York, Washington, London, or Geneva.

Education may be a great defense against slavery, but education requires funding. When communities are poor, funding for education must come from national governments. When those governments are bankrupt, education is not funded and never reaches those that need it most. India has a law that forbids child labor but no law that requires children to attend school. When economic improvement is linked to better education and a growth of democratic institutions, slavery falls. But when rich nations turn a blind eye to the internal affairs of lucrative trading partners, profits shore up the position of slaveholders. Resolving economic and social vulnerability has many strands, yet this is where we turn full circle and come back to public awareness. For organizations like the World Bank or the World Trade Organization to build antislavery measures into their policies, the powerful countries that control them must order it. For those countries to insist on these measures, their citizens have to demand it from their politicians, and for that to happen the citizens must know what they want. Otherwise, indifference rules.

That indifference can be seen in the United States. We all have an occasional chuckle when we read about some quaint old law still on the statute books, but how about this one: "all goods . . . produced or man-ufactured wholly or in part by . . . forced labor . . . shall not be entitled to entry [into the United States] and importation is hereby prohibited." That is the Tariff Act of 1930, the basic law regulating imports to the United States. It seems a reasonable idea, even if done for the strictly self-ish reason of protecting American workers from competing with slave labor. But how do we know if slaves made any of the goods that pour into America? Do you remember any customs official asking you that question as you passed through an airport? The rugs that Raj made as a slave were not for local consumption; they traveled to Europe or the United States and may be in the stores where you shop. We will explore this question in depth in chapter 7.

GLOBAL SOLUTIONS, LOCAL HEROES

Stand back a little, and you see that many factors are propping up slav-ery. Some of these are intentional and criminal, like the corrupt police who capture and return runaway slaves. Some of them are unintentional but misguided, like World Trade Organization policies that ignore human rights. Some are located in the local village, others in a nation's capital, and still others in the international headquarters of the World Bank and United Nations. All this begs a simple question: *who* should be doing *what* to stop slavery? Some of these supports for slavery can be knocked away by antislavery campaigners and activists, but other sup-ports, like the effect of the global economy, are way beyond their reach. But that is not a counsel of despair. The task we face is to understand dif-ferent levels of action and to figure out how to work effectively at every level. Public awareness is part of it, as is putting pressure on politicians, but we also need to get to know our frontline workers. At the local level, antislavery workers are liberating slaves. They are doing the legal work and the rehabilitation that governments should be doing. Their pay is low, their hours are long, and they are sometimes in real danger. You will meet a number of these heroes in this book. They are acting out our moral belief that slavery is wrong.

One thing that has been lacking is a close link between those of us in the rich countries of the world and these frontline workers. People in Europe and North America can support and protect people in the devel-oping world. Groups like Free the Slaves have found that supporting lib-erators financially, and letting local officials know the rest of the world is watching over them, can literally bring freedom to slaves and keep antislavery workers safe. Slavery reaches us through the global economy; we have to reach out across the globe to those people who are combating slavery where it lives.

FALLING BACK INTO SLAVERY

We know one more thing that we must do to stop slavery—effectively rehabilitate freed slaves. For every one of the millions of slaves alive today, liberation is not enough. Although it is not well studied, we know that rehabilitation is essential to sustained freedom. When bonded laborers have been freed in India but given no support to rebuild their lives, some have fallen back into slavery. Incredibly, some even return to slavery by choice. Some years ago I met a bonded farmworker named Baldev, an Indian ploughman whose family had been in bondage for generations. Baldev had inherited debt and slavery from his father, his father had inherited the debt and slavery from his father, and before that no one could remember when the slavery had begun. I wrote about Baldev and his family at the time because he was, in many ways, the classic bonded laborer: cowed, destitute, uneducated, exploited, and resigned.[5] Some time later I visited Baldev again and found him working in the fields. As we talked I was amazed to discover that Baldev had, after generations of bondage, paid off his family's debt and gained his freedom. A distant relative had died and left him some money, just enough to wipe out his debt. I was even more amazed when Baldev told me that his freedom had lasted only a few months because he had *voluntarily* put himself back into slavery. When I asked him why he had done this, his reasoning was clear:

All I have ever been is my landlord's ploughman, just like my father and grandfather before me. When I paid off our debt, our landlord no longer gave us the daily grain allowance we had as bonded workers. I began to worry; what if something happened to me or to my family? Who would care for us? Where would we get food? I was free, but now I was worried all the time. So I went back to my landlord and asked him to take us back. I didn't need to borrow any money, but he still agreed that I could be his ploughman again and that we would belong to him.

Baldev was dropped into freedom and found only insecurity. With no one to help him into a new life, he could not make the transition himself and soon fell back into the safety of letting another person control his life. Without rehabilitation Baldev chose the devil he knew, and in doing so he may have sentenced his children to a life in bondage.

Compare Baldev's situation to the graduates, like Raj, of the Mukti Ashram. These children return to their villages equipped with the skills and education to make their way in the world. Equally important, they return feeling empowered and committed to stopping bondage and child labor. These children often become village leaders. The adults come to rely on them because they may be the only people in the village who can read and write and because they show no fear in confronting landlords or local police. The example and influence of a single rehabilitated slave can dramatically alter a whole village. In one village I visited in India, an activist from an antislavery organization helped a handful of women form a tiny credit union. They slowly saved enough to pay off some of the illegal loans that held their families in bondage. When the first families gained their freedom, a real awakening came to the village. When other families saw that freedom was possible, they didn't bother to pay off their loans; they simply renounced them. Acting in concert, they were able to stand up to the threats of the slaveholders. With the village freed, the children were no longer required to work all day with their parents. The villagers quickly constructed a shelter to be used as a school and asked the activists to provide a teacher. It may have been only a pole-frame hut with a thatched roof, with logs to sit on and one battered chalkboard, but the adults glowed with pride as they showed me their school and their children's lessons. It would take an armed invasion to return this village to bondage.

TAKING A HARD LOOK

We know some things that we can do to stop slavery—education, honest government, and rehabilitation—but what we don't know would still fill an encyclopedia. In the rest of this book, I'll take a hard look at people and organizations—working locally, nationally, and internationally—that say they are trying to stop slavery, and some that don't say that but should. Slaves are coming to freedom every day through a number of means. For thousands of people every year, slavery is coming to an end. This book is a blueprint for expanding this liberation to millions of others.

If education works, then we need to find out how much it will cost to provide that education. We have some idea of how much this would be.

Many top-notch economists have spent years figuring out how much it will cost to provide every child in the world with a basic education—a U.N. Millennium Development Goal by 2015. Their estimates range from $9 billion to $28 billion. Let's assume it would cost the top end of this estimate. Yes, $28 billion is a lot of money, but put it in perspective. That is the same amount that charities in the state of Michigan spend in a year, it is the personal worth of the man who started selling those confusing self-assembly bookshelves at IKEA, and it is the amount that tobacco company Philip Morris was ordered to hand over to a woman who sued the company in Los Angeles.

We need to estimate the other costs of getting the job done: anticorruption campaigns, debt reduction, police training, rehabilitation, and training and paying the antislavery workers. This book will provide some of those estimates. It will also point out something surprising: there is profit in ending slavery. That may sound strange at first, but when you set millions of people free to work for themselves, to buy food and clothing and shelter and education and medicine and even toys for their children, you unchain productivity. The result is a freedom dividend of significant proportions.

Slavery is complex and widespread, but it is also simple and narrow in its violence and greed. Starting in the next chapter we'll look at how slavery ends, for individuals, for communities, and for whole countries. We'll look at both successes and failures. At every level the same question will be asked—if this ends slavery, how do we expand it to all slaves?

3

Rescuing Slaves Today

The setting sun casts long shadows across the dusty streets of Nai Basti, a village in Uttar Pradesh in northern India.[1] Women are carrying jars of water from the village standpipe, and tiny fires are being tended in the brick braziers, where supper will be cooked. Crisscrossing the open space at the center of the village are children are at play as well as dogs, goats, and a couple of cows in the slow and patient search for something edible.

Some of the larger houses of the village have one or more additions, shedlike rooms about six feet by eight feet built onto the side or back of the house and fitted with one or two narrow slit windows and a stout padlocked door to the outside. The only sound that comes from these windows is the soft rustling and clicking of a carpet loom being operated. Inside one room sits a child of nine squinting in the failing light at the tiny knots he is tying over and over into the weft of a rug. He pulls the warp strings, threads and ties the knot of colored wool, presses the knot tightly into the forming carpet, and then repeats this movement again and again. He has been knotting at the loom since dawn, and as the light fades twelve hours later, he still has another hour or more of work. In midmorning he was given a small bowl of lentils and allowed to empty the tin can that was his toilet. Sometime in the afternoon he was visited by his master, who gave him a slap in the face for a poorly tied knot. Wool dust coats his throat, lines his nose, and is rubbed into the abrasions on his fingers where he pulls and knots all day long. The dust is slowly building up in his lungs, and as he works he coughs and spits, careful to spit away from that part of the floor under the loom, where he sleeps.

As the village slows into the rhythms of evening, tired men and women walk back from the fields, rough hoes, mattocks, and shovels on their shoulders. Inside a dusty old car near the edge of the village, three men sit in tense silence. They sweat as they fidget nervously in the closed car, its tinted windows hiding them from view as they watch the village. In a few moments, they will try to find and free slave children. Within an hour any one of these men could be injured or dead, or absolutely nothing will happen and they will just have to drive away. They know where the slave children *should* be, but there is no guarantee the children haven't been moved since they received this information. As the sun goes down, a drab green jeep with two police pulls alongside the car. One carries an old rifle, the other a stick the length of a broom handle. Slowly they climb from the jeep and saunter to the car, surly and grumbling as they come.

One of the men in the car is the ashram coordinator.[2] Three weeks before, the ashram coordinator had been eating his midday meal at his desk at the Bal Vikas Ashram when a slight and poorly dressed woman was shown into his office. The woman told the coordinator what she had seen in Nai Basti. Her message was short and simple: looking through the slit windows of the sheds housing looms, she had seen slave children. A few whispered words were all she could manage, but two of the children had told her they were from Araria, a district in the state of Bihar, some five hundred miles away. After hastily relaying her message, she left, quickly blending into the crowd of poor people walking along the road outside the ashram. The woman is poor, illiterate, and lower caste. She confides in no one that she sometimes reports cases of slave children to the coordinator. Every time she does make a report, she takes a risk. The men who control the looms, the slaveholders, are the most powerful people in her district. Their families are rich, their thugs ready to make life horrible for anyone who disrupts their business. And the police know which side of their bread has all the butter. Without the help of this brave, nameless woman, and others like her, many slave children would never be found.

You might think that armed with this knowledge the coordinator would spring into action, racing to rescue the children—but he can't. From the minute he learns about the children, his effort to save the children from slavery is like swimming up a waterfall. Arrayed against him are the forces of the powerful families, police who just want a quiet life, and the district government itself. Indian law is clear: these children should be rescued immediately. But the coordinator has to assume at every turn that if word leaks out, someone will warn the slaveholders, and the children will be shipped off to another village. Most of the police feel they have nothing to gain from rescuing children and much to lose if they come to be seen as working against the loom owners. But this dereliction is not complete; the coordinator has found a couple of people he can trust. With them, and his co-workers, he begins to plan a raid.

The coordinator has been raiding looms and other places where slaves are held for years, and he knows that every step must be carefully planned. A co-worker is sent to the village to look around and later make a map of the sheds most likely to hold slave children. The coordinator schedules an interview with a district official he can trust to begin the process of getting permission to carry out the raid. As in the United States or Europe, a private citizen smashing down someone's door, no matter the reason, can end up in court, and slaveholders often use lawsuits against anyone who tries to free their slaves. Once the coordinator has permission, he needs to get the police involved. In what is the Achilles heel of the whole operation, no raid can be carried out without the police coming along. As soon as he shares the information with the local government and police, someone may warn the slaveholders. When he is making arrangements for the raid, the head of the police keeps asking, "Why are you doing this? What is the point? What are these children to you?" The administrators drag their feet, and the paperwork takes weeks, with every day that passes offering another opportunity for someone to warn the slaveholders. When police are finally assigned to accompany the coordinator on the raid, he knows the risk is especially high. Some of the police take payments from the slaveholders. If one of these is assigned to the raid, a tip-off is certain. Five or six times a year a raid collapses for this reason. After weeks of preparation, the raid finds no children at all; they have been moved to another village. When a raid turns up empty, the police complain that their time is being wasted, and the loom owners, whose sheds have been broken into, threaten lawsuits, criminal charges, and violence. The whole lead-up to the raid is nerve-racking. Children's lives are at stake, but the outcome cannot be controlled. The corruption of police or the thugs of the slaveholders can sabotage the rescue at any time.

RACING THE DEVIL

By the time the police amble over to the car, the coordinator and his co-workers are getting out, shaky with anticipation. They may have been noticed getting out of the car, or the arrival of the police may have been noticed, so from this moment every second counts. Asked if they are ready, the police answer with agonizing slowness—their reluctance to be here and their disinclination to help this raid succeed are palpable. Finally, with a surly nod, they give their assent, and the ashram workers turn and race into the village.

The ashram workers know that the next sixty seconds can mean life or death to the slave children of this village. With the metallic taste of fear boiling up in their mouths, they run as fast as they can. Have the slaveholders been warned? Are the thugs waiting? What will happen to the children if they are not able to reach them?

At the door to the first loom shed, the coordinator pushes hard while his colleague calls through the slit window. The brutalized and brain-washed children have been told again and again that if the police come they must hide in the rafters or underneath the loom, that the police will hurt them or kill them, and they have come to believe it. In the frantic, desperate moments outside the door the coordinator tries to keep his voice calm, telling the child inside that he has nothing to fear. For the slave children the raid is terrifying. Addled from malnutrition, stupefied by the repetitive mindless work, terrified by beatings, they are shaking in fear when a stranger bursts through the door, grabbing them. Some of the children freeze, others scramble to the roof beams to hide, others begin to scream and fight their rescuers. Grasping the child gently but firmly, the coordinator has to ignore the cries, because to stop to comfort one child now could mean failing to set other children free. Handing the first child to a co-worker who will gather the children together in the center of the village, he races to another hut and another. By the time he has pulled four children out of their sheds, the police have finally arrived and are standing around looking bored. Meanwhile, some villagers are pouring out of their houses, trying to stop the raid and to take back the children who are huddled together on the ground in the center of the village.

"This is my child!" shouts a woman as she tries to grab one of the children out of the growing group. The children are squatting in the dirt, pressed together in fear, some sobbing, others staring, eyes glazed. The coordinator dashes back and steps between the children and the woman.

"We'll find that out soon enough," he says; "if this is your child, he will be returned to you." The policeman nods, and the coordinator races to another hut, now throwing stealth aside and kicking in the door. Within five minutes nineteen children are huddled in the dirt, trembling and crying. As the growing and increasingly vocal crowd of villagers begins to press in on them, the children bury their heads, squeezing together more and more tightly. One of the workers goes from child to child, gently trying to penetrate their panic and shock. Squatting beside a child he almost whispers through the noise—"It's okay, . . . we're here to help get you back to your parents. . . . What's your name?" The boy cannot answer at first: he simply cannot think.

Turning from the children, the coordinator hurls a challenge at the police. "You know who this house belongs to . . . these children were locked up in there . . . the owner should be arrested!" The police turn slowly away, shaking their heads. They have to come along for the raid, but they are not about to get themselves in trouble with the rich men who run the village.

Ten minutes have passed, and all the huts have been searched. The nineteen children seem to be all the slaves in the village. The coordinator would like to do a much more thorough search, but now he has to safeguard the children who have been rescued. More villagers are gathering and, despite the presence of the police, some of the slaveholders' thugs are turning up. They look on menacingly, but none have moved yet to attack the rescuers. The ashram workers have to get the children up and into a van that has rolled to the center of the village. They have only a few minutes to get these children out before the thugs will try to take them back by force. Quickly, firmly, they help the children up and into the van; other co-workers are there to sit with them and guard them. Finally the van rolls off, throwing dust onto the crowd of villagers. From the van windows peer the children's smudged, tear-streaked faces, full of both fear and wonder as they see the world again after years at the looms. Twelve minutes have passed since the raid began.

FREE BUT NOT SAFE

The van drives straight to the police station. Here the children are photographed and their names are gathered for a "First Information Report," which includes their condition, the locations of the houses where they were held, and a list of all the people taking part in the raid. The police, resentful, drag things out, while ashram workers collect more information from each child and try to hurry the process along, knowing the children are still not safe. Now that the raid is over, the slaveholders are reemerging and will be sending messages to the police they bribe, asking them to stall and obstruct while they plot. In a few hours the reports generated from the raid will be copied to the slaveholders, and another race will begin.

As soon as the report is filed, its contents can be accessed freely by anyone, including the slaveholder or his lawyer. The name of the person filing, the names of parents, the names of the children, their location, and the names of their home villages are all there. While the police drag their feet, the slaveholders intimidate some witnesses, bribe others, manufacture evidence, and make the children they still control disappear; if they think it is necessary, they file legal countersuits entangling the ashram workers. Although the children who have been rescued are generally safe, filing a report can tip off slaveholders to hide any other children they control.

Antislavery workers have learned that to file the First Information Report they have to send someone who is literate, familiar with the system and rules, and unwilling to take no for an answer. If at all possible, they send a lawyer. Yes, the coordinator can get his reports filed, but how many people have been sent away from police stations empty-handed and end up being denied justice? Hundreds? Thousands? No one knows. And, of course, most parents never make it to the police station in the first place.

Everyone wants government to be open, but when criminals and slaveholders have more sway than victims, that openness can be more harmful than helpful. For ashram workers part of the problem is that the First Information Report is required both to initiate an investigation and prosecution of slaveholders and to provide the necessary recognition that these children are, in fact, former slaves and thus eligible for special grants and care. Any person (not an organization) can file this report, but that doesn't mean that it is easy to do. Imagine that somehow the father of one of these children, against all odds, manages to find out where his son is being held. Now imagine that, in spite of desperate poverty, he makes the five-hundred-mile journey from his home to this village in Uttar Pradesh. By some incredible combination of luck and perseverance, this father finds his son and makes it to a police station to report the enslavement. Like everyone else in his family, he's illiterate, so he has to ask the police officer on duty to help him. He has no idea that a particular report has to be filed, so when he is told, "Sorry, you're in the wrong station" or "You must have two witnesses," he walks away. As soon as he leaves, the police officer might go to the slaveholder and tell him which child has been discovered and who and where the child's father is. If he does, that night the child is moved to another loom. That night the father is visited by thugs. No report has been filed. No report, no case of slavery. End of story.

Even with the children moved to the safety of the ashram, the legal process drags on and on. Every report filed can lead to a case that will last three years on average, and sometimes much longer. Only the person filing the report is allowed to carry the case forward, so if anything happens to that person, the case dies. The coordinator explained that he could take on only one or two cases each year because the time they burn up means that other important jobs, like rescuing children, get neglected. And between the bribed and threatened witnesses, disappearing evidence, and countersuits by the slaveholders, a victory in the courts is rare. For that reason, many antislavery workers don't even bother trying to get slaveholders convicted and concentrate instead on rescuing children and reuniting them with their parents. That course is, needless to say, the devil's own trap. Children are free, but the slaveholders are also free—to continue turning children into slaves. In chapter 8 we'll see what can be done to stop the supply of children flowing into slavery in the looms.

For the children who are now safe, a new life begins. On the outskirts of the nearest big city is a place of safety and care, the Bal Vikas Ashram. Bal Vikas Ashram is a care and rehabilitation center for children rescued from slavery. (*Ashram* is a Hindi word meaning "a place of shelter or a retreat," and *Bal Vikas* means "child development.") The children's immediate needs are far beyond what their families can provide, and most come from villages hundreds of miles away. What's more, finding the families can sometimes take days or weeks. Many of the boys enslaved in the carpet looms were kidnapped four or five years before, and their families, poor and illiterate farmers for the most part, often migrate to other parts of India looking for work. These are not families who leave a forwarding address, and the activists from the ashram have to do detective work to trace them.

AFTER LUNCH, MORE LUNCH!

The children who are brought to the ashram are terrified, usually sick, malnourished, and often deeply traumatized. Very little is expected of them when they first arrive. They've already been checked over by a doctor, so they are given a bed and shown where the toilets and dining room are and are left to look around and mix with the other children. If there is a magic medicine that draws them back to reality, it is the smell of food cooking.

In slavery the food was poor and scarce, and the children arrive skinny, often stunted, and deeply, deeply hungry. When asked about their time in slavery, many children talk not about the violence they endured but about the bad food:

I was always sleepy when I was on the loom, and my work would get spoiled. The whole morning I would be weaving and I would only get a little food at about 12:30. The food wasn't good. I didn't like it at all. The food was so bad I didn't want to eat it. Every day I had to make myself, force myself, to eat it because it was so bad. The loom owner would give us wet half-cooked rice. The dal or the lentils I would get would not be well cooked and full of water—not at all what dal was supposed to taste like.[3]

A person can survive on two small daily helpings of beans and rice, but just barely. Visitors come to the ashram with images of children learning to be free, gaining skills, coming out of their shells. They see all this, but often what they remember best is the sight of children eating and eating and eating: big plates of food and happy greasy faces. A few hours later, more plates of food and more happy faces. The children are shoveling it down, and as they do, they begin to grow.

The children of the ashram form teams to cook the meals. After being locked up for most of their childhood, they need to learn many practical skills, including cooking. They are taught to cook also because the teachers want to counter the strict sex roles that plague Indian society. Getting them into the kitchen is not difficult; these kids are motivated. Cooking meals is a time of happy chatter as the kids peel potatoes, chop vegetables, and pat out the dough for their flatbread. The children grow much of this food in a large garden at the ashram. At the nondenominational prayer time, visitors can hear children praying for guidance and strength when they return to their villages to plant new gardens to feed their families.

A few years ago I followed the progress of two boys, Huro and Shivji, who were rescued from the looms. When they arrived at an ashram near Delhi, they were traumatized, malnourished, and stunted, and I wondered if they could ever fully recover. Six months later my friend Brian

Woods returned from the ashram with filmed interviews.[4] Instead of two frightened, sickly children I saw two confident, literate, motivated boys, who looked as if they had grown nearly a foot since I had seen them. It was an important lesson for me about the resilience of children.

This resilience is nowhere more apparent than in the classroom. These children are as starved for mental stimulation as they are for food. In the classroom they are attentive and diligent, and the speed with which they make up for lost time is simply amazing. Huro and Shivji were pre-schoolers when they were kidnapped and taken to the looms; they were eleven-year-olds when they were rescued. I had worried that it would take years for them to catch up, if ever, but six months later they were working at nearly their own grade level. Knowledge is power, and these kids really demonstrate the power that knowledge brings. Shivji said, "If you are illiterate, anyone can cheat you. If you are literate, no one can cheat you." This was no slogan; Shivji was talking about how to stay out of slavery, how to recognize the lies told by the men who trick children into slavery. At the Bal Vikas Ashram, the children learn practical skills as well as regular school subjects. A boy there talked about his class in electricity: "I like it. I like the electricity idea. I like the fact that [the teacher] gives us notes and lessons that we have to memorize and figure out how it works. He asks me questions in class, and when I'm able to answer, it feels good."[5]

The academic and skills education they get is important, but in the world where these children live, what they learn about human rights, power, and community organizing may be even more important. In many ways this is therapy as well as education. Imagine a circle of thirty children sitting on the ground with their teacher. The teacher asks question after question: "How many of you were enslaved in the looms?" "How many of you were beaten when the rugs weren't perfect?" When the children see everyone's hand going up, they realize they were not alone in their experience, a realization that literally changes their lives. By bringing their pain and their abuse out in front of everyone, they take control of it. By sharing in the experience of others, they learn that their enslavement was not their fault but a pattern of abuse and exploitation in which they were simply victims. And by sharing their pain and anger, they also begin to see their own power to put a stop to slavery. As the outdoor class goes on, the teacher leads them to radical new ideas—that they have rights as human beings, rights that cannot be taken away and can only be denied or violated, rights that should be supported by the whole structure of government. For children who have been told again and again that they are worthless, who have come to blame themselves (as abused children often do) for the suffering they've endured, this is a new universe of release and empowerment.

ROOTS, SNAILS, AND LEAVING TOWN

Freed slave children spend about six months at the ashram. Some who need more support and care stay longer, and some have nowhere else to go. After a rescue, Bal Vikas's staff begin the search for the children's families, but some children's parents or relatives cannot be found. In that case, the children are placed at foster homes or boarding schools. Of the children who go home, many come from the neighboring state of Bihar.

It is difficult for us in the rich countries of the developed world to comprehend just how poor these families are. The families of rural Bihar live at the subsistence level, on the edge of starvation, and many villages are barely holding on. Annual floods wash away homes and push families to camp on elevated roadsides. Many of the men are gone when the floods come, searching for work in other states, and the women and children, exposed to the elements, are reduced to eating roots and snails for much of the year. Nearly all are illiterate, and all are at the mercy of the local landowners who control everything—work, land, government food relief, and the police.

For such families, the possibility of money arriving from a child who has gone off to work in another state could mean the difference between life and death, and "recruiters" are ready to take advantage of these destitute families. Since the idea of migrating for work is normal for the men of the village, the smooth-talking recruiters can weave a story of a good job in Varanasi that will not only give a boy a skill and plenty to eat but make it possible for him to send money home as well. With the local landowner vouching for the recruiter, mothers give in, and children disappear into the looms.

The ashram graduates who return home are often the only people in the village who can read and write. Though they may be only nine or ten, they are often looked to by the adults for advice and leadership. In the past the landowners would control government notices about food or work programs, but the ashram graduates can read these notices aloud to the village and then suggest appropriate action. The returned children become watchdogs, keeping recruiters out of the village and convincing parents not to send their kids away. A rescued child slave at Bal Vikas Ashram explained:

No, no, I will absolutely not let my parents send any of my brothers to the loom. When it comes to the loom owners, I was badly beaten. . . . In fact, they made us work day and night on the loom. I will make sure that none of my brothers get caught in the same trap. [And if you spotted a trafficker in your village?] Yes, I will go to the police station right away, I will file a report and inform them about the presence of such a man.[6]

Bal Vikas Ashram does an amazing job, rescuing more than one hundred children a year, but this is just a small fraction of the thousands of children kidnapped and tricked into the carpet looms. (We estimate that more than 100,000 children are enslaved in carpet making.)[7] The villages face enormous problems that foster slavery—poverty, corruption, caste discrimination, and woeful ignorance. Schooling can help keep children out of slavery, but even if a village is lucky enough to have a functioning school, for these families keeping the children enrolled is a low priority compared to fighting off starvation. In rural Bihar more than 90 percent of children drop out of school by age ten, and two-thirds leave school at age seven or eight.[8] Many of the villages worst affected by trafficking have no functioning school at all. The slavery of a single child can end with a rescue; stopping slavery in a village requires some big changes. In chapter 8 I will examine how villages and towns and countries can make themselves immune to slavery. The bad news is that there are hundreds of thousands of villages and towns that need to be slaveproofed. The good news is that, like a smallpox vaccination, once inoculated against slavery, villages almost never go back.

FISHING OR BAIT?

Villages in Ghana are also trying to bring their children home and keep them there. In the 1960s, a dam built on Ghana's Volta River slowed the vigorous flow of water and destroyed the livelihood of nearby fishing communities. Families either migrated upstream above the dam or dispatched their children to stay with relatives, where the children were able to send proceeds from their work home. In this impoverished environment, fishermen and traffickers took advantage of the situation and recruited children for paltry sums of money (around $30 to $90) to work in dangerous conditions, with false promises of skills training and education. Children remain trapped in these conditions for many years.

A few years ago, Monika Parikh, a researcher for Free the Slaves, traveled to the lake formed by the dam, Lake Volta, to explore rumors of children being enslaved in the fishing villages there. Lake Volta is one of the world's largest lakes and for a time was a source of fish for both the national and export markets. In recent years overfishing has meant a drop in fish stocks. The resulting economic pressure has pushed some fishermen to enslave children rather than pay adult workers. These children, some as young as three, work long hours mending, setting, and pulling nets; cleaning and smoking fish; and rowing the fishing boats. They must also dive deeply into the lake to retrieve snagged nets. Sometimes the children have weights tied to them to help them descend more quickly; some never make it to the surface again. Much of the work goes on during the night, and in the dark depths the children get tangled, trapped, and drowned. A local man explained, "The bodies of children wash up on the shores of our village, but the police typically attribute the deaths to drowning, a natural cause."[9] If not drowned outright, the children suffer from shock when forced down into water that is too cold for diving.

When Parikh was able to speak with some of the enslaved children, she found them hollow-eyed, gaunt, and grim. They reported that they were fed fermented corn and cassava flour, but only sparingly. Two little boys reported eating some of the small fish they had netted, but for this their master beat them with a cane. If sick or injured, the children receive no care or treatment. Exhausted and staggering from lack of sleep, they often hurt themselves in their work. While most of the enslaved children are boys, some girls are used for domestic work and to sell the fish in the market. Like other trafficked girls in Ghana, they are likely to be sexually abused as well.

As with the Indian children enslaved in the looms, these children often come with the initial cooperation of their parents. Fishermen visit villages in the surrounding countryside in order to recruit children. With schooling hard to obtain and family incomes around the starvation level, parents will sometimes agree to let their children go in order to gain a 200,000 cedi (about $28) "advance" on their child's labor. Normally, the fisherman promises that another 400,000 cedis will be paid to the parents over the next year. It is usually a lie, of course, and away from their home villages the reality of slavery descends on the children. Fishermen, when asked, will frankly state that they have "bought" the children, and once at Lake Volta, the treatment the children receive makes this assertion clear.

For all the horror these children suffer, a happy ending to this story is unfolding. After Parikh's work was completed, she circulated her report to a number of local and international agencies. Around the same time, the local relief organization Association of People for Practical Life Education (APPLE) began to work directly with the fishermen and children.[10] The APPLE workers directly approached the fishermen, explaining why the children should be freed by pointing out the damage to the children and the illegality of the fishermen's actions. They also began a dialogue in the local villages with a goal of building community pressure against the use of children. Although this approach may sound too mild, keep in mind that many of the fishermen were themselves on the edge of starvation; at that time also Ghana's laws against slavery were so inadequate that the relief group had no power to force them to free children. If the people of the local community made a conscious decision to renounce the practice, it would be much more likely that no more children would be enslaved to replace those who were freed.

Meanwhile the International Organization for Migration (IOM), an intergovernmental organization, began to bring its resources and expertise to bear. With a grant from the U.S. government, the IOM worked with APPLE staff to set children free and reunite them with their families. To prevent any recurrence, the IOM began to help some fishermen move into other types of work if they promised to stop enslaving children. Once the children returned home, some of their families were also helped to find ways to increase their income, thus relieving some of the pressure that drove them to "sell" their children in the first place. Though the problem is still widespread and needs more resources to resolve, by 2006 some six hundred children had been freed. One fisherman released thirteen children in 2003 and then set up a poultry farm with IOM assistance. "Too many children were dying," he explained.[11] Now he helps IOM by speaking out against child slavery to other fishermen.

We can take away some lessons from Lake Volta. The rescues of the fishing children show how a single antislavery researcher gathering facts can mobilize groups to free children. It also shows that real progress can be made when economic alternatives are developed for both those who would enslave and those who are vulnerable to enslavement. Developing alternatives to the practices that tempt some fishermen to exploit children is important, but more important is helping the families who are vulnerable to get the education, income, and skills that can protect them from slavery. We have also seen that the movement of children into slavery in West Africa can be stopped—a crucial lesson because child slavery is widespread and deeply rooted in the region. In Ghana alone, children are enslaved for growing cotton and cocoa, mining gold, and serving in markets and homes, as well as for fishing in Lake Volta. Work aimed at helping children enslaved in farming in Ghana has begun, but for most, like the enslaved children of northern India, at the moment there is no hope of rescue. Notice that three of the commodities just named— cotton, cocoa, and gold—flow into the stores of North America and Western Europe and from there into our homes. What we as consumers can do about slave-made goods is taken up in chapter 7.

One of the challenges we face is to plan and build systems that will find all of these enslaved children, take them to safety, and help them to recover. But we also face challenges where child slaves can be even harder to find and liberate—places like America.

"HE THOUGHT HE OWNED HER SOUL"

I don't subscribe to the myth of pure evil, the idea that a slaveholder is somehow a fundamentally subhuman beast who lives only to enjoy causing suffering in others. I've met and talked with slaveholders as they played with their grandchildren or cared for their animals, and even though they are criminals who have committed terrible acts, they still seem to love their kids. I hold on to that belief because I dream of a world in which slaves are free *and* slaveholders are cured of the evil sickness of slavery as well. Still, some slaveholders make it hard to hold on to that belief, and one of these is José Tecum.

Originally from Guatemala, José Tecum lived with his wife near Naples, Florida. Having done well in America, Tecum also built himself a fine house back in his village in Guatemala. Here he lived like a prince and soon came to assume the powers of feudal lord. Power corrupts, and the power that comes with riches in a country where even the law is for sale can warp and destroy a mind. The abuse of this power, especially to take young women for sex, is an old story. Recall the degraded villain of *Uncle Tom's Cabin*, Simon Legree, who buys young females with the intention of using them as sex slaves. Foreshadowing José Tecum, Legree takes his new fifteen-year-old slave, Emmeline, into his house to rape her and can be heard telling his distraught wife, "I'll do as I like!"

José Tecum liked Celia, a young woman in his remote village in Guatemala. We'll never know why Celia became the focus of his attention, but as Tecum watched her, he became obsessed. Celia's family was poor and dared not cross this powerful man. Still, as Tecum badgered her father to allow him to take Celia as a maid, her father continued to refuse. Finally, Tecum tried another tactic. Visiting Celia's home, he brought bottles of liquor and got her father drunk. In a drunken stupor, the father did not stop Tecum when he grabbed fifteen-year-old Celia and dragged her to the next room, where he raped her. Celia's brother cowered with his father, tortured by the shame of what was happening but feeling powerless against Tecum. The rape marked Celia by the notions of her culture as spoiled and unmarriageable. A few days later, Tecum offered money and a chance for Celia to go to America, and her family, in their shock and shame and with the fatalism of the oppressed, gave in.

Tecum had taken control of Celia's life, but before leaving for America he made his control absolute. Taking some of her hair, he performed a voodoo-like ritual that tied her to him. In Celia's village people believe that a person with enough power and the right ritual can literally take your soul. Celia believed this completely. From that moment not only her present life but also her eternal life was in the hands of her rapist, and any resistance could damn her forever. To further increase his control over her, Tecum told Celia that if she crossed him, he would have her family killed.

Celia's shock increased in America. Growing up in a village with no road or cars or phones or electricity, she was baffled by many aspects of her new life. She had never seen a bridge, for example, and panicked when they drove over one in a car. Celia was isolated by language as well, normally speaking the indigenous language of her village, K'Iche, and rarely using the Spanish that most Guatemalans speak. At home in Florida, Tecum spun a tale to his wife to explain Celia—a distant relative who needed work. And at first his wife went along with this. After all, Celia was a free domestic servant, docile and obedient. When his wife left the house, Tecum did what he liked with Celia.

One day Tecum's wife came home early and found Tecum and Celia in the bedroom. She exploded, but like Simon Legree, Tecum insisted he could "do as he liked." The screaming match turned into a fight, and soon Mrs. Tecum was thrown against the wall. Injured, she managed to get to the neighbors and call the police, which in their case was the county sheriff's office. A deputy was dispatched to the scene, and he investigated and arrested Tecum on a domestic violence charge. When the deputy wrote up his report later, he mentioned that there was a young woman on the scene who was crying but that the only information he could get from her was her age—fifteen. He never realized he was standing next to a slave.

Good police and sheriff's departments have a victim assistance officer, sometimes called a victim's advocate, and the next day the local victim assistance officer paid a visit to the Tecum house. She described what she found as Mrs. Tecum opened the door:

I immediately noticed this female sitting by the window. She was dressed in her native clothes, and she appeared very sad—a very sad female. . . . I identified or saw that she was the same female that was talked about in the report. Then after I spoke with Mrs. Tecum, she pointed at Celia and said that it was all her fault—for sleeping with her husband.[12]

The young woman looked terrified, and the officer sensed that something was wrong. Mrs. Tecum didn't want Celia to talk to the officer and tried to stop her, but the officer explained that it was her job to talk to everyone, and she took Celia out to the yard where they could speak by themselves. Celia told her that she wasn't in school and that

she had to work to pay Mr. Tecum 8,000 quetzal [just over $1,000]. And that's because she had to pay for the trip. At that point she started crying again, and she told me she felt like a slave. . . . She explained that all she did was work for him and that she had to obey him. She advised that she was scared of him, that all she wanted was to go back to her family in Guatemala.

Faced with a minor who "felt like a slave," who was not related to the family, who was working but not getting paid, and who was clearly distressed, the officer still wasn't sure what to do. She left and explained later:

When I left, I left kind of concerned about her statements, so then I . . . talked with the sergeant and a lieutenant, and they basically told me that they couldn't do anything and that I should just go ahead and call border patrol and have her deported. But then I immediately thought that that was not the solution for this situation, that there was something more to it.

We have to admit that there was a serious flaw, not in the work of this officer but in the American law enforcement system that finds it difficult to remember and enforce our antislavery laws even when a slave stands in front of an officer and says, "I feel like a slave." We can be thankful that this woman officer bucked her superiors and kept going back to Tecum's house. She knew something was wrong but couldn't fit whatever it was into the categories provided by the system. The officer explained what happened on her fifth visit:

So at that point I went back [to Tecum's house] with the Children and Families investigator and we told Celia that she was going to go with us. . . . Mrs. Tecum became very upset. She kept talking in her dialect to Celia, intimidating her—we could notice by the body motions. A deputy was keeping Mrs. Tecum on one side while we went to assist Celia, thinking that she had a bag of clothes and everything. We were kind of surprised when we saw Celia picking up a very small plastic bag—a Winn-Dixie bag—and all she had in that bag was a pair of underwear, a pair of shoes, some sandals, and that was it. So basically the only thing she had was her native dress that she was wearing. I told her that she was going to be fine and everything; she gave me a hug, and she thanked me for taking her out.

It took five visits before Celia was brought to safety, and luckily José Tecum did not make Celia disappear after the first or second or fourth visit. If anyone deserved a hug, it was this officer, for sticking to her guns and bringing Celia to freedom. She did great work, but it wasn't on the basis of training or experience in handling slavery cases. It wasn't because her superiors were keeping her up to date on American antislavery laws. It was because her gut told her "something here is not right."

"LIKE STARTING FROM ZERO"

If we compare the liberation of Celia with the freeing of the child slaves from the carpet looms that opened this chapter, we find the same cause for concern. In India police corruption is a key problem, but in the United States where police corruption is rare, the rescue of a slave still happens more by accident than intention. What if a different officer had gone to Tecum's house? What if the officer had done as her superiors suggested and just had Celia deported? What if the Tecums had had the sense to hide Celia? How many of us—police, meter readers, shop workers, or hospital staff—have stood next to a slave in America (or Canada or Europe) and never known it? There are none so blind as those who will not see.

This notion of vision, of being able to see the slavery around us, is crucial. While this woman officer was straining to see the slave before her, officials in India were saying children couldn't be slaves—they were just migrant workers. Children in West Africa weren't being taken into slavery; they were being "placed" with families so they could earn a little and learn a trade, something like an apprenticeship. Those who are benefiting from slavery are creating smoke screens to obscure our vision; most of the rest of us just live in a fog of ignorance. Is it any surprise that the crime of slavery is wrapped in many layers of rationalizations, justifications, and plain bald lies? Part of our job is to pierce this fog of lies and ignorance and to recognize the slavery around us whether in our own communities or in other countries. Later, the woman officer said that building up an understanding of Celia's case was "like starting from zero." So it is with most of us; we abhor the idea of slavery, but we're not sure what it looks like in the real world.

THE BLUEPRINT

This book not only tells the stories of people in slavery; it also presents the beginning of a plan for the eradication of slavery. In this chapter I've told three stories about people with little power and few resources who are *getting people out of slavery*. These people may be heroes, but they are also people just like you and me. These are ordinary people who just couldn't wait for someone else, some agency or government, to take action. The people in these stories and other individuals who have helped slaves to freedom didn't set out to be liberators. Usually they just responded in compassion to another person's suffering. They felt in their gut that something wasn't right. Maybe they didn't understand that the person they were helping was in slavery, but they did know that they couldn't leave that person in that situation one more day. And one rescue often leads to another. Many of these individuals have found that after a few years they've liberated dozens, even hundreds, more slaves. To their own astonishment, they find they have become a focus for other ordinary people who hate slavery and want to take action.

These people's heroism is inspiring, but is supporting them the way, or one of the ways, to bring slavery to an end? Is it effective? That is, do slaves come to real and sustainable freedom? Is it efficient? Is it good value for the money? If we have some money to spend on ending slavery, should we support these liberators and others like them? Those questions may sound cold after the warm way in which I described these liberators, but I am going to ask those same questions of every group working to bring slaves to freedom. The United Nations, national governments, states and districts, human rights organizations, churches, clubs, families, and individuals—all who are trying to end slavery—have to be accountable. We have to find the most effective and efficient paths to freedom and then spread them around the world.

This grassroots work of bringing slaves to freedom one by one is certainly effective. No gradual process takes place here, no long-winded policy development process; a moment of liberation happens, and usually an understanding that the ex-slave needs support in the transition to a life in freedom. This hands-on liberation is also good value for the money. To the slave, freedom may be priceless, but it still costs something, and small groups like Bal Vikas Ashram are bringing people out of slavery at a relatively low cost. One estimate across a number of such groups in northern India (by Ginny Baumann, Free the Slaves partnership director) puts the cost at around $100 per slave liberated, and sometimes it is a good deal less than that. Even in a high-cost country like the United States, the liberation of Celia probably cost no more than $1,000, counting the wages of the officer and deputy and the costs of running the sheriff's department. Yes, the subsequent investigation, arrest, trial, conviction, and imprisonment of Tecum cost taxpayers more, but Celia was freed after the deputy visited five times during a single long day's work. In all these cases, of course, protection and rehabilitation add further costs.

What about the cost of freeing the children in Ghana? Even though Ghana is a poor country with low wages and low overhead, freeing the children there can be more expensive than in India. Every liberation is an equation with a new set of variables. In Ghana one variable is that the traffickers lie to the parents about where their children are being taken. The children normally end up some three hundred miles from their homes, and much effort and expense are needed to find them. Add to that the costs of wresting them away from the fishermen who hold them, of medical care and rehabilitative support, of returning them home, and then of working with their families to build up their understanding of trafficking and their earning potential so that no child will be taken again. This is what it takes to make this liberation effective, to make sure no more children will be taken from the home village and that the freed slave children will go on to receive an education and lead productive lives.

This liberation equation is still being worked out, but it looks as if real freedom for child slaves in Ghana will cost about $500 to $600 per child.[13]

Is the cost of bringing slaves to freedom one by one efficient? Does it represent value for the money? One way to answer that question is to apply that cost to all the slaves in the world. What if we have to pay $500 a slave to free all twenty-seven million people trapped in slavery today? The answer is a big number, $13.5 billion, but it is actually a small number on the global stage. Thirteen billion dollars is the amount New York City will receive from the U.S. government over the next few years to spend on roads, buses, and subways. It amounts to about $47 for each U.S. citizen.

MAKING IT HAPPEN

Money alone will not solve the problem. We have to change minds, laws, customs, and our way of doing business to bring slavery to an end. In the case of these individual liberators, we must do a number of things to support them and expand the field of their work. These brave men and women reach out to slaves and pull them to freedom. What can we do to help them? We know that, at the least, the following six actions will keep the liberation of individual slaves on track.

PROTECT THE LIBERATORS

Most of us know about the terrible dangers faced by the "conductors" on the Underground Railroad before the American Civil War. Some will remember Elijah Lovejoy, killed by a mob for being a conductor and publishing an antislavery newspaper, or Amos Dresser, whipped through the streets of Memphis for working to free slaves. There were martyrs to the cause of abolition then, and sadly there are martyrs today. In India, antislavery workers are threatened, beaten, falsely imprisoned, and sometimes killed. In Pakistan, Nepal, and across North and West Africa, they face the same violence. The work of many liberators is disrupted by the need to find safety when the thugs come. On the front lines of liberation, these workers must run for cover every few weeks or months. We can do better than this. We know that when people around the world learn about a prisoner of conscience locked up in a dictatorship, the attention, letters, and pressure brought by average citizens can save the prisoner's life. When a school or church or town "adopts" a person held unjustly and keeps the bright light of public attention focused, torture and disappearance are much less likely to happen. The liberators who are risking their lives around the world need this same protection. Since they cannot always rely on the normal protections of the police, and sometimes the police are a threat, they need our help. We must identify them by name and do what is necessary to ensure their safety as they bring slaves to freedom. Yes, there will always be risks—theirs is a dangerous job—but we need to help make it as safe as possible.

GIVE THE LIBERATORS THE TOOLS THEY NEED TO DO THEIR JOBS

I have visited liberators all over the world, and I know they need more tools, which are often little things that most of us take for granted. In Brazil, the work of freeing slaves would have been made much more effective with a few additional cell phones and some jeeps. In India, the Sankalp organization has been freeing whole villages from debt-bondage slavery, reaching these remote rural slaves *by bicycle*. When a recent grant included about $3,000 to buy Sankalp three motorcycles, the number of villages that could be reached by three of its workers more than doubled. Money for salaries for more workers and for more motorcycles would double that again. Functioning schools can keep children out of slavery; in most of the developing world, you can keep a village school going for less than $5,000 a year. Some office space is needed here, a working telephone there, some training for this worker, and a restful holiday for that one. (Once an antislavery worker builds up skill and experience, the last thing we need is to lose the person to burnout.) The end of slavery will be built, in part, on these small expenditures. At the same time, these expenditures have to be efficient, to provide good value for money. Dumping cash on anyone is a recipe for disaster. The heroes fighting slavery deserve the right tools and a decent life. Our goal has to be the right amount of money to the right liberators at the right time.

WRITE AND ENFORCE EFFECTIVE ANTISLAVERY LAWS

Slavery is a crime, and we can rightly ask: why are a bunch of charity workers expected to do all the work to end it? In every country of the world, there is some sort of law against slavery, but many, perhaps most, of these laws are outdated, hard to apply to modern slavery, and inadequately enforced. For example, although the United States amended its Constitution more than a hundred years ago to abolish legal slavery and passed other laws against such things as peonage, it didn't have a clear law on human trafficking and slavery, with adequate punishments in force, until 2001. Given the seriousness of these crimes, the small penalty mandated by laws around the world is astounding. If murder is the most serious of crimes, slavery follows close on its heels. Slavery is kidnapping and torture and theft and assault and often rape all rolled together. In spite of that, in many countries the crime is punishable by a few years of imprisonment and a fine. Almost no country faces up to the question of compensation to ex-slaves. When we remember that slavery is the theft of a person's labor, of the person's economic potential, it seems obvious that the antislavery laws should point to ways to make some restitution for what was stolen. We need better laws and rigorous enforcement so that charity workers don't have to do the work of government and police. Help is available to write such laws; international legal scholars have spent years developing model laws. The richer countries are ready to share resources to educate officials and the public and to promulgate the laws. When a local liberator can turn to the police and point to a clear and specific violation of antislavery law and when the police know exactly how to enforce that law (and get the support of their boss), the flow of slaves to freedom will dramatically increase.

TRAIN, MOTIVATE, AND MOBILIZE LAW ENFORCEMENT

Police at the local level are slow to enforce antislavery laws. Think of Celia in south Florida, where slavery is a hidden crime. If you are not aware that the crime could be happening on your turf, you may not see it even when you are looking right at it. America has a good law, but many police have not been adequately trained to enforce it. A policeman I met in California said, "If I find a bag of cocaine, I know what to do, but if I open the back of a truck and find ten people, are they smuggled? Are they trafficked? Which one is the perpetrator and which are the victims? And the chances are that they will speak a language that I don't know, and the important first minutes of investigation will be blocked." Just as law enforcement had to get up to speed and stay abreast of computer crime, police need training and help to bust the crime of slavery.

Today, the rate at which we are cracking down on this crime is nothing to be proud of. Note that the FBI reports about seventeen thousand murders every year in the United States. Not surprisingly every police department of any size has a homicide unit. Now compare that situation to the fact that the government says about seventeen thousand people are trafficked into slavery in the United States every year. When it comes to murder, more than twelve thousand of those seventeen thousand homicides will be "cleared," that is, solved and brought to trial. How many slavery and trafficking cases were brought to trial last year? Slightly over one hundred. Imagine the public outrage if America's police could solve only one hundred murders a year out of the seventeen thousand committed! The day will come when most police departments have a slavery and trafficking unit next door to the homicide unit, but every day that passes until that happens is another day in hell for thousands of slaves.

If a rich country like the United States, with generally good law enforcement, is so far behind in addressing this crime, imagine the situation in poorer countries with indifferent law enforcement. Those countries will need a lot of help. But money spent there will stop the crime in Europe and North America. Most people in slavery in the richer countries are trafficked from poorer countries. This supply of slaves can be choked off at the source if we help other countries to train and motivate their police. I'll discuss this more in chapter 5 and will show how U.S. government programs that already exist can easily be adapted to this need.

CLONE THE LIBERATORS

Of course, we can't literally clone these heroes, but we can say, "Where there is one liberator today, there will be three next year." With no shortage of people ready to do this work in spite of the danger, this is simply a resource question. We need to find the best liberators and then invest in giving them apprentices, in that way extending their reach and activity.

More liberators will emerge as people come to know more about slavery in their own countries. Louis never set out to be a hero, but he rescued slaves in Maryland all by himself. A recent in-depth analysis of a number of slavery and trafficking cases in the United States showed that Joe and Jane Public were crucial to freeing slaves in one-third of the cases. These Good Samaritans usually had no idea they were dealing with slavery, just that a person needed help and needed it right away. When every citizen knows how to recognize a possible slavery case, the number of freed slaves will dramatically increase.

HELP FREED SLAVES HEAL

For many freed slaves, liberation is just the first step on a long road. The mental and physical violence of slavery leaves deep scars on the body and the mind. Incredibly, we know next to nothing about the best ways to help freed slaves. Whole research centers and institutes and journals and specialists are devoted to helping victims of torture, but for the victims of slavery, who are often tortured themselves, there are none. This true emergency needs an emergency response, and we will have to learn as we go. There are some experienced people around the world, like the staff at Bal Vikas Ashram, but they tend to spend all their time helping freed slaves. In the same way that we want to provide the best liberators with apprentices, our initial goal must be to provide the best rehabilitators with helpers and people who will document what works best and then spread that knowledge around.

We must also ask freed slaves what they need. Too often, we view ex-slaves merely as victims, expecting them to be pathetic and grateful but not to actively participate in their own rebirth to freedom. Sometimes, when you ask ex-slaves what they need, the answer is "forty acres and a mule" or its equivalent in Africa, Asia, South America, or Europe. Slavery feeds on poverty, insecurity, and ignorance. Every freed slave who has economic options and understands human rights is a beacon of hope to enslaved or enslavable neighbors. Later, in chapter 8, I will look more closely at how to reduce the poverty that supports slavery.

Are these six actions everything we can do to help those individuals who are liberating slaves? Of course not. We need to spend more time asking the liberators what they need, and watching closely as they go about bringing slaves to freedom. I have asked a number of liberators what they think needs doing, and their answers are often not about their situation or the local conditions but about much larger factors in their country or the whole world. The next chapters expand the focus, looking at what needs to happen in communities and countries around the globe to eradicate slavery, and they ask what we can do as consumers and businesspeople. But while we are achieving those goals, slaves will still need to be freed. This means these liberators must be properly supported and have the resources they need. Many people in slavery today will not survive, especially if they must wait for a fifth visit or for people's realization that they are standing next to a slave.

A final question has to be answered about these individual liberators: if we expand their work as much as we can, how many people come out of slavery as a result? In India alone I can think of individuals in four separate regions who have freed thousands of slaves on a shoestring. Others are doing this dangerous work in Pakistan, Nepal, Ghana, Thailand,

Laos, Brazil, and on and on. We won't know till we try, but I suspect that hundreds of thousands of people could be freed in this way in a relatively short time if we put the right resources into the hands of the right people. This is not the way to end slavery for good, but it is the job that needs doing now. These liberators are like the emergency aid workers fighting an epidemic. When people are dying *today* someone must act *today*. There are slaves waiting to be freed. As we begin the long process of turning the giant supertankers of government and building the international alliance against slavery, usually these liberators alone stand between slaves and a lifetime of slavery.

WHAT WE CAN DO AS INDIVIDUALS TO FREE MORE SLAVES

This chapter is about the power of individuals to liberate slaves and to help them achieve lives of dignity. Every one of us, no matter our position in life, has a role in the eradication of slavery. Here are five things individuals can do to help end slavery.

1. Know the warning signs of slavery and human trafficking, and report suspicious behavior to your local antitrafficking shelter, social services provider, or police station. Or call the twenty-four-hour National Human Trafficking Resource Center hotline (1-888-373-7888) or the U.S. Department of Justice's hotline (1-888-428-7581, during regular business hours).

2. Help educate people in your community about how to identify slavery and trafficking, particularly people like law enforcement officials, medical workers, restaurant inspectors, transit workers, and service station employees who are most likely to come in contact with victims. A community member's guide to fighting human trafficking and slavery, a guide that includes the warning signs of slavery, is available from Free the Slaves.

3. Adopt and clone the liberators both overseas and at home by giving a regular contribution to an antislavery organization that frees people from slavery and helps them rebuild their lives. See www.freedomdirect.net.

4. Bring the antislavery message to your faith community or other community group; use your moral leadership to help others in your community join in this inspiring opportunity to make history. One good way is to share this book with others.

5. If you are a community leader, or just a concerned individual, make your city one of the inaugural Slavery-Free Cities. See details at www.slaveryfreecities.org.

Children work fifteen hours a day on the expensive carpets. Their fingers are dipped in oil and lit with a match when they begin to bleed. (Free the Slaves | Peggy Callahan)

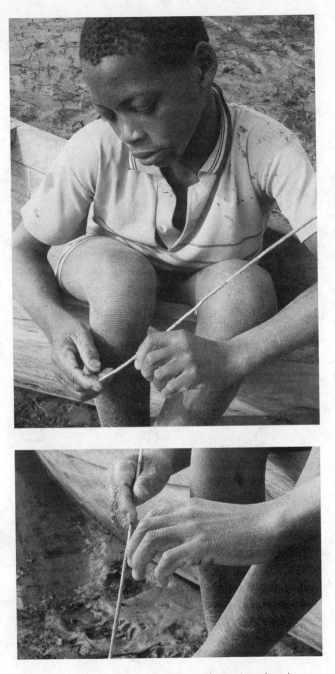

This boy in Ghana had spent days in the water when he was
discovered by an antislavery worker from APPLE. Hungry and
tired, with hands and feet swollen and cracked, he continues to
work. (Free the Slaves | Lookie Amuzu)

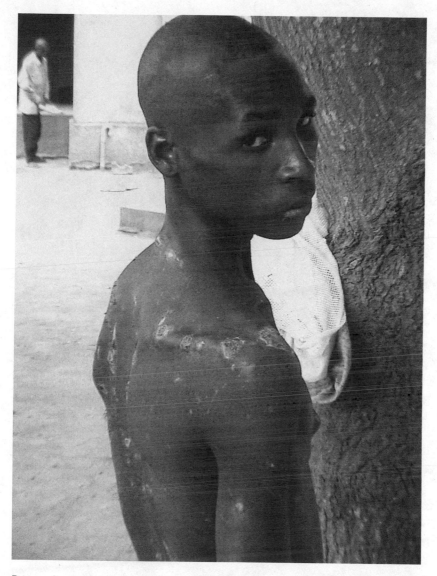

Drissa, after being severely beaten not long before he was freed from slavery on a farm in the Ivory Coast. (True Vision | Brian Woods)

Rambho being freed from the looms. Once he was freed, traffickers contacted his mother and told her that he had been thrown in jail. (Free the Slaves | Supriya Awasthi)

Activists from Bal Vikas Ashram are traveling to remote villages in northern India where traffickers prey on young children. (Free the Slaves | Peggy Callahan)

This couple (pictured with their grandson) was trapped in debt bondage slavery their entire lives. Upon being offered a chance for freedom, they expressed concern about the loss of their home, the hut behind them. (Free the Slaves | Supriya Awasthi)

Children at a village training in Ivory Coast organized by the International Cocoa Initiative. Their signs explain to their parents that they are too young for heavy and dangerous farm work. (ICI | Katherine Owen)

Activists from Bal Vikas Ashram in a remote village where children are trafficked. Not long before this photo was taken villagers felt powerless to act against traffickers. (Free the Slaves | Justine Schmidt)

Street theater is a powerful tool used around the world to educate villagers about trafficking. In Nepal hundreds of people turned out to see this play about sweet-talking traffickers who force young girls into sex slavery in India. (Free the Slaves | Peggy Callahan)

A freed slave, a graduate of Bal Vikas Ashram, back home in Bochi village with his mother and a cow he bought with his rehabilitation funds. (Free the Slaves | Supriya Awasthi)

Freed slave children at the Bal Vikas Ashram load their plates at lunchtime. Good nutrition and plenty to eat are crucially important to children who have been malnourished for years. (Free the Slaves | Supriya Awasthi)

Ramphal, now freed from slavery in the quarries in Sonebarsa. He was one of eight men jailed when a slave owner was killed there. (Free the Slaves | Peggy Callahan)

Children freed from slavery in the quarries in Sonebarsa, now attending a village school. Seated in the middle is Ramphal's son. (Free the Slaves | Peggy Callahan)

Rose was enslaved in the suburbs of Washington, D.C. She ran away after years of abuse. A Good Samaritan took her in and then with Rose's help rescued more Cameroonian slaves. (Free the Slaves | Peggy Callahan)

4

Home-Grown Freedom

We're never going to get there, unless we all go together.

FANNIE LOU HAMER

Fannie Lou Hamer is one of my heroes. The granddaughter of slaves, she grew up as a sharecropper in rural Mississippi. In 1962, when she was forty-four years old, civil rights workers came to her little Delta town, and she learned a secret that had been kept from her all her life: she had a constitutionally guaranteed right to vote. When the civil rights workers asked for volunteers for the dangerous job of going to the courthouse to register to vote, her hand was the first to shoot into the air. For trying to register to vote, she was thrown off the land she farmed, shot at, threatened, beaten by the police, and jailed, but she, and many others in her community, never gave up. She later said, "The only thing they could do to me was to kill me, and it seemed like they'd been trying to do that a little bit at a time ever since I could remember." African Americans in towns like hers all across the Deep South began to organize nonviolent resistance, including boycotts, sit-ins, and teach-ins, and they kept turning up to register to vote time after time, no matter how much abuse they suffered. Fannie Lou Hamer may be best known for her statement about life under the segregationists in the South: "I am sick and tired of being sick and tired!" But the words that I remember best are her pronouncement on freedom: "We're never going to get there, unless we all go together."

It really wasn't so long ago that American citizens like Fannie Lou Hamer were fighting for basic freedoms. Their experiences can help us understand how slave communities around the world are fighting for their freedom today, and what we need to do to help them achieve that freedom. Chapter 3 was about individuals who help slaves come to freedom; this chapter is about communities and groups that join together to end slavery. Some of these communities are almost all slaves, and this raises an important point about how we understand slavery and freedom.

It is easy to think about slavery in the simple terms of evil slaveholders and innocent slaves, a crime that is truly black and white in its moral contrast. Often, from this viewpoint, slaves are victims—helpless, dependent, a little pathetic—who need to be rescued, and we expect them to be grateful for a chance at freedom. What this view misses is the resilience and strength of people caught in slavery, their endurance, intelligence, and compassion. Yes, some slaves are so beaten down that they find it hard to get up. Others, like Fannie Lou Hamer, have been denied the knowledge of their own rights and freedoms. But a tiny seed of knowledge can grow into a powerful, unstoppable push to freedom. If we are going to help slaves make this push, we need to recognize and respect the power that resides in every person in slavery, especially when slaves join together and make a collective decision that they are leaving slavery for good.

THE SILENT REVOLUTION

Fannie Lou Hamer risked her life for the right to vote. In northern India, a village of slaves risked everything to come out of slavery. In the state of Uttar Pradesh, open pit quarries for gravel, building stone, and silica sand (used for glass making) are dug out by hand. The quarries are ugly scars on the land, and most of them are in national forests that are supposedly under government protection. To stand there you would never dream you are in a forest, for there are only a tiny handful of trees as far as the eye can see. Before Indian independence in 1948, a great sweep of this land, hundreds of square miles and hundreds of villages, belonged to a nobleman, the Rajah of Shankargahr (*rajah* means "king" or "prince"). When India achieved freedom from British control, the vast feudal holdings of local royalty became part of the new nation, and all over the country the forests and mineral deposits were taken over by the national government for protection. All except in Shankargahr, that is;

somehow after independence the rajah's family managed to hold on to 120 square kilometers of land containing forty-six villages, many of them involved in quarrying. Not long after, a local judge handed the rajah a lease to the mineral rights for all this land in perpetuity. Obviously, a prince is not going to dig in his own quarries, so for a cut of the profits he subcontracted the control of villages and quarries to other people.

About forty families lived in one of these quarrying villages, a dusty place called Sonebarsa. All of these families were Kols, an ethnic group near the bottom of India's steep ladder of caste and discrimination. All the families of Sonebarsa—every man, woman, and child—were slaves, locked into hereditary debt bondage. Most of them had no idea what freedom meant. One of these was Ramphal, a young man who was the son and grandson of slaves in the quarry and whose children had been born into debt-bondage slavery. He described his life then: "If I would move in my house or out of my house, if I wanted to sit somewhere or get up, if I wanted to eat, if I wanted to drink—anything I wanted to do, I required permission. Freedom of movement was something I was not aware of; I didn't know it existed. And it wasn't just me; my mother, my father, my grandparents, had to live through this, generation after generation. It was deep in our minds."[1]

Every day Ramphal, his wife and children, and the other families of the village did the hard work in the quarry. The men broke stone with primitive hammers and spikes. Without protective clothing or goggles, the sharp flying chips of rock peppered their skin and cut into their eyes. Smaller and younger workers moved the rocks, dragging them to be broken, pounding small stones into gravel or sand, or hauling away the pieces. From the age of three or four, children marched with baskets of gravel or sand on their heads and dumped them into piles or waiting trucks. There was little to eat, infant mortality was high, and old age came quickly as lungs filled with mineral dust. Tuberculosis, malaria, and silicosis were constant companions. As they worked, the villagers destroyed the environment they lived in, the "protected" forests were cut down to get at the minerals underneath, and the strip mining speeded up the erosion of the remaining soil. Over many generations lush woodland became barren desert. For all their work, the villagers received a mixture of food and a few rupees, barely enough to keep them from starving. For the citizens of Sonebarsa, life was unchanging and unchangeable.

Legally, these families could simply walk away from these bogus debts and their bondage, but practically they could not, for several reasons.

Like all slaves, they lived under the threat of violence. If families tried to move away or even to find a new master in hope of better treatment, the slaveholder's thugs would retaliate with beatings, rape, and destruction of their huts and few possessions. Families were completely vulnerable to these attacks because no law, no police, no group would protect them, and they had no knowledge of their rights. If a family survived the beatings and left the stone-breaking work, they were likely to starve. In this deeply impoverished area, they would find no work, and the devastated natural environment offered no way to make a living. For the handful who got away, without access to jobs, health care, community support, or credit, independence was impossible to sustain. If they needed medicine or food, if they needed clothes, or even if they needed to bury someone, they would be drawn into illegal debts and bondage. Any family crisis could tip them back into slavery.

Like many of the villages nearby, Sonebarsa was a machine for slaveholders to make money, but that machine began to break down in the late 1990s. The grit that first began to jam the gears of this moneymaker was a quiet visit one evening by a worker from the Sankalp organization, which was formed to help the poorest of the poor. At first, Sankalp sent health care teams to visit villages like Sonebarsa, provided child care while the parents were in the quarries, and helped some adults learn to read at night. This work made the lives of the slaves a little better, but it soon became apparent that this was a Band-Aid fix on a gaping wound. Giving the slaves health care and other support simply increased the profits made by slaveholders and did nothing to change the repression endured by the slaves. For a while the organization was puzzled; clearly these slaves needed health care and other support, but how could that help be provided without subsidizing the slaveholder? A friendly lawyer tried bringing a suit under Indian law against bonded labor slavery, but that didn't help either. The main result of the case was that the slaves named in it were thrown out of their homes and left to starve; meanwhile the case went nowhere in the local courts.

The breakthrough for Sankalp came in 1998 when bonded families in a village some miles from Sonebarsa asked a simple question: why don't we get our own mining lease? Although many mining leases are controlled by the rich and powerful, under Indian law public land can be made available for mining by the very poor as a job creation program. The slaves of this village may have been illiterate and uneducated, but they knew how to run a quarry. After all, they'd been doing that for generations. Why not use the craft they knew, use their own skills to build better lives? The foundation of basic education, and the knowledge of rights provided by Sankalp, had prepared the villagers to figure out their own solution.

Their idea made sense, but it was also a scary and radical one. Getting their own lease meant going into direct competition with the slaveholders, the other mineral contractors, local government officials, even the rajah himself. No one had ever tried such a thing, and if they failed, they would face starvation, violent retribution, and a return to slavery. What's more, leases aren't free. Where was the money going to come from? Typically, a family would have a few pots and cooking utensils, one or two wooden bed frames strung with rope, and not more than two sets of clothes for each person. That's it. Together the villagers made a desperate gamble. From their tiny purses came the widow's mite, a bit of jewelry here, and a few rupees there. Tools, even the beds they slept on, were pawned to raise the down payment on the lease. With help from Sankalp for the legal necessities, the lease was awarded, and a revolution occurred, but not before the villagers suffered even more abuse.

The months between applying for the lease and getting a response became a hungry, frightening time. When the contractors found out about the lease application, they threw the villagers out of the quarry. For several months the villagers scraped by eating weeds and roots, hoping but not knowing if their gamble would pay off. Finally the news came: the lease was theirs! Facing down threats and attacks from the slaveholders and the contractors, they took over running the new quarry for themselves.

If you have ever known the difference between working for yourself and working for an uncaring and greedy boss, you won't be surprised that the villagers' productivity and profits shot up dramatically. Cutting out the contractors and middlemen, the quarry workers began to sell their stone and sand to whoever offered the best price, and they kept all of the proceeds. From day one, they took their children out of the quarry and put them in school. Then they began to pay taxes on the earnings from their quarry. The local tax officials were amazed. The slaveholders and contractors had rarely bothered to pay the taxes they owed; it was simpler just to bribe or bully the officials.

One of the women of the village talked about her experience:

As bonded laborers, we were completely under the control of the contractors. Always we had to work—even when we were sick, we were forced to work. Then we got familiar with the laws and formed a self-help group. When we became free of the bondage of the contractor, they stopped giving us any food or any kind of wage, and we reached a point of starvation. We used to live on these mustard leaves. We would share even a small amount of rice among all of us. This went on for six months. After we got the stone quarrying lease, we started earning much more. Now we get 100 rupees a day.

Witnessing the profound change that came with the mining lease, Sankalp and its local allies knew they had found a way forward. These slaves didn't need job training; they just needed a chance to do the work they knew well. Working for themselves, families could gain better conditions and freedom. Soon, Sankalp's workers were fanning out to other villages of quarry slaves with the story of how bonded workers had freed themselves by taking control of their own quarry. One of these villages was Sonebarsa.

Sonebarsa was known for the misery of its inhabitants. A woman of Sonebarsa said, "Life under the slaveholders was complete hell." Ramphal agreed: "Each time I look back at the life I lived in Sonebarsa, my heart is filled with grief and with sadness." Women and girls were assaulted and raped by the slaveholders, and no one could stop them. Ramphal explained, "You have to understand, what they wanted to do they could do. For example, an eight-year-old girl was sitting in her house, and the landlords came and set fire to the house. The girl died." For the families of Sonebarsa, life was unremitting toil mixed with intervals of terror.

The first Sankalp workers found families completely cowed, broken by the cruelty of the slaveholders, but they took time and kept talking, gently and slowly introducing the ideas of freedom and self-reliance. When the slaveholders and quarry contractors learned that their slaves were holding meetings, they had the Sankalp workers beaten up and thrown out of the village. Although barred from the village, the Sankalp workers had already sparked a determination among the workers, who said they would not stop their meetings. In retaliation, the slaveholders increased their attacks on the women and girls of the village. "The people of Sankalp came repeatedly, they would talk to us, and awareness spread," said Ramphal. "On the basis of what they said and what we thought among ourselves, we started walking the path." Quietly, the first self-help group was formed, careful plans were made, and for the first time in their lives, the people of Sonebarsa began to dream a little.

Feeling their strength growing, the villagers organized a meeting to elect someone to be the village head. Sankalp workers knew that such a public meeting would be the moment when the slaveholders would try to smash the movement once and for all. Liberation is more a process than an event. As slaves move to freedom, as their minds open to liberty, their masters may not notice at first, but when freedom erupts publicly, slaveholders know they will need to use force to snuff it out. In every liberation comes a moment of crisis, physical threat, and potentially violent struggle. For Sonebarsa, that moment had come.

Fearing violence, Sankalp workers had asked freed slaves from other villages to come and support Sonebarsa in its first steps, and thousands turned out. Sonebarsa's reputation for violence and atrocities had spread through the region, and neighboring villages wanted to do what they could to bring this terror to an end. From sixty villages, some 3,500 people came to join in Sonebarsa's first public meeting. Faced with such a crowd, the slaveholders could do nothing to prevent the gathering, but when the meeting was over and people starting leaving, armed thugs began to beat some of the women. As villagers ran to protect the women, a vicious melee broke out, and villagers began to throw building stones at the thugs. When the fight was over, one of the slaveholders was dead.

Scapegoats had to be found. Ramphal and seven other villagers were falsely accused of the killing and put in jail, but the retaliation didn't stop there. Within days the slaveholders, contractors, and their thugs attacked again. This time the large gathering of people from the other villages was gone, and the thugs did their worst. Armed men stormed through the village, dragging people from their homes and beating them, looting homes, and throwing the villagers' possessions into a great bonfire roaring in the center of the village. Then they torched the houses, destroying everything the villagers had except for the clothes on their backs. The villagers fled, many of them frightened that they had lost all of the rice and other food they had stored to feed their children. One village woman, Jyothi, explained the shock and sadness she felt: "Not only were my eyes weeping; my very soul was shattered. It was almost as though it were ripped apart." With eight of the men locked up, the women and children suffered. One of Jyothi's children died after the attack, yet she and the other women held on. "My husband was in jail, my children were homeless, but even then, because of the change that had come, I knew something was going to happen. I knew it," she said.

Scattered in all directions, the villagers found that the self-help groups in other villages, also made up of recently freed slaves, were ready to take them in and feed them. The other groups also began to collect money, food, clothes, and tools for the scattered families. Slowly, the families of Sonebarsa began to find their way back together. Sankalp arranged for lawyers to press for the release of the men who had been imprisoned. After eight long months, the men were freed. More months passed as the families scraped together what little work and food they could. Most of the families had relocated to a plot of national forest land near the now-destroyed village of Sonebarsa, but they faced continuing violence from the slaveholders. In spite of all this, they had hope. Sankalp workers were pushing hard for a mining lease for the people of Sonebarsa. Finally, a full year after the destruction of their village, the lease was awarded, and the villagers had a foundation on which to build new lives.

With control over their livelihoods, the villagers quickly began to see change. As their incomes increased, they got more and better food, and they immediately pulled the children from work in the quarries and put them in school every day. Emboldened by their freedom and emerging power, they decided to build a new village near the quarry. Using stone from their own quarry, they constructed new homes, and they started planting trees around the village. When they were finished, they met to choose a name for their new home. The name was not to be *Sonebarsa*, the village of their slavery. Instead they chose a new name, *Azad Nagar*, which means "Land of Freedom."

Quarry work is still mind-numbing and backbreaking, but hard work in freedom is light compared to that in slavery. Ramphal talks about his work now: "The work is the same, but there is a fundamental difference. I'm master of my own mind, my own destiny. That is a big difference. Today I am free not only to live as I want to live but to hope for a better tomorrow." Jyothi adds, "My children are in school, I have food in my stomach; ever since we started to hold the hand of Sankalp, I love my life."

GETTING FREE AND GIVING BACK

Those of us who live in rich countries may feel that we can learn little from the poor of the developing world. This may be one of our greatest failings. Yes, there are sad, harmful, and backward aspects to the cultures of many poor nations. But if we are honest, we will see that among our wealth and sophistication there is also sadness, harm to our children, and selfishness that is backward and cruel. We have high ideals and great gifts to offer; ex-slaves have great gifts to share as well. What has amazed and humbled me when I have met freed slaves is their dignity and remarkable lack of bitterness. While you might expect them to devote their lives to recrimination and revenge, they simply seem too busy building their new freedoms to hate anyone.

The citizens of Azad Nagar have certainly been busy. The village education committee meets to oversee and improve the local school. The villagers work together to make sure there is a free school lunch every day, ensuring that every child has the nutrition needed for learning and that someone is there to make sure the teacher is doing a good job. Some adults study with their children at night, learning to read and write. The education committee is also the springboard to other issues. In it the women plan community improvements, work to build up their local school, and chart their campaign to get a government clinic built nearby. The major role played by women in the village is no surprise to Sankalp workers. One explained: "You know, when slavery exists in any area, the victims of slavery are primarily women. They have been victimized so severely and deeply that when empowerment is started, they rise up. They are more open to the idea of freedom, and they are more open to the idea of forming groups." As the women of Azad Nagar began to push for change on their own, the Sankalp workers knew that their main work was nearly done, that it was time for them to move on to the next village in need of liberation. While a worker still drops in regularly to check on them, he explained. "That's what we want. If they are independently able to ask for their own demands and rights, and without my direction, then I am free to move on to someone else." Sadly, he won't need to go far.

There are hundreds of villages in Uttar Pradesh in slavery, and thousands and thousands of slaves. India has the largest number of slaves in the world; the government gives no clear estimate, but most experts suggest there are eight to ten million. Most are in some form of debt bondage. Sankalp works in only one area of one state, and that work is dangerous. "I have faced pressure, threats to kill me, threats to beat me up," said one worker. "But you know, if we have taken up voluntarily the responsibility of bringing about a revolution, then the danger is something we have to accept as a part of life. That's it." Sankalp's advantage is that freedom spreads like a virus. Once introduced into a community, fear, danger, violence, hunger, and death must be faced, but slaves are drawn to freedom the way the starving are drawn to the smell of food. Ramphal knows it can take a long time for this desire to burst out in a community, but he says, "That doesn't matter. We keep telling them [people in other villages], showing them our life, the life we lead now, and they are keen to get out of bondage, so it will happen. It's just a question of time."

GETTING OUR HEADS TOGETHER

In order to understand how communities can join together to free slaves, we have to look closely at how that conscious collective decision to *do something* comes about. Anyone who has ever tried to organize something as simple as a neighborhood bake sale knows that reaching agreement and consensus can be a drawn-out, frustrating experience. Yes, if your family is in slavery, you are motivated. Then again, if you have grown up in slavery, chances are that you have no idea about how to start bringing people together. Slaveholders everywhere work to isolate and disempower their victims. Slaves are denied the right to make even the most fundamental decisions—what to do, whom to marry, what to eat, where to live. On the other hand, perhaps because of their lack of experience, they are able to more easily follow the first small steps. Ending slavery in a village, a region, a country, or in the whole world takes not one but hundreds of linked decisions. There has to be the first life-changing, bet-the-farm decision of commitment, the decision in which all of us, slave and free alike, have to say out loud, "The end of slavery starts *now!*" But then what?

For the villagers of Sonebarsa, the decisions grew like the beautiful layers of a pearl. The tiny grit, the gentle, agitating voice of a Sankalp activist, was the seed around which that pearl of freedom could grow. The layers were added as more and more villagers, especially the women, thought things through and decided together that other goals had to be turned into realities. The things they were desperate to change are not hard to imagine: an end to the rapes and attacks, food for their families, the chance of education for their children, dignity for their men. Like Fannie Lou Hamer, they were "sick and tired of being sick and tired." They had nothing to lose but their lives, and they decided that freedom was worth the gamble.

These were slaves deciding to organize as a community to get themselves out of slavery, but it is also true that communities that are not enslaved, like our own neighborhoods, towns or cities, also have to make a commitment to rid themselves of slavery. We know for a fact that there are slaves in more than seventy American cities, and the number is likely to be much higher than that.[2] Now you might think that it must be easier to bring about the collective decision to end slavery in a country where people are used to making decisions together, where you don't have to put your life on the line to get something done. If only that were true! San Diego had to face up to slavery on its doorstep, and struggled to find the right way forward.

A WAKE-UP CALL IN SAN DIEGO

About thirty minutes north of San Diego is the town of Oceanside, where strawberries and other fruit grow in fields bordered by beds of golden reeds. Waving gently in the ocean breezes, the reeds concealed an ugly business. Pimps pushed paths through the tall reeds, and hollowed out small "caves" along the paths. There on the ground, with scraps of clothing, bits of blankets, used condoms, spit, empty bottles, and trash, teenagers were on their backs, forced to have sex with the two hundred men a day who prowled these paths.

One of these girls was Reina. At the age of fifteen, Reina was slipped across the border from Mexico by human traffickers, who lured her with the promise of a job. She was quickly put to work, forced to have sex with itinerant farmworkers in the reed caves. Because she was pretty, more men wanted her and used her every day. In Reina's case, and for the girls enslaved with her, we have something very rare—an independent witness, "Patricia," a Mexican doctor who supplied condoms and care to these girls. Like other HIV/AIDS workers around the world, Patricia was allowed into the darkest holes of slavery only if she promised not to intervene. She explained to the newspaper El Universal,

> If I wanted to help these girls I had to develop a relationship with the pimps. I learned that in the city of Guadalajara, where I worked for many years. I had to convert myself into someone who doesn't judge, who doesn't express opinions, but only listens. . . . When I came here, in one hour I counted that one little girl had been with 35 men, one after the other. She just lifted her skirt. . . . Generally they do this to the girls who are no longer virgins. They spend six months being transported back and forth through the various camps.[3]

Virgins are too valuable to put out in the dirt for the migrant workers to use; their degradation is more likely to begin with a gringo. Patricia explained that local American men contact the pimps looking for a "cherry girl." Later, once she has been broken in by the men Patricia calls "red-necks . . . white American men," the girl will be shuffled from camp to camp.

This was Reina's life, though she was not a virgin when she was brought to the United States. Born in Puebla, Mexico, Reina lost her mother when she was seven, and her education ended after the second grade.[4] For a while she was cared for by her grandmother, but her grandmother died as well. She was left with her father, and her life turned ugly. When she was eleven, he gave her as a gift to the local police chief, who raped her again and again. In time she became pregnant and gave birth to a little girl. Then, aged fourteen, she met pimp Arturo Lopez. In an age-old scam, Arturo convinced Reina that he was in love with her and that he could take her away from the abuse she was suffering. He persuaded her that if she would just leave her baby with some of his relatives, he would take her to the United States and fix her up with a good job.

Taken to Tijuana, Reina was forced to become a sex slave. When she resisted, she was told her baby would be killed. Soon a coyote slipped her into the United States. She was lodged in the town of Vista, California, and during the day was sent into the reed beds or other sex camps for migrant farm workers. Shattered emotionally and in great pain, she readily turned to the drugs and booze the traffickers offered her. For her the drugs offered a moment of oblivion and relief; for the slaveholders they were another tool used to control Reina and the other girls.

Perhaps it was the thought of her baby in the hands of the pimps; perhaps it was Reina's moment to be "sick and tired of being sick and tired." We don't know for sure, but after seven months, Reina made a run for it. Caught, she was beaten savagely by her pimp, Arturo. After a few days, she tried again. This time she made it and managed to reach the local police station. The police in turn called social services, as well as the county sheriff, who was known to be investigating human trafficking cases. Because Reina didn't fit the guidelines for child protection, social services called Marisa Ugarte of the Bilateral Safety Corridor Coalition (BSCC), who interviewed her at the police station. Marisa later described the girl she found: "She wore a tiny miniskirt and a jacket and was so overpainted that you almost couldn't recognize her real face. She looked to be between ten and fifteen years older than her real age. Her hair was short and dyed brown, her mouth was small, she had the eyes of a dreamer and a very seductive attitude. When we began to interview her she broke down and out came an agonized human being, drowning in pain."[5]

Marisa didn't know Reina, but she knew all about her situation. For months Marisa and the other members of the BSCC had been telling anyone who would listen that there were sex camps in the fields around San

Diego. At first the Mexican consulate didn't believe them, so they turned to the United Nations Children's Fund (UNICEF); then the consulate asked for a formal complaint supported by concrete evidence. A few weeks later, Reina escaped. Soon the BSCC was helping to coordinate a raft of agencies in building a case against Arturo and his employers, the Salazar crime family. In Mexico, the police and social services stepped in to rescue Reina's daughter. Reina began to heal slowly, but her recovery was rocky. Although the infections and injuries of her body could be treated, her mind was much more difficult to mend. At times she could tell her story and testify; at other times her mind would crack and she would regress to childhood, losing touch with reality. Many of her abusers melted away, and with Reina swinging between clarity and confusion, she was deemed an unreliable witness. Other girls, fearing for their families, refused to testify. Two of the three Salazar brothers went to prison for lesser crimes; the oldest brother remains free.

CROSSING BUREAUCRATIC BORDERS

With a case like Reina's, the community of San Diego knew they had a problem. Like citizens of many American cities, San Diegans had a hard time saying, "There is slavery in our town." Who wants to face up to that? It was obvious that standing so near the border, there were going to be more human trafficking cases, and something had to be done. But who was going to take responsibility? If people are brought across the international border, that was for the federal government to worry about, right? What about the state and local crimes that were being committed? And what about the vibrant community of Latino Americans who felt these crimes so personally? A girl like Reina needs a lot of help, including medical care and counseling, and clearly she's not going to get that from an FBI agent, however sympathetic the agent might be.

San Diego discovered with Reina that human trafficking is complex and crosses bureaucratic boundaries. With no set plan for how to deal with a trafficking case, local government, the media, social service agencies, and law enforcement all began to get involved. Confusion ensued, based on the laws that had been broken, about which agency should take the lead in Reina's case: Immigration? The FBI? The county sheriff? The San Diego Police Department? Which agency should be responsible for making sure she had a safe place to live, enough to eat, and the medical and psychological care that she desperately needed? And there was one question that all the groups and agencies were asking: who is going to pay for this? No one was holding back or asking for money up front, but every social service agency, every police department, is working on a tight budget. Much to their credit, the different agencies of San Diego rushed forward to help. With sixteen to twenty-two agencies involved at any one time, the resulting commotion occurred for all the right reasons, but it brought duplicated efforts and wasted time. Nor was San Diego unique; at the end of the 1990s, as the country "discovered" human trafficking, other American cities were experiencing similar confusion as agencies and jurisdictions tussled over victims.

Clearly something had to be done. Feathers had been ruffled, but cooler heads realized that everyone needed to sit down and talk things through, away from the pressure of a case like Reina's that required immediate action. The idea was simple: work through who should do what when a trafficking case broke, and at the same time look for funding to do the fundamental work, such as researching the size of the problem and raising community awareness, that everyone agreed had to happen. It was a simple idea but not an easy one to pull off, especially since some of these agencies had been struggling with one another for years. Charities supporting the rights of immigrants often found themselves in conflict with the federal Immigration and Naturalization Service. Law enforcement had one agenda, social services had another, and both were regular competitors for slices of the city budget.

As the first meetings were convened, tension was rife, and diplomacy was needed to keep the focus on the needs of people enslaved in the community. Like the bonded families of Sonebarsa, San Diegans had to overcome the barriers of fear and ignorance to work together to get free from slavery. Unlike Sonebarsa the choices were not so simple and not so immediately critical. When sheriff's deputies or social workers chose to act on a slavery case, the fundamental nature of their lives, their livelihoods, or the lives of their children would not be threatened. That is not to say that people in San Diego were less interested in the welfare of trafficking victims, just that as communities make the collective decision to end slavery, they come to that decision with different needs and experiences. To bring an end to slavery everywhere, we have to find a way for all communities, no matter what their starting point, to arrive at the same conclusion.

In San Diego this meant talking and talking. As the players got to know one another, trust emerged. Around a long table, munching doughnuts and sipping coffee, they decided step-by-step what the response should be when a trafficking case arrived. They discussed different scenarios: What if there were a lot of victims? What if the victims were all minors? What if they spoke a language the workers did not know? What if they were HIV positive? After a while it seemed that a case would never come and they would be stuck planning forever. And when the case did arrive, it had a few wrinkles that they had not planned for.

In late November 2003, the FBI and the new Immigration and Customs Enforcement agency (combining the old Customs Bureau and the Immigration and Naturalization Service) warned social service providers that they were about to raid a human trafficking operation.[6] Staff from the three agencies that had agreed to lead the response met to await the rescued victims. When they arrived, at a facility run by Immigration, the victims were interviewed by law enforcement and then immediately handed over to Spanish-speaking staff from the social service agencies. Initially the plan operated perfectly, with staff doing their assigned jobs. What derailed the plan was that each of the women victims had a small child in tow. A scramble began to find appropriate housing; the emergency shelters wouldn't work for mothers and small children, so an alternative had to be found. And one of the victims, showing signs of tuberculosis, needed to get to a doctor right away, for treatment as well as to determine if hers was an active and transmittable infection.

Within hours of the raid, law enforcement handed custody of the trafficking survivors to the social service agencies. Although transferring custody sounds simple, this was a huge step because custody carries legal responsibilities; handing the victims over demonstrated the trust that had developed between community members. It also meant that the victims, now called "clients," would get more of the help they needed sooner and in a setting that helped them to feel safe and cared for. When it came time to go to court, law enforcement and the service providers were working together, and the clients felt able to testify against the traffickers. Women who had been victims left the courtroom as survivors who went on to get jobs and bank accounts, put their children through school, and build new lives.

I hesitate to call the San Diego experience a model for other communities in the United States or Europe, but it certainly has some important lessons for us. At a time when agencies confronting human trafficking and slavery in other cities were still squabbling over turf and budget, agencies in San Diego squabbled too, but they also put a plan in place that paid off for trafficking victims. Every time a new case is discovered, the plan is refined a little more. And every time ex-slaves can safely testify against traffickers and go on to build lives with dignity, San Diego has something to be proud of.

THE TASTE OF CHOCOLATE

While sophisticated San Diego had to squabble and struggle, backcountry villages in Ghana have been able to achieve community consensus almost from the beginning. In the experience of these poor villages, there may be another model for all of us, one that shows how groups and communities can get it right from the get-go and begin to rid themselves of slavery and the conditions that lead to slavery. A good place to start is the village of Sika Nti, in Amenfi district in Ghana. Sika Nti is a long way from where most of us live, but it is linked to our daily lives in a special way. On the little family farms that surround the village, people grow yams, okra, melons, and squash to eat, but to make a little cash they grow lovely small trees with big bean pods—cocoa. That cocoa goes into the world market and ends up in the chocolate we eat.

This scene took on an ominous cast a few years back when a film was being made based on my book *Disposable People*. The filmmakers found that in neighboring Ivory Coast young men and boys, usually migrant farm workers, were being enslaved on cocoa farms. Other researchers, trying to determine how much slavery was going on, found another problem—children from farm families doing dangerous jobs, using sharp machetes on the trees and spraying insecticides and herbicides without any sort of protection. A new group was formed, the International Cocoa Initiative (ICI), with support from the world's major chocolate companies, to see what could be done (more about this organization and the role of the chocolate companies in chapter 7).

None of us want slavery or child labor in our chocolate, and the villagers didn't want that either, but they were small farmers barely getting by on what they could raise and didn't need rich foreigners parachuting into their villages to tell them how to run their farms. Telling a family that the children can't work on the farm anymore doesn't make a lot of sense if withdrawing their work means that the family income falls to the point that the children start to go hungry. It was important to find a way to change things without hurting families.

Catherine Owen and Peter McAllister, who made up the new ICI staff, understood the farmers' point of view. Peter had worked in Africa for years, and Catherine had helped rural communities in Haiti. Trying to find ways to take the slavery and child labor out of chocolate, they had to resist pressure to rush in and make those villagers toe the line. They knew that real change had to come from within the community. For change to happen, the community itself had to make a conscious collective decision. They also knew that no foreigners, or even local government officials, would be able to uncover child and slave labor in these remote, close-knit villages. Cleaning up chocolate's supply chain meant getting the farmers on board.

Consumers were clamoring to get slavery out of their chocolate *now*, but Peter and Catherine stuck to their guns and began to build a system that helped communities cleanse themselves of child labor and slavery. Peter and Catherine made sure that they had good local partners: people the villagers would understand and trust, people who shared their farming background and experience. Then they chose twenty-four communities in three districts of the country. Rather than coming in and telling the villagers that they had a problem, the ICI workers started by talking separately with the men, the women, and the children of the village about what problems the villagers wanted to solve. Not surprisingly, many of these problems overlapped with our concerns as chocolate consumers. In Sika Nti, children said they were poorly protected on the farm. They complained there was not enough time for schoolwork after doing their chores on the farm, that their palms were badly swollen after weeding large areas of land, and that they didn't like being exposed to chemicals when they sprayed the cocoa trees. The mothers were worried about their children handling dangerous tools, machetes and poisonous insecticides. They wanted to be able to provide better parental care and support, additional ways to earn money, and a community clinic. The men of the village said the community needed a primary school. They were concerned about the heavy loads of cocoa beans children were carrying and about child trafficking.

The ICI workers made it clear that they couldn't solve the village's problems, but they promised to help the village set and reach its own goals. With the problems out in the open, and with the community deciding what needed fixing, getting agreement on what to do next was easy. In the first meetings the adults agreed that the children had to come out of the dangerous jobs and worked out a labor-sharing plan so that neighbors could help cover the work that had previously been done by the children. Then the ICI workers ran workshops on how to use farm chemicals safely. In much the same way that Sankalp workers in India had helped the village of Azar Nagar get a mining lease, the ICI workers helped the villagers lobby the government to build and staff a primary school in the village. As trust grew, villagers began to report young people who had been trafficked into Ghana and exploited on farms. These self-policing communities were infinitely more effective at rooting out slavery than the overstretched and understaffed government agencies.

Tony Dogbe is one of the ICI workers who help communities get organized. He explained that before the community faced up to the problem and made a decision to act, child labor had been seen as normal:

In terms of child labor, they definitely admit using children on the farms, and they see it as a normal practice. . . . This bottom-up approach is excellent, but it has its challenges, and it requires everybody involved to be patient. We can't go faster than the community is willing to go. It is quite a gradual process. But it's a deeper way of dealing with the problem; you are uprooting it rather than just cutting off the stem or the branch.[7]

This patient approach is critical because cocoa is not only the site of slavery; it is also the only way many families get ahead. Peter McAllister explained, "Cocoa is the lifeblood of hundreds of thousands of smallholder farmers and indeed a major export earner for the country of Ghana at large." Cocoa is the cash crop that pays for many farm children to go to school and get the education they need to get ahead in life. At the same time, because it is a valuable crop, some farmers will do everything they can to increase their earnings. The challenge faced by communities in rural Ghana is that while most families count on cocoa to pay for school, some children end up enslaved.

One of those children, Abdullah, was turned over to a cocoa farmer when he was thirteen years old and his parents were facing extreme poverty and feared that they could not feed him. He had attended school for a time but had dropped out of primary school some time before. The farmer agreed to care for Abdullah in exchange for his labor growing cocoa. Three years later, when ICI staff met him, Abdullah worked on a cocoa farm in Ghana's Western Region, far from his family in the north. Other boys from the north were on the farm, and most of them had never had a chance to go to school. Abdullah and the other boys, like poor migrants around the world, had only their muscle power to earn their keep and no family resources to fall back on. They also had no real protection against any unscrupulous farmer who wanted to exploit or enslave them. Although they might want to go to school, they were not able to. Even if they weren't caught in slavery, they still had to work all the time just to live. When ICI staff met Abdullah, he was trying to combine work with study, not easy when schools are few and far between.

Abdullah and his co-workers are the reason why community-based projects like those run by ICI need dramatic expansion. Because of high birth rates in recent decades, they represent a swollen generation of migrant youth who are vulnerable to exploitation and enslavement. It is a story that is repeated in the histories of most countries, including nineteenth-century Europe and North America. Victorian fiction is full of stories of children abandoned, left at workhouses, or making their way on the streets, and gathering these children into schools took decades and enormous resources. In Ghana the national government says it is too poor to mount school programs extending to all rural areas, but if the government can't reach to every village, the job can get done in other ways. The important thing is the transformation that comes when a local village decides to confront the conditions that lead to enslavement. Does it really matter whether this collective decision is the result of a government program, a local coalition, or the input of a group like ICI? Our job is to make sure that this transition takes as little time as possible.

NO TURNING BACK

This chapter has looked at tiny villages and big cities. Some were enslaved; others were trying to rid their community of traffickers and slaveholders and to set free and care for those who had been caught up in slavery. In these communities, across different continents, languages, economies, and governments, the same story keeps unfolding: no matter how powerless and poor, with just a little help, people will do whatever is needed to get slavery out of their lives and homes. Over and over, when a community believes there is a realistic possibility of freedom, it becomes unstoppable—even when there is risk.

Understanding that fact is crucially important, because when it comes to ending slavery community-based freedom may be the best strategy of all. Rescuing individual slaves can leave the criminal slave-based businesses intact, and soon a new slave has taken the place of the freed one. But when a whole community drives out the slave traders and the slaveholders, freedom is firmly set in place. Breaking the cycle of slavery will also free a community to smash through other problems that support slavery, like illiteracy, poverty, and disenfranchisement. Slavery is a blood-sucking parasite that leaves a community paralyzed and stupe-fied. Get rid of slavery and, with a little help, a village can actually slave-proof itself. The process of confronting and defeating slavery shifts power to the community, which means achieving community goals like good education and economic stability becomes possible. In turn, edu-cation, economic stability, and learning to work together are a vaccina-tion against slavery. Without slavery incomes go up, children go to school, and corruption falls. There will still be problems, of course, since every community is made of people who have different interests and goals, but now the community is moving forward without the dead weight of slavery holding it back. Families are the building blocks of this change, moved to act by what may be the most powerful of human desires.

THE BONDS OF FAMILY

In the weeks after the end of the American Civil War, African Americans set out on one of the greatest internal migrations in history. White wit-nesses were astounded; many said it seemed as if every black person in the country was suddenly on the road. No one knows how many of the four million ex-slaves walked away from the scene of their bondage, but hundreds of thousands were driven by a common need. The countryside was in ruin, farms burned, stores empty, railroads destroyed, and sick-ness and hunger were everywhere. Yet in that place of devastation, in that "year of jubilee," ex-slaves were in motion. Being able to move freely was intoxicating, but that feeling wasn't what drove freed slaves on long and hungry treks across the country. What moved nearly every mother, father, brother, sister, and child was the intense desire to find family members who had been sold away. Most slave families had been torn apart, children sold from mothers, married couples split, family bonds smashed on the auction block. The anguish of forced separation and the dream of reunion burned in millions of hearts. For ex-slaves, preserving the union was not political; it was personal. It was about family.

In the 1930s when thousands of ex-slaves were interviewed, that pain and that search were still clear in their memories. Delia Garlie was an elderly woman in Alabama when she was asked to tell the story of her life in slavery and after. Garlie was born in Virginia, the youngest of thir-teen children. In her voice you can hear the pain of families broken on slavery's wheel:

I was grown up when the war came, and I was a mother before it closed. Babies were snatched from their mothers' breasts and sold to speculators. Children were separated from sisters and brothers and never saw each other again. Of course they cried; you think they didn't cry when they were sold like cattle? [My family] was all put on a block and sold to the highest bidder. I never saw brother William again. Mammy and me was sold to a man by the name of Carter, who was the sheriff of the county.

One night the master come in drunk and set at the table with his head lolling around. I was waiting on the table, and he looked up and saw me. I was scared, and that made him awful mad. He called an overseer and told him: "Take her out and beat some sense into her." I began to cry and run and run in the night; but finally I ran back by the [slave] quarters and heard mammy calling me. I went in, and right away they came for me. A horse was standing in front of the house, and I was taken that very night to Richmond and sold to a speculator again. I never saw my mammy any more.[8]

This story reminds us that between parents and children, between brothers and sisters, the bonds of family may be the strongest of all human ties. Almost any parents will tell you that they would sacrifice anything to be with and care for their children. It is a deep and fundamental truth of the human family. When slavery has destroyed almost every other part of a person, this powerful drive remains. Slavery can crush ambition, self-reliance, and independence of thought, even a sense of self, but it can only depress, never destroy, parental and family love. When children are trafficked away from their families today, the pain of separation is no less than it was when a family of slaves was sold off to different owners in the antebellum South. In nearly every community we have looked at in this chapter, antislavery workers have unleashed the power of parental love. That love has fueled great changes. When a seed of outside help allows families to connect with their deep desire to get their children back and to never let another child go, then a community changes for good.

Those of us living in the rich half of the world need to think about this carefully. Giving public talks, I am often asked, "How can a mother sell her child like that?" Confronted with the story of a parent who has let a child go with a trafficker, the listener recoils and assumes the parent has to be a monster. I have heard people say, "*We* love our children so much that we would never allow them to be taken away, but people *over there* feel differently; children don't mean as much to them." Don't believe that for a second. Parents everywhere will do everything in their power to protect their children. But in extreme poverty parents get caught in horrible situations and have to make impossible decisions. Often it boils down to "Do I take a chance that this person's offer of food and a job is real, or do I risk keeping my children here and watching them starve?" The fact that sometimes parents make a bad decision doesn't mean that they don't love their children. All parents want their children to be safe and educated.

At the beginning of this chapter, we saw the enslaved families of Sonebarsa go through hell to get free. When they finally established their new village and, for the first time in their lives, had some money to spend and the freedom to decide how to spend it, they spent it on their children. Before the adults bought anything for themselves, they took their children out of the quarries and put them in school, then put food in their mouths and clothes on their backs. The same story is played out over and over whenever families come out of slavery. Jyothi was one of the mothers in Sonebarsa who lost a child in the violence that came with their liberation. She is clear about her priorities: "My dream for my children is that they grow to be 'big' people, who can read and write, who can live in cities, and have a job. All I want is that nobody remains a slave. That every child is free, free to study, free to learn, free to live their own life." Like new immigrants in the United States who would make any sacrifice to support their children's education, freed slaves are newly arrived on the shores of freedom. They understand knowledge is the power their children must have.

THE WAY FORWARD

Using the power of governments or the United Nations would seem to be the way to end slavery once and for all. But while governments, in time, may indeed be the most powerful forces against slavery, today they are not. At present, the most efficient engine for freeing slaves and keeping them free is when a community makes a conscious collective decision to do just that. As far as I can tell, more slaves are freed every year through community organization than any other way; they are also freed more efficiently, and their freedom has more permanence. What's more, the critical and needed rehabilitation after liberation happens more quickly and with greater power when it grows from the community. Recent local elections in India demonstrate this.

I have always been amazed and moved by the resilience of freed slaves, but I was stunned when the election results were announced in rural Uttar Pradesh in early 2006. In the preceding months the Sankalp and other activists in the antislavery movement had been helping hundreds of slaves who had recently come to freedom, some of them the people in the village of Azar Nagar whom we met at the beginning of this chapter. We knew that these ex-slaves would be working hard to better their lives, but when I heard that ninety-nine freed slaves had decided to run for office, I was astounded. I was also a little worried that the disappointment of election defeat would be a real setback for them. Then, two weeks later, I heard the news that floored me: of the ninety-nine running for office, seventy-nine had been elected. In a groundbreaking change for rural Indian politics, thirty-one of the newly elected ex-slaves were women. This rapid transformation from slave to elected official demonstrates how powerful the community approach can be. Looking at other ways to end slavery, today and in history, I have found nothing like this. Yes, some ex-slaves were elected to office in the Deep South after the American Civil War, but they did so with an army of occupation to back them up, and as soon as that army pulled out, they were quickly pushed to the side or worse.

The local self-help groups of ex-slaves are also having a profound impact on the natural environment. Remember that the slaveholders destroyed the national forests with illegal strip mining. Now in villages like Azad Nagar, villagers are replanting the forests. Free the Slaves helped Sankalp and the villagers raise funds, and now more than ten thousand trees have been planted. And these are not just any trees; the villagers are planting the five species of trees that Mahatma Gandhi recommended for village prosperity—trees that supply food, fuel, fodder, fiber, and flowers. When whole villages come out of slavery, it seems miraculous. Now I feel I need a word for "more than miraculous" when I see recently freed villages replanting forests; landscaping strip mines into watersheds, ponds, and irrigation systems; building schools; putting an end to child trafficking and "slaveproofing" their villages; electing their members to office; and starting new businesses. What powerful forces for freedom are locked up in every slave! It is up to us to find the best ways to set those forces free.

MAKING IT HAPPEN

Fannie Lou Hamer was right; we are not going to get there unless we all go together. Every time communities free themselves or bring freedom to

others, a seed, a catalyst, has started the ball rolling. It might be someone too persistent to ignore, like Fannie Lou, or the antislavery worker
who slips into a village at night to spread the idea of freedom. Freedom
is viral; you can catch it from other people, but you have to have that
first person infected with liberty to emerge within or to reach into your
community and infect others.

A conscious and collective decision has to be made to effectively bring
slavery to an end, and this idea applies beyond local communities as well.
To achieve global eradication, conscious collective decisions have to be
made at every level—from the family all the way up to national governments and whole societies. We know how to do this. Remember that
national decisions start with small groups. Consider the little group of
Quakers and others that Adam Hochschild describes meeting above a
bookstore in London one May afternoon in 1787:

> A somber-looking crew, one man in clerical black and most of the others not
> removing their high-crowned blade hats, filed through its doors and sat down
> to launch one of the most far-reaching citizens' movements of all time. Cities
> build monuments to kings and generals, not to people who once gathered in a
> bookstore. And yet what these particular citizens did was felt across the
> world—winning the admiration of the first and greatest student of what
> today we call civil society. What they accomplished, Alexis de Tocqueville
> wrote, was "something absolutely without precedent in history. . . . If you
> pore over the histories of all peoples, I doubt that you will find anything
> more extraordinary."[9]

That afternoon these twelve invented the antislavery movement, in a
world where slavery was the economic equivalent of the automobile
industry today, and where slavery was not just legal but a major government policy for economic growth. They were fortunate that they lived in
a time and place where they could dream and build without too much
threat to their well-being. Today, we need to support the dreams and
plans of slaves and ex-slaves. If we are going to help these communities,
what are the actions we need to take? What are the ideas we need to
grasp? The following six points should move us in the right direction.

THINKING FREE AND BEING FREE

Liberation projects all over the world have taught us that one fact is
inescapable: when slaves make a conscious decision to reach for freedom,
that freedom will be more durable than when they do not. Of course, we
can't wait for that thinking process when immediate rescue is the right

thing to do; slaves who are locked away need to be liberated. But the rescue should be followed by a chance to think through the process of slavery and liberation, to give ex-slaves the chance to own their freedom. When slaves are rescued in police raids, redeemed through purchase, or snatched by activists and not given a chance for learning and decision making, they have a greater likelihood of falling back into slavery. To stay out of slavery, people need both the mental tools to grapple with a life in freedom and the economic tools to keep themselves in control of their own destiny. We know this can be done. The children at the Bal Vikas Ashram, who have been rescued from slavery in the carpet looms, graduate and become leaders in their home villages. At home, they are often the only people with the confidence and knowledge to stand up to the local landowners and moneylenders who prey on their families. The result is that they become change agents who help slaveproof their villages. As we build new programs for liberation and help existing programs to improve, we must ensure that each program creates the opportunity for slaves and ex-slaves to come to a true and conscious decision to be free.

ONE SIZE DOES NOT FIT ALL

Every slave's bondage is unique. The fundamental facts of slavery are the same, but the way those facts play out varies enormously. The strategy that gets one person out of slavery won't necessarily work for another. If we look closely, we see that people in slavery have specific needs that must be met if they are to escape and survive independently. The cookie-cutter solution simply won't work. Whoever is working for liberation, whether government or activist groups, has to take time to watch and listen, to understand the texture and nuance of each slavery experience. With that understanding, the right answers can be brought to bear.

The things that stop people from leaving slavery can be surprising. One elderly couple was in debt bondage, living in a crude hut on the slaveholder's land. They had an intense desire for freedom, but they were fearful to risk the little security they had. They suffered brutality and exploitation, but they couldn't break loose of "home," the one place that was theirs together. They simply could not imagine a place where they could have a safe home. The antislavery worker found that for this elderly couple, the key to freedom was to show them a place where they could reerect their hut in safety. Sometimes we need to ask people what they are worried about. They may be seeing obstacles to liberation that are invisible to our eyes.

Another way to gain an insight into the lives of slaves is by creating helpful services—services that may not directly address slavery. Such a service could be simple health care, advice about agriculture, or help in setting up a credit union. Slaves find it hard to trust people, and for good reason. But we have discovered that if slaves learn to trust antislavery workers, to know that they are not leaving, and to believe that someone is truly interested in their lives, they will begin to see the alternative to slavery. That vision of freedom feeds the collective decision to act, to take responsibility for their own liberation. And above all, sticking close to people in slavery can give antislavery workers the chance to really understand the issues slaves face and what it will take for them to conceive of a life in freedom. Then they can build the right services to improve economic stability, literacy, access to credit, and skills training, all of which are needed to lock in freedom.

CLONE THE LIBERATORS (AGAIN)

To really get to know and gain the trust of communities in slavery requires people who are willing to live in remote and depressed areas. Finding people who are willing to live in these rough conditions is a challenge, because the very people who are trained and speak the local languages have often spent their lives trying to get *out* of those same boondocks. With education and exposure to the bigger world, they would prefer to live where they can surf the Internet and live the life they had hoped for. The solution could be as simple as making sure that antislavery workers are well paid and provided with the right mix of opportunities for growth, so that they will want to go where they are most needed and stay there.

We could also make it easier for people who *want* to work in remote areas to help free slaves. The U.S. Peace Corps has about eight thousand volunteers and trainees. These are people who have chosen to live where conditions can be rough. Many of them are working in countries where slavery is prevalent, and many them are doing exactly the jobs that are needed to build communities and ensure that freedom survives. We could take the small step of saying that in the next Peace Corps intake there will be a call for volunteers who want to receive training to work with people in slavery, a step that could probably be accomplished with a single line added to the next Peace Corps appropriations bill in Congress. A good training program would need to be assembled, but many experienced antislavery workers would be overjoyed to teach those skills. Other similar groups, such as the British organization Voluntary Service Overseas, could do the same. Finding enough volunteers should not be a problem.[10] Every year I speak at a number of universities and meet thousands of students, and at every stop students ask me about how to become anti-slavery workers.

PREPARE FOR THE BACKLASH

Ending slavery requires that oppressive power relations are brought to the surface and reversed. This is a fundamental confrontation. This is the world turned upside down. In every liberation there is a moment of danger, and the point when the slaveholder's power and profit are threatened and violence is sure to follow. Sometimes the moment of danger is brief, as when a well-conducted raid whisks a child out of slavery and into safety. But when a whole community seeks freedom, they can't just run and hide, and the result can mirror the tragedies that rained down on the people of Sonebarsa: loss of livelihood, violent assault, and destruction of their homes and few possessions. Although the former slaves of Sonebarsa are now free, their liberation was marked by tragic losses. To make sure this doesn't happen means preparing antislavery workers and organizations, as well as communities in slavery, for the fact that this crisis will always come. Together they have to decide if the risk is worth it and if it is, when and how they should take that risk. When liberty comes, the slaveholders will react; the question is how to manage and mitigate the force of that reaction. For this we need to bring in the experts, the specialists in conflict resolution who can analyze and explore the best ways to defuse potentially explosive situations and make sure that everyone gets to freedom alive. We must make sure that everyone concerned understands the possibility of danger in the moment of liberation and find ways to bring about that change as safely as possible.

PLAN FOR THE WORST

While our eyes are on the prize of freedom, we need to think through all the possible steps and missteps along the way. Given the volatile and unpredictable nature of liberation, we have to engage in a special kind of disaster planning. We have to ask: When the houses start burning, what are we going to do? When the slaveholder drives a family out of their home, where will they be housed? The more we engage in planning to deal with worst-case scenarios, the more successful liberations will be. As we will see in chapter 5, triumph can morph into disaster.

We already know some of the key ingredients to avert catastrophe. Safety in numbers, for example, can be critical. One slave is easily intimidated, but it is hard to turn twenty slaves. In the case of Sonebarsa, the presence of people from other villages deterred the slaveholders from attack when the moment of crisis came, but the lack of a worst-case plan meant that the atrocities and destruction occurred when the villagers were left alone again. Forging connections with some powerful person or group that will back up slaves in their reach for freedom can be important as well. In little villages the big landowners can do pretty much whatever they like, but introduce a judge, a lawyer, or a politician from the city, and they back down. The presence of foreign observers has saved lives more than once. It's important to make sure that workers who are at the sharp edge of liberation forge these connections and alliances before they need them.

WE ALL GO TOGETHER

Slaves are marginalized and downtrodden, but that does not mean that they are free from prejudices of their own. Cultures that foster slavery are also likely to harbor racism, religious discrimination, and devaluation of women. The trafficking and enslavement of women and children often grows out of cultures where physical and sexual violence against women and children is both prevalent and shrouded in silence. In this situation the first step toward ending slavery is for women to come together to resist violence within their own homes. Experiencing the power to resist violence and knowing that they have a right to be safe gives women the confidence that they can protect themselves and their children from traffickers.

When freedom applies to everyone, remarkable powers are unleashed. Again, this can mean turning the world upside down, a situation that may not always be comfortable. One of the ex-slave women elected to local government in India wouldn't come out of her house for an interview because her in-laws were in sight.[11] She may have been on the village council, but she was still operating under the rigid local customs that dictate how a woman shows respect and deference to her in-laws. When organizers included her in planning for freedom, they unlocked potential long suppressed not just by slavery but by sexism as well. When a community reaches for freedom, it needs every bit of energy and brains it can muster.

BRASS TACKS

Many of the points just made are about big ideas and the shape of community change, but now it is time to get down to brass tacks. As communities make the collective and conscious decision to throw off slavery, go through the moment of crisis, and take the first slow and careful steps toward autonomous life, we can see the essential ingredients of a sustainable future. If a community of ex-slaves is going to survive in freedom, it will need the following:

IMMEDIATE ACCESS TO PAID WORK Ideally, ex-slaves will be able to generate income themselves, doing jobs they know, and not depend on handouts. They may need to be given a bag of rice and some emergency supplies, but the sooner the ex-slaves are working for themselves, the sooner the community gains stability. Once they are doing paid work, they can take steps to diversify income by moving into other types of work, thereby broadening the economic base of the community as a whole.

A CHANCE TO BUILD UP SAVINGS For the poor and vulnerable, owning assets can be the difference between a problem and a catastrophe. Slavery is often the result of having nothing to fall back on in a crisis, and sliding down into debt and bondage. When a family has something in reserve, even if it is just a flock of chickens or a goat, they have the resilience to bounce back when the next setback occurs.

ACCESS TO BASIC SERVICES Having a school means children are kept out of the workplace today and are building human capital for tomorrow. Having a clinic within a reasonable distance means minor illnesses don't worsen and become debilitating and lives are saved by simple vaccinations. Because women and children often spend three and four hours hauling water each day, providing access to clean water near the home means hours of productivity added to the lives of ex-slaves. Planning for freedom has to include asking both women and men what services exist and which are needed.

WORKING WITH THE EARTH You need a lot of pillars to hold up freedom, and one is a productive environment. Slaves are often forced to work in ways that are environmentally destructive. From the Brazilian rain forests to the Indian quarries and West African lakes, slaves are used to wreck the environment in order to line the pockets of slaveholders. This destruction has the greatest impact on the poor and is itself a force that drives more families toward enslavement. Building a sustainable community in freedom means sustaining the natural environment as well. The tree-planting projects run by ex-slaves around Sonebarsa are a perfect example. Many ex-slaves say that one of the first things they want to do in freedom is to clear and plant a garden plot. Nutrition and health can make rapid gains with fresh vegetables and beans, and what is not eaten can be sold to diversify income. It is a small thing, but seeds and a hoe can make a big difference.

MORE BRASS TACKS (THIS TIME FOR FUNDERS)

The chain of events that leads to communities being able to throw off slavery often starts with a charity, a foundation, or some other grant-making body. The activists and community workers who provide the seed for liberation need to get paid and meet the other expenses of their work. Governments should be supporting antislavery work, but for the most part they don't, so it is important to examine how funders help liberators help slaves to freedom. Having seen the relationships that exist between funders and antislavery groups around the world, I want to suggest a few specific things that antislavery workers and organizations will need to have in order to best stimulate and sustain communities fighting slavery. Charities and foundations that support antislavery work are doing the best they can with the resources they have to share, and antislavery workers are doing the best they can for the people in slavery. The funders need the activists and the activists need the funders. Unfortunately, the fact that one side of this relationship has the money and the other has to ask for it can bring tension and confusion. It is important to recognize that fact and then to step back and find ways to help funders and antislavery groups work well together.

RELIABLE FUNDING

Antislavery groups need the same stability for themselves that they are helping ex-slave communities to build. They don't normally need large amounts of money, just money they can count on. Although it can be immediate for individuals, for many communities liberation takes time. People in slavery live with a great deal of insecurity, and antislavery groups must be reliable in everything they do with the communities they support; they can't be running out of money in the middle of a liberation project. For those of us who are making individual donations to antislavery groups, we can help by planning our giving so that it is long-term and reliable. More important than the size of the gift is the regularity with which it comes.

FLEXIBILITY

We've seen that local antislavery groups need to listen carefully to discover the needs of slave communities. To be responsive to those needs,
local groups need funders that understand flexibility. For example, six
months into a project the antislavery workers may realize that the health
care they are providing is good but that to get people out of slavery,
microcredit will be needed. An antislavery movement needs to *move*,
always in the direction of ending slavery, and if that means changing
course from health care to microcredit, then so be it. The destination
always has to be freedom, not a project that, though "successful," deliv-
ers less than that. To keep moving forward, the antislavery workers need
the flexibility to adapt and navigate, and funders need to be flexible
enough to support a needed change in direction.

ASSEMBLING THE TOOLKIT

Many antislavery groups grow out of the grassroots. They may know a
lot about local power relations but very little about national laws that
could act as levers in their own communities. Every antislavery group
needs a good understanding of and the ability to use whatever antislavery tools and laws exist. Building up that expertise among antislavery
groups is something the rest of us need to support.

CRITICAL THINKING, CRITICAL FUNDING

Local antislavery groups need the space to think critically and forcefully
about how to get the job done. We can help create that space by improving the relationship between antislavery organizations that ask for funding and nonprofit groups and foundations (including governments) that
supply funding. In the current system it is easy to replicate a culture of
patronage. On the ground the antislavery group is saying, "We always
get a grant from the Bloggs Foundation to run a clinic, so we need to
keep asking for grants to run clinics." But the antislavery workers know
that in terms of stopping slavery, another clinic isn't going to help. What
is really needed here is for antislavery workers to identify the crucial
blockage on the road to freedom and then to be able to say to the Bloggs
Foundation, "The tool we need to open the blockage is *this*." That
sounds easy, but when antislavery workers are stuck down in the village
and their funder has rules about what they support and how they fund it

and there is not even a category on their application for the tool the workers really need, the workers will be tempted to go for what they can get—another clinic grant. Big foundations need rules for grants; giving away a lot of money requires rules, because giving away money responsibly is much harder than most people imagine. Our challenge is to find the way to increase the level of understanding and trust between the workers on the ground and the funders in their boardrooms to the point that, in working together, they are faster, smarter, and more powerful than the slaveholders.

FIRST A SEED, THEN A TREE, THEN A FOREST

All of these ideas point to ways in which communities can bring an end to slavery. For almost every community struggling with slavery, there is another still held so tightly in slavery's chains that struggle is impossible. But we know this: the best and most viable solutions to slavery will be created within the communities where slavery is being experienced. People in slavery know best what they need to reach freedom. Outsiders can share ideas, protection, and resources, but the actual solutions have to first convince and then be owned by the people fighting to leave slavery.

Eradicating slavery in one community is achievable; there are many examples of that. We know less about how to translate the experience in one village to a whole state or region. How do we build organizations and coalitions that will have a wider impact? Three steps seem to be needed. First, successful community-based solutions need to be *scaled up* as much as possible. To do that, antislavery groups and their funders need to be always thinking about incubating new strategies and then multiplying them. Once a successful strategy is tested, it should be proactively offered to the world as a freely available, "open-source" program.

Second, antislavery groups need to join together and cooperate, forming a wider movement with a shared identity. Joining together in the world of human rights can be difficult because groups often feel themselves to be in competition for recognition and resources. Being human beings, even altruistic antislavery workers can have egos that make them want to be leaders or that make it difficult for them to cooperate. We must recognize that some grassroots workers chosen for special attention by the media have had their lives and their effectiveness severely disrupted by demands far in excess of their workload, jealousy from other workers, and increased visibility to slaveholders and their thugs.

Third, scaling up successful antislavery programs also means shifting more of the responsibility to government. *Government accountability* for the enforcement of antislavery laws and for provision of preventive and rehabilitative services needs to be *intrinsic* to antislavery strategies. To end slavery, the culture and purpose of government must support human rights rather than sectional interests. If government is on board, it can adopt the successful methods and extend the effects of local projects. Although the value of state or regional policies will depend on the ability of the government to function efficiently, at the least it can make useful tools and methods more widely available.

The collective decision making of communities is crucial to throwing off the yoke of slavery. Some of the causes of slavery, however, go beyond the reach of any individual community. A village may be able to drive out traffickers, but it needs to join with other groups to change government policies that may support slavery. One such policy is the treatment of women enslaved in prostitution as criminals and not victims. Laws exist in many countries that require a woman found in prostitution to be arrested and locked up, regardless of how she came to be in that situation. Clearly, treating a victim of slavery and serial rape as a criminal is not the way to deal with the problem. In India, women were being kidnapped from towns and villages, raped, and enslaved in prostitution. The horror story told by one victim who made it home might have moved her neighbors but would have little effect on national law. Some problems can't be solved by a single community. In this case, it took years to build a network of survivors, women's rights groups, antislavery and antitrafficking groups, and international nongovernmental organizations (NGOs). Acting in concert, they were able to penetrate some of the preconceptions that blinded politicians. Recently, the law was changed and, with luck, slaves in prostitution are now being freed instead of incarcerated. Building networks like this takes time and needs a strong sense of affinity and trust. Those facing slavery on the ground have to find ways to reach, convince, and enlist people whose lives are far away from situations of slavery. When slavery is linked to exports and products, this could mean joining with industries; or when the influence could help change government policies, this could mean connecting with international bodies like the United Nations. Ending slavery means acting locally *and* globally.

OUR TOWN

No matter what laws are passed or U.N. resolutions are promulgated, slavery ends when local communities first decide it will end and then take

WHAT WE CAN DO AS COMMUNITY MEMBERS TO FREE MORE SLAVES

This chapter is about the power of groups and communities to liberate slaves and to help them to achieve lives of dignity. We all belong to a community and to groups within that community, and most groups can play a role in the eradication of slavery. Here are six things our groups and communities can do to end slavery and especially to help other groups and communities fighting to end slavery.

1. In your book club, Sunday school, scout troop, women's group, MeetUp, senior center, Rotary Club, other community group, or library book discussion list—whatever is right for you—offer to show a DVD, discuss this book, or give a presentation to help others learn about contemporary slavery.

2. When schoolchildren learn about modern slavery, they become unstoppable in their determination to end it. Give them the opportunity to join the anti-slavery movement by sharing with them, and letting their teachers know about teaching packs from Free the Slaves. Help children in other ways to turn the act of ending slavery into deep learning.

3. Build an antislavery library in our schools and filing cabinets. A vast store of knowledge about freeing slaves is scattered around the world, little of it collected and organized. As a result, wheels are being reinvented and hard lessons learned over and over again. We can make sure that everyone has access to information about modern slavery and what to do about it. Collect books, movies, and information and create a central repository in your community. This will help our own communities and groups to become seeds of freedom for others around the world.

4. For groups like the Peace Corps, Voluntary Service Overseas, and faith-based organizations, train your volunteers to recognize the warning signs of slavery and trafficking and to be of service to antislavery workers in all sectors.

5. For all of us, through the charities and development groups we support, provide remuneration and recognition needed to attract and retain skilled frontline antislavery workers for the communities that need them most. Help them be trained in conflict resolution to make communities' transition to freedom as safe as possible.

6. For funders, provide flexible, long-term funding for stable, efficient grassroots groups; foster and participate in a dialogue with other funders, freed slaves, and antislavery workers to plan better support for communities that are freeing themselves.

action. Slavery is woven into the fabric of life at the intimate level of our neighborhoods. Slavery has to be cut out of that fabric by those who best understand where its threads are hidden and how they are knotted together with the strands of corruption, indifference, racism, or greed. If you or I live in a community without slavery today, it is because someone in the past turned to a neighbor and said, "This must end." Slavery is too big to be stopped by any individual, no matter how powerful, charismatic, or clever that person might be. The end of slavery is within our grasp, but only if we join together to make it so.

5

Governments
Carrying the Biggest Stick

The vast Himalaya Mountains rise up over the city of Kathmandu, Nepal. Strangely, they seem to lift the city as well, pulling it up from its smoky valley toward their snowy peaks. The mountains mirror both the lofty aspirations of the people and the immovable and stony indifference of the royal family to those hopes. The people of Nepal need their mountains, if only to cling to when the next shock comes, for waves of change have smashed into Nepal in recent decades. I was part of a small one that set slaves free, and then condemned some of them to death.

To get an idea of what Nepal is like, imagine that in the Middle Ages the island of Britain had come under the sway of an irresistibly powerful king, a king so powerful and paranoid that he and his descendants sealed off the country from any communication and then lived like gods on the backs of millions of serfs. It sounds like a strange fantasy film, but in Nepal this actually happened. A land without roads, remote from the bustle of neighboring India and China, it was seized in 1846 by a man who renamed himself Rana and instituted total control over the population. His family's grasp on the state began with a wholesale massacre of the nobility in the courtyard of the royal palace, followed by a purge across the country. The king was retained as a puppet, and the Ranas settled in as hereditary prime ministers, closing the borders, and awarding themselves and their children lives of unimaginable luxury, while the people toiled and died in medieval drudgery and squalor. At a time when much of the world was being transformed by industrialization, the invention of flight, even the birth of nuclear power, Nepal was frozen in a dark age. Only when the British left India in 1948 and ended their support for the Rana autocracy did the country open its doors. The first foreigner in Nepal in more than a hundred years arrived in 1951 and found a feudal land of powerful nobles who owned the peasants along with the land they farmed. The country was basically without electricity, roads, schools, and—outside the palaces—any machine not known in the Middle Ages. There were nine doctors in the whole country, and they served the nobility; the millions of serfs and peasants had no health care at all and were tormented by disease and plague.

Now imagine medieval Europe suddenly flooded with the technologies and ideas of the twentieth century, and you have an idea of the electrifying change that swept the capital and reverberated through the countryside. Many of the changes, such as the public health care brought by foreign medical teams, were positive. Others were less so, as the powerful families gained a taste for instruments of even greater power and embraced modern forms of corruption. The bonded and enslaved peasant workers in Nepal are known as *kamaiyas*, and fulfill the role of medieval serfs. With the shock of modernization, from which the kamaiyas were mainly excluded, their masters learned new ways to exploit them. Before 1950, the bonded-labor slaves were simply owned by their masters, but when the expectation of change arrived, their masters quickly converted that relationship to one of ostensible "debt" that left intact the hereditary slavery and control over their lives. When "democracy" made its appearance, slaveholders also used their enslaved workers as a vote bank, ensuring dominance over local institutions. Opening markets to the rest of the world also opened new ways to exploit slaves. Reports by the United Nations point to the redeployment of enslaved workers into quarries, cottage factories (making things like matches), brick kilns, carpet looms, and, particularly ugly, the sex trade. Kamaiya girls were sold to sex traffickers from India and put to work in the brothels of Mumbai and other Indian cities, where Nepali girls, viewed as exotic and especially beautiful, are in high demand.

The precise numbers of enslaved workers in Nepal are not known because it has helped successive governments and their powerful supporters in the countryside to conceal the extent of slavery since it was abolished (on paper) in 1926 after pressure from Great Britain. Piecing together reports from different sources and talking it over with experts in Nepal, I estimate that there are around 2.5 million people in slavery in Nepal today. The lives of slaves, however, are also reeling from the changes that have rocked the country.

Rapid social and economic change has been disruptive, and even some of the ostensibly positive changes have had mixed results. As public health improved and the death rate, especially for children, plummeted, the population exploded, and the agricultural carrying capacity of this stony and mountainous land was quickly reached and surpassed. Indigenous food supplies could not keep pace with demand, and food imports became necessary. Many of the elite, and the political parties, simply lost interest in the countryside, and investment and government concern for rural peasants evaporated. Control of the country shifted from the king to parliament to hand-picked cabinet members and back to the king again, but without disturbing the underlying domination of the richest families. For the common people, a dawning knowledge of political rights and the possibility of a better life has set off a revolution of rising expectations, expressed most strongly by the Maoist groups who call for land for the peasants and who now occupy large areas of the countryside.

I HELP PAVE THE ROAD TO HELL

Just after the millennium celebrations in January 2000, John Montagu and I set off from London for Nepal. We had the best of intentions, hoping to help local antislavery groups in their fight against the debt-bondage slavery that was pervasive in the countryside. We were traveling primarily as representatives of Anti-Slavery International, but we both had other roles that we hoped would help us when we reached Kathmandu. As a university professor and specialist on contemporary slavery, my job was to bring a global view and suggestions for reform to the groups working with Nepal's enslaved workers. As a longtime worker in developing countries, John brought a real expertise and understanding of the region. He also carried something that opened certain doors in the Kingdom of Nepal: his title as the Earl of Sandwich. To many ears this title has a comical ring, but this is a very old family whose thread runs through the whole fabric of English history. Yes, one of John's ancestors was the eighteenth-century hell-raiser who supposedly would not leave the card table to eat and called instead for meat between slices of bread, thus giving his name to the snack. Some of his other ancestors led the great British navy and served the government in other ways. The nobility, and especially the royal families, of those few countries that remain monarchies tend to stick together, and John's title and seat in the House of Lords would open doors for us that might otherwise have remained closed. Inheriting a title can actually be a great burden, and it is to John's credit that he took it on because he felt he could use it for good in the fight against slavery and social injustice.

Just getting to Nepal proved tricky. Fog in New Delhi diverted our plane to Mumbai, where we were stuck incommunicado in a transit holding lounge for nearly forty-eight hours. Awaiting our arrival in Kathmandu were a clutch of journalists and a room set up for a press conference, but we never appeared, nor could we even let them know where we were. When we finally arrived, we were swept up in a whirlwind. Meetings had been scheduled with nearly every government minister, every senior politician in the opposition, and all of the nongovernmental organizations concerned with kamaiyas. We attended a reception at the British embassy and other receptions, teas, and dinners. At every meeting we stressed the importance of the government making a clear statement and instituting a comprehensive law that would not just ban debt-bondage slavery but also include supports for those coming out of slavery to help them attain autonomy and full citizenship. The debt-bondage law across the border in India had shown how well this rehabilitation program could work—on those few occasions when the law was properly enforced.

The highlight of these meetings was a conference of activist organizations that were gathering together to try to find a unified plan of action. In and of itself, this meeting was a breakthrough. Just a few years before, activists had been thrown in prison for pushing radical ideas like democracy. Activist organizations were marginalized and, excluded from true participation in civil society, they tended to fight among themselves. Denied a legitimate role, ideological differences grew in importance and took up time and energy. The conference brought together feuding groups and gave them a common goal beyond their differences. Our presence, especially John's, opened doors to government officials that had been slammed in the faces of NGO leaders. There was a palpable buzz as groups found strength in numbers and recognized common goals. A longtime antislavery worker from India named Swami Agnivesh also joined us in Kathmandu. As a Hindu priest and respected human rights worker, he brought a special legitimacy to our visit. Although our views were respected, we were foreigners visiting from the very country that had supported the Rana dictatorship. Agnivesh was a Hindu visiting a country that is 98 percent Hindu, and as a holy man he could not be suspected of pushing a private agenda for personal gain. John and I could say, "You can do it," and be encouraging, but when Agnivesh said, "You can do it, I know, because I am like you, and I was able to do it, and here is how . . ." then the activists began to plan and act. But in a little over a week, John, Agnivesh, and I were gone, having stirred up and advised and encouraged and pressed for change. Among the local groups, a newfound hope was taking root that big changes were possible—a deeply felt belief that would have triumphant and disastrous consequences.

RISING EXPECTATIONS

In the early nineteenth century, Alexis de Tocqueville looked at how revolutions and democracies came about.[1] He noted that under extreme dictatorships revolutions rarely happened; it was only when people began to have a vision of something better that they would rush toward change. He noted how it was only after reforms occurred or economic prosperity arrived that popular revolt began. Though de Tocqueville never used the phrase himself, the idea became known as the "revolution of rising expectations." The human rights workers we met in Nepal were already feeling that change was in the air. Ten years before, the king set out to smash the Movement to Restore Democracy, and more than fifty people were killed by police gunfire and hundreds were arrested. Working for change at a time when the king had dissolved parliament and suspended democracy, many of the activists had spent months or years in prison. By the time we reached Nepal, everyone was excited about the emergence of democracy and civil society, but they were also looking over their shoulders in fear of a crackdown.

For the activists in Nepal, finding a common and unified approach was exciting and empowering, and having our support and suggestions seemed to be helpful. The result was a little like lighting the fuse on a bottle rocket, as new sparks began to pop everywhere. In the capital, previously antagonistic groups joined together to pressure parliament. In the countryside, workers began to push for big changes. A few days after we left the country, on January 14, 2000, an honest local official in one rural area announced there would be a required minimum wage for agricultural workers. Immediately a bonded-labor slave named Nepal Chaudhari brought a petition to the local official demanding that he be paid back wages for all the years he had been enslaved. Chaudhari's slaveholder, taken by surprise, refused to pay, but fearing legal problems he waived Chaudhari's bogus debt and set him free. News of Chaudhari's liberation spread to the local kamaiyas, and with rising expectations they pushed for freedom as well. A deal worked out at the next higher level of government allowed slaveholders to voluntarily release bonded families whose illegal debts were below a certain sum, and twenty-two enslaved families were freed. The rural district of Kanchanpur in the far west of Nepal became a center for action as kamaiyas, with the help of activists, began to push hard for change. In March, eighteen families filed a petition against their slaveholders. In May, forty-eight families in six areas of Kanchanpur filed petitions demanding freedom. Within days one official had issued a "freedom certificate" to a family—following a practice that is common in India but that lacked legal backing in Nepal. The same month a series of demonstrations broke out in the neighboring district of Kailali. Some of the bonded-labor slaves marched in protest all the way to the capital in Kathmandu, a distance of some three hundred miles, arriving in early July.

These rapid changes uncorked the bottle of frustrations and expectations, and events began to take on a distinct whiff of revolution. In the same Kanchanpur district that had seen the petitions filed by bonded workers, an unheard-of mass meeting was announced for July 8. The meeting was remarkable because it included government officials, local officials, judges, enslaved kamaiyas, activists, *and* slaveholders. The result was the Kanchanpur Declaration, which outlined a formula that would ultimately emancipate all the enslaved families in the district. By July 14 (aka Bastille Day, marking another revolution), some 1,600 kamaiyas had registered their petitions for freedom in various offices of Kanchanpur, Kailali, Bardiya, Banke, and Dang districts. The petitions asked that the "loans" owed to the slaveholders be declared null, as they had been forced onto the people and were illegal. On the same day, journalist Pratyoush Onta, writing in the *Kathmandu Post*, noted that "Even as more than 100 Kamaiyas have arrived in Kathmandu to advance their movement toward freedom, Nepal's government maintains a complete silence regarding their demands." Onta blasted the government and the major political parties for failing to speak to the needs of enslaved workers and asked why it took risky action by the kamaiyas to even get them talking about the issue. Onta finished the article on an ominous note, pointing out that petitions and requests for help "were once tried by political activists who now call themselves Maobadis [the revolutionary Maoists in armed revolt]. One can only hope that we do not have to endure the same tragedy twice because the government has not learnt the cost of its previous silence."[2] After hundreds of years of slavery, a lightening bolt of change and possibility had struck the countryside, igniting hope and action. With injustices that were deep seated, the yearning for freedom that had been bottled up for so long was ready to burst.

PLUCKING DISASTER FROM THE JAWS OF VICTORY

We will probably never know what went on behind the closed doors of the royal palace in early July 2000, but I can venture a few guesses. For a monarchy with a tradition of almost total dominance, the feeling must have been palpable that things were getting out of control. In a land where rules come from the top, the idea that a local district could issue a declaration setting out how the age-old kamaiya system would be demolished must have been seen as just short of rebellion. Bonded laborers, the silent and ignored slaves who had propped up the local landowners—and by extension the royal family—for generations, were now shouting slogans outside government offices in the capital. Foreign television crews were filming slaves crying for freedom in view of the royal palace. For the power elite, this was a threat, an embarrassment, and worse. The specter of two million enslaved workers rising up and joining the armed Maoist revolutionaries in the countryside was the stuff of nightmares.

In parliament discussions had been proceeding on a law that would both free and rehabilitate slaves, but its passage was still months away. In a true democracy, the law would have been moved to the fast track, and public statements would have emphasized that the new law was coming. But in a monarchy like Nepal's, there is a way to short-circuit the democratic process, and on July 17 the king ordered, by royal edict, that debt-bondage slavery was abolished. The action had the effect of making a law without discussion by parliament or input from civil society. It also meant that the emancipation proclamation, though welcome, came without provisions for its implementation. The royal edict said little more than "keeping a family in debt slavery is now an offense, and the debts are now void." It did not include the wording of any new statute, instructions on how the law was to be enforced, any indication of where the funding was coming from, or whether there would be any compensation or rehabilitation for ex-slaves. The NGOs, the activists in the countryside, all government agencies (as well as the slaveholders)

were caught by surprise, completely unprepared to act on the new "law."
Still, for ex-slaves like Kashiram Chaudary, who had joined the movement to end bonded-labor slavery just as the edict was announced, the
moment was sweet:

*I was just moved from one master to another; this wasn't my choice. Some
were very bad; I was beaten and there was nothing I could do about it. We
were like prisoners before, we worked all day in the field. The landlord was
always telling us what to do. Now I know I am poor, but so are lots of people.
At least we are not hungry. Now I am a free man.*

Despite the lack of substance in the law, a cheer went up around the
world. I, and many others, hoped that since the government had clearly
declared that hereditary debt slavery was finished, the laws of implementation and support would follow. In a mix of joy and hubris, I wrote
to my friends and colleagues with the good news. At that moment the
idea of emancipation sweeping across the whole country moved me
deeply. The idea that my work might have been a small part of this
emancipation thrilled me. I remember typing with tears of joy welling up
in my eyes, for I believed that I had contributed to a momentous and
wonderful event. In my mind's eye, slaves were stepping into the golden
light of freedom.

THE SLAVEHOLDERS RESPOND

Pride goes before a fall, and I feel shame about my pride and the fall that
followed the emancipation of slaves in Nepal. The Nepali parliament
scrambled to make it sound as if it had played a major role in the declaration ending debt-bondage slavery. In the ensuing media rush, several
politicians from different parties were interviewed, all of them explaining
how their party was the pioneer in antislavery work and how much they
wanted to offer support (sometime in the future) to the soon-to-be ex-
slaves. If the lightning bolt of demands from previously quiescent slaves
had rocked the western districts, the promulgation of the royal edict
declaring all debts cancelled and slavery at an end was sheet lightning
from border to border. The problem was that some people heard the
thunder before others.

Radio is critical to communications in Nepal. Because of the mountains that block television signals, the lack of roads, and the fact that
newspapers are concentrated in the capital, radio is the best way to get

news around the country. But slaves don't have radios; around the world today, slaves are one of the few groups of people who are still unconnected to the great web of electronic media—which is key, since keeping slaves in the dark is crucial to keeping them slaves. When the news of the royal edict broke, slaveholders were the ones who heard it first. All over the country on the evening of July 17, slaveholders were spitting up bits of their evening meal and turning red in the face as they heard the news that the *king* had just wiped out the "debts" they were owed and smashed the bond that held their workers in thrall. Having no warning of this drastic move, they felt panic and urgency sweep over them. This was their livelihood, their life, their legacy from their parents, and their future legacy to their children. Many of the slave families they controlled had been owned by their parents and grandparents and so on, back through the generations.

Although the slaveholders were concerned about losing the money that they had "loaned" the enslaved workers, they had two greater worries. The first worry was that several politicians were saying that the freed kamaiyas should be given the rights to the huts and garden plots they occupied. The second worry was that the law clearly stated that holding kamaiyas was now a serious criminal offense. No guidelines had been given by the government for either of these points, so slaveholders assumed the worst—that the huts and land that they owned would be taken from them and that they were now liable to be arrested on the charge of keeping slaves.

The slaveholders' response was immediate and deadly. Simultaneously, on thousands of farms across the country, slaveholders came to the same conclusion: if the kamaiya slaves were thrown out of their homes and driven away immediately, there would be no one to claim the huts or report the slaveholder to the police. On the morning of July 18, widespread forcible evictions began. A slaveholder drove four families from their homes in Kailali district. It was necessary, he explained, because, "What if the government should decide that my land should belong to the kamaiyas?"[3] The evictions came as a shock to many kamaiyas. Slaves who lived near towns might have known something was happening, but for the majority of kamaiyas living in the more rural areas, the evictions and seizures came as a complete surprise. In a neighboring district, the slave Janjira Khuna and his family were thrown out of their home because the slaveholder feared that they might gain rights to his land. Not willing to waive Khuna's "debt," the slaveholder seized his elderly father to hold until the sum was paid. Slaveholders seized the meager contents of thousands of slave homes—cooking pots, string beds, the occasional hoe—as compensation for the money they were "owed."

FRYING PAN STOLEN, JUST THE FIRE NOW

Emancipation and eviction arrived together, and while happy to be free, the kamaiyas were suddenly homeless, jobless, and hungry. In 1865 slaves were freed in the United States and dumped into the economy without access to credit, education, or political participation. Although what was done to them virtually guaranteed their long-term second-class citizenship, they were rarely evicted and robbed at the same time. In Nepal, the picture quickly turned ugly. Some forty thousand people were freed in the five western districts, and most were turned out of their homes. Suddenly the roads were filled with families seeking food and shelter. Some families moved into abandoned livestock sheds; others clustered under trees. Many families walked to the nearest village or town in hopes of help. By early September there were thirty-seven refugee camps in the districts of Kanachanpur and Kailali alone. In the camps, families built shelters of brush and, if they were lucky, received a sheet of plastic from activist agencies. All over the country the nongovernmental organizations mobilized every penny and person, but the food rations fell to starvation levels. With autumn came the monsoon, and soon the wretched camps were flooded. Within days of the coming of the rains, disease broke out, and people, children in particular, began to die of pneumonia, dysentery, malaria, and encephalitis. Hemlata Rai sent this dispatch from a camp three weeks after the emancipation:

As the Dhangadi sky bursts open, Saraswati Chaudhari picks up her baby boy from the muddy ground and rushes into her hut with its blue plastic covering. She places him on the charpoy (rope bed), and in a mechanical motion picks up her family's ration sack and then the handful of kitchen utensils scattered all over the floor to pile them on the other end of the string bed. She hurriedly collects the firewood and that too goes on the bed. All her belongings now safe from the water soaking the floor rapidly, she herself perches on the bed with the baby on her lap. Since she left her "owner" two weeks ago, the plastic-covered hut has been this former Kamaiya family's only protection against the raging monsoon. And when it pours heavily, the only dry place for her family is the bed.

But Saraswati is among the lucky ones. Angani Chaudhari has been living with his family of eleven inside the skeleton of a hut hoping the government will provide him with at least a plastic sheet to cover it "someday soon."[4]

The government response to this huge internal refugee crisis was practically nonexistent. Some local officials distributed rice, while others refused to give out food. A half-hearted scheme was set up to register ex-slave families, but the enumerators missed as many as half of the families. Families that had not been kamaiyas but were friendly with local officials were registered for relief they didn't deserve. Seeing that they had little to fear from the government, the slaveholders began to organize. In one district they brought a lawsuit to prevent human rights groups from aiding the ex-slaves. In other areas they used corrupt police to threaten ex-slaves and extort money to pay off the "debts" owed by the evicted families. In September the central government in Kathmandu announced that the kamaiyas would be resettled in October 2000, which was then extended to January 2001, extended again to May 2001, and again to June 2001, until finally they just gave up announcing deadlines. The government also announced that ex-slaves would be entitled to ten khattas of land (0.6 of an acre); then they reduced the allotment to five khattas. A family needs at least ten khattas to survive. The size of the entitlement hardly matters, however, since only a handful of ex-slaves ever received land.

By 2007, seven years after the abolition of debt-bondage slavery in Nepal, the situation is still dire. The precise numbers are still unclear, but of the forty thousand freed kamaiya families, about two-thirds have never had any help at all. Many have not received an identity card that allows them to claim help and land, while perhaps one-fifth have been given certificates for land to be awarded in the future. One-third are still living in refugee camps. The majority of kamaiya children are not in school, since many camps have no school and many families need the labor of even their smallest children to ward off starvation.

It doesn't have to be that way. A remarkable program set up by the International Labor Organization has reached some fourteen thousand ex-kamaiyas in western Nepal.[5] In five districts where support has been targeted, literacy is improved, health care and vaccinations now cover most of the population, more than 70 percent of ex-kamaiyas now have secure farm land, and all have their own homes. Incomes are up, livestock ownership is up, access to clean water is up, and half now have radios. The success of this program begs the question—why hasn't the government of Nepal extended it to the remaining kamaiyas?

Just like the American emancipation of 1865, the abolition of slavery in Nepal in 2000 was botched. Though he was speaking of another time and place, the actions of the government of Nepal are perhaps described best by Frederick Douglass: "Whether we turn to the declarations of the past, or to the professions of the present, the conduct of the nation seems equally hideous and revolting."

SOME THINGS ARE HARD TO LIVE WITH

It has been more than six years, and it still hurts me to think about Nepal. It probably always will. Working with groups in Nepal in early 2000, talking with government ministers, I kept pressing them to bring in a new law abolishing debt-bondage slavery. I hammered at the point that all around the world people, organizations, and governments were watching and waiting for a law to be passed as a clear sign of Nepal's commitment to end slavery. I wanted something to happen *now*, something dramatic that would kick-start liberation. I was a fool.

In my pride and eagerness, I thought that my perspective was clearer than that of people who knew Nepal well. I thought that after hundreds of years the kamaiyas could step easily into freedom and that the government, so long the tool of landowners and slaveholders, would support them. Some of these slaves, and slave children, gained their freedom only to find increased suffering and an early death. I wasn't the only person to get this wrong, and I had no control over the actions of the king when he abruptly announced the emancipation and set off the tragedy of a botched abolition, but I have to bear part of the blame. I was wrong to push for immediate action. I should have learned from the experience of America in 1865 and shouted from the rooftops that a clear and funded program leading to economic and social autonomy and citizenship must be in place for each ex-slave.

No one knows exactly how many people have died in the refugee camps, but the truth I have to bear is that some died because I pushed too hard and thought too little. I learned a lesson, and others paid for that lesson with their lives. Liberation has to be followed by a chance to build a new life in safety, knowledge, and dignity, or it is a cruel mockery. I hope I have put that heart-breaking lesson to good use. It certainly has important things to teach us about how governments should respond to slavery. But first we will look at another Asian country, this time a rich country whose record in freeing slaves is equally dismal.

THE TROUBLE WITH JAPAN

Nepal is a poor country suffering from the tremendous medieval legacy of powerful landowners and slavery. Given that Nepal is lurching into the present and tripping over the stumbling blocks of corruption and future shock, it is not surprising that things got into a mess. But it is surprising that there are also many slaves in modern, highly educated, and economically prosperous Japan.

Japan is one of the most law-abiding countries in the world, so how do we explain the high level of a serious crime like slavery? Robberies in Japan, for example, occur at the rate of 1.3 per 100,000 population (the rate in the United States is 233 per 100,000). Unlike Nepal, the slaves in Japan are not agricultural workers trapped for generations, but young foreign women imported in large numbers to meet the demands of Japanese men for sex and "entertainment." That the importation of these young women has gone on for years with government acquiescence is even more puzzling until you dig a little deeper into Japanese culture.

The sale of sex in Japan is vast in scale. In 2001 it was thought to generate $20 billion a year and was known to be growing rapidly. That amount takes the world's largest car maker, Toyota, four years to earn. The sex business itself is in the throes of change. Fading out are the old-fashioned brothels, strip clubs, and "soap lands" (staffed by naked prostitutes offering soapy massages), whose relatively high overheads meant that the average price of sex was $300 to $500. Quickly replacing them are the "fashion massage shops." Their overheads are much lower, as one business writer explained, because they are "staffed by heavily exploited foreign workers."[6] The cost for sex in a fashion massage shop is $50 to $90. Moving down the ladder, sex with foreign women is being sold on the street for $8 to $10. In Japan, all this commerce in sex is quaintly known as the "entertainment industry." No one knows for sure how many people work in this sprawling trade, but in addition to several hundred thousand Japanese women, there are estimated to be at least 150,000 to 200,000 foreign women who fill the most dangerous jobs and who are most likely to be enslaved. You might assume that prostitution is legal in Japan, but it is not. On the other hand, Japanese law defines only intravaginal heterosexual acts as prostitution, nothing else. Any

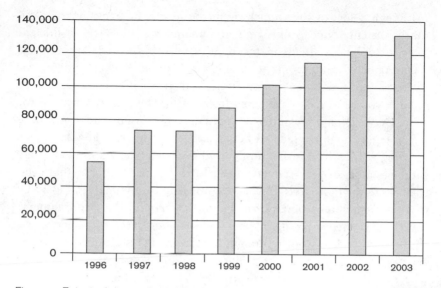

Figure 2. Entry to Japan on "entertainer" visas, 1996–2003

other form of sex for sale is legal and is not regulated. In addition, the key law against prostitution punishes solicitation—so it is prostitutes, not the men who use them, who are arrested and punished, although the government doesn't really do much of anything to combat this generally illegal business.

Actually, the Japanese government does a great deal about the illegal sex trade—to support it. For more than twenty years the government has opened the country to human traffickers by giving them a special means of entry all their own. As we have seen, the sex industry in Japan is called the "entertainment trade," and there is a special visa for young foreign women, established by the government, called the "entertainer visa." The visa is supposedly given to singers and dancers who will be giving performances in theaters and nightclubs. If this were true, then Japan would have more professional entertainers than any country in the world. In reality, an increasing torrent of young women is being brought to Japan to be forced into prostitution. (See figure 2.)

What other country is so in love with entertainment that it is necessary to import 133,103 singers and dancers in a single year? And are the Japanese such jaded theater goers that the 123,322 singers and dancers imported the year before ceased to be entertaining after a few months?

Although a few of the women might be legitimate entertainers, obviously, the entertainer visa is a gift to human traffickers from politicians who are willing to do favors for organized crime. In 2003, 80,000 of the "entertainers" came from the Philippines; another 6,000 to 7,000 came from each of the United States, China, and Russia. Over the years some 40,000 young women have come from Latin America to Japan on the visa. Under intense pressure from human rights groups and other countries, Japan finally agreed to better police the entertainer visa system starting in March 2005, but no figures have been released showing a fall in the number of "entertainers" brought to Japan. Of course, that is little help to the thousands of women controlled by criminals in Japan. Of the half a million women brought into the country as "entertainers" over the past ten years, no one knows how many remain in slavery.

If the trafficked women brought into Japan on government-approved visas were the only ones, the problem would be vast by the standards of the rich nations. By comparison, the U.S. government believes that between 14,500 and 17,500 people are trafficked into America each year. Sadly, entertainer visas are just one part of the harvest of young women swept up by Japanese organized crime. According to government estimates, about 220,000 illegal residents had overstayed their visas in the country in 2004, and hundreds of thousands more will arrive each year on tourist visas. Both categories include a significant number of women trafficked and held against their will. In addition, while the rate of marriage by Japanese women to foreign men has remained fairly constant, marriages of foreign women to Japanese men have skyrocketed to more than 30,000 a year. An investigation by the Organization of American States found that while many of these marriages are legitimate, some are known to be "phony marriages arranged by traffickers and used to move foreign women into the Japanese sex trade or the underground labor force."[7] Sometimes, trafficking a young woman into Japan will include manipulation and fraud at several levels. Take the case of a girl from Thailand named Sri:

> Sri was approached by a woman she knew from her province, who . . . told her about a well-paid job opportunity in a Thai restaurant in Japan. Sri decided to take up the offer because her parents needed money for her younger brother's schooling. Sri applied for a passport herself, but was called to an office to meet a "boss" who had many passports at hand and chose one for her. She had silicone injections in her face to make her look more like the picture on the passport. However, she barely carried the passport herself, entering Japan with a man posing as her "Japanese boyfriend," who took her passport after they passed through immigration.

Sri believed that the passport may have carried a visa for a Japanese spouse. At the airport in Japan, the "boyfriend" rang another man who came to pick her up by car, and took her to a bar, where she was told she had to repay a debt of 4.8 million yen [about $40,000] to cover the costs involved in bringing her to Japan, and that she would have to work as a prostitute. The bar was in the countryside, without any sign advertising it as such. There were many other women from Thailand and China, but Sri was too frightened to talk to anyone. She had her hair dyed yellow. Clients paid 10,000 yen for 20 minutes. Sri had to pay 45,000 yen a day on her debt, 1,000 yen for food and another 1,000 yen for a bodyguard. She needed ten clients a day to repay her debt, but managed only three or four.[8]

Sri had one advantage. Unlike most trafficking victims in Japan, she could speak some English. After a period of sexual exploitation in the brothel, she used her English to get a taxi to take her to the Thai embassy.

The basic rule of human trafficking is that victims flow from poorer countries to richer countries. Japan is by far the richest country in Asia and the largest destination for the young women duped and coerced by criminals. No one knows for certain how many trafficking victims are in Japan. The U.S. Department of State says that "There are no clear estimates on the number of trafficking victims in Japan, but most agree the number is significant and many women will not come forward for fear of reprisal by their traffickers."[9] The first time I tried to make an estimate in the late 1990s I pulled together what information existed and conservatively suggested 5,000 to 10,000 slaves in Japan. Having now spent time in Japan and talked the problem over with researchers there, I now believe that estimate should be increased. Given the number of "entertainers," the 150,000 foreign women thought to be part of the sex industry, the explosion in foreign women getting "married" to Japanese men, as well as the numbers of illegal residents overstaying their visas, I believe the number to be much, much higher, at least in the tens of thousands.

THE GOVERNMENT THROWS ITSELF INTO INACTION

The Japanese government got a shock in June 2004 when the U.S. government issued its annual *Trafficking in Persons Report*.[10] The report investigates how well countries are doing in the fight against human trafficking. It ranks countries into three groups, or "tiers." Tier 1 countries are doing a good job of responding to trafficking and slavery; Tier 2 countries are trying but not doing enough; and Tier 3 countries have serious trafficking problems and are not doing anything about them, or are even making matters worse. There is also a special "Tier 2 Watch List" for countries that need a warning to get their act together. Being on the Watch List means a country is in danger of being relegated to Tier 3. Relegation is serious because a country placed on Tier 3 can be sanctioned in a number of ways and will suffer as a result. A certain amount of politics plays into the list each year. Countries that are "friends" of the United States tend not to end up on Tier 3, even if they aren't doing that much about trafficking. Countries that the U.S. government defines as "enemies" are not only more likely to end up on Tier 3 but tend to suffer sanctions as well. Although it shouldn't be a big surprise, in world history slavery has always taken a back seat to political expediency. Suzanne Miers has written an amazing study of slavery in the twentieth century, and a pervasive theme of her work is the constant sacrifice of antislavery ideals on the altar of political and financial interest.[11] Japan, of course, is a "friend" of the United States, so its relegation to the Watch List, joining corrupt dictatorships like Serbia and Tajikistan, was quite a shock. For the Japanese it was more than just a bad score. In a culture that avoids embarrassment at any cost, this public shaming by a friend left politicians reeling.

For a country that donates relatively large sums to combat poverty and disease around the world, the sudden exposure as a center of trafficking and slavery was humiliating. In response, the government leaped into a flurry of talking. By December an "action plan" was approved, which actually contained very little action. For four years a nonbinding U.N. convention with provisions on human trafficking had been awaiting ratification by the Japanese parliament, so that was rushed through. Getting tough on crime, the parliament placed a whole series of proposed laws "under discussion," and one was even enacted—a provision recommending that the number of entertainer visas be reduced. But this recommendation was met with sharp protests from the "entertainment industry," and the politicians backed off. A government delegation went off on a junket to the United States, Thailand, Colombia, and the Philippines to discuss human trafficking. Airport inspectors were told to tighten up, but there is no record that they were given any training on detecting human trafficking.

The results of all this activity were about what we would expect. In 2004 the number of victims found and protected quadrupled from six to twenty-five. The number of prosecuted offenders rose from thirty-seven to forty-eight. Some seventy-seven victims were identified in 2004, though the government has not said how many of those were helped and how many were just deported.[12] If there are tens of thousands of slaves in Japan, the government has managed to find far less than 1 percent of them. This extremely low level of surveillance and detection might be expected in some poor and rural countries, but Japan may be the best-policed democracy in the world.

Japanese police operate what is known as the *koban* system. The *koban* is a one-room mini–police station with a territory of about one-fifth of a square mile, an area most city dwellers would think of as their local neighborhood. There are thousands of these *koban* in Tokyo in addition to the district police stations. Police officers are in the *koban* around the clock as well as patrolling the neighborhood. It is an extremely labor-intensive system that basically means the police know everyone and their business, and very little happens in any Japanese city without the police knowing about it. On the other hand, one researcher has noted that Japanese police are "tolerant" of organized crime, a euphemism I think we have to read as "on the take."[13] In the report on human trafficking to Japan written for the Organization of American States, the researchers noted that groups trying to help trafficking victims report that "policemen return women, who came to seek help [at the *koban*], to the traffickers." Although a system of *koban* exists in the rural areas as well, the report goes on to note: "For women who are working in remote areas of Japan, such as the isolated islands in Okinawa, it is almost impossible to escape."[14] Police inaction in dealing with trafficking is demonstrated when we compare the numbers trafficked into slavery with the number of murder victims. Both are extremely serious crimes, trafficking actually incorporating a bundle of crimes often including rape, kidnapping, torture, assault and so forth, but the (low) estimated number of enslaved victims in Japan outnumbers murder victims many times over. In the United States the estimated ratio is about one to one. Something is terribly wrong in Japan when victims fear the police, the crime is both pervasive and officially ignored, and the flow of victims, by a number of indirect measures, is increasing.

WHISPERING THE F WORD (FOREIGNER)

To fully understand the acceptance of slavery in Japan, we must look even deeper into the country's culture. Below the polite and polished surface of Japan's rich hospitality lies a disturbing core of racism. No law prohibits racial discrimination in Japan. Although Japan is not exactly the world of Jim Crow, it does echo Alabama in 1960. Outside restaurants, bars, public baths, apartment buildings, and nightclubs are signs denying admittance to non-Japanese. Foreigners are regularly discriminated against when it comes to jobs and housing. A core concept of superiority and purity in Japanese culture often translates into racist exclusion.

Given the extensive slavery in the sex industry, the general view held by Japanese men that women are inferior is no surprise. "Japanese men see women as second-class," said Sumiko Shimizu, a member of parliament and head of the Japan Women's Council. "This attitude underscores the tacit acceptance of women as sexual objects to satisfy men." As with racial prejudice, no legal recourse is available for systematic discrimination against women, whether by the government, businesses, or other institutions. This is a country in which a young woman is expected to give up her job if she gets married and will be sidelined at work and pressured to leave if she doesn't. Few women are employed above the lowest levels; the first woman ever to be named to run a major corporation took her post in 2006. Women are paid significantly less than men. Behind the lack of laws and the job discrimination is the subtle and constant expectation, deep and pervasive in the culture, that women should be meek, agreeable, and willing servants of men. You don't have to speak Japanese to see this. On the nightly television news I would watch the man and woman who were the anchor reporters. The woman presenter would be constantly bowing to the man, or giggling and covering her mouth to make a point of her inability to understand the weighty issues that men must consider. That deference is humiliating, but it can also be dangerous. Domestic violence is an unmeasured and ugly current in Japanese families. There was no clear law on spousal abuse until 2002, and police still routinely ignore assaults on women by their husbands. Combine deep-seated and unquestioned racism with a cultural belief in the inferiority of women, and the resulting cocktail can be deadly.

In 2006 I traveled around Japan meeting with antitrafficking groups and government officials. Although nearly all the officials were polite and welcoming, they also tended to speak only in generalities and excuses. When I asked about foreign women enslaved in prostitution, they would say, "Yes, an abuse like that would be a serious matter." If I asked why there was no official shelter for women freed from slavery, they would say, "The government is discussing this matter carefully so that we will make the right decision." On the other hand, when I spoke to the women who were actually dealing with the handful of enslaved prostitutes who had escaped, they spoke of their experience in detail and with desperation. They faced an uphill battle. Since the public tends to see the whole issue of the abuse of foreigners as distasteful or embarrassing, the hard-working organizers who help traumatized young foreign women are snubbed and ignored (in a very polite Japanese way) by the average person. The police are no help and are often a hindrance. Many of the local male politicians have been using these young women sexually in the strip clubs and brothels, and some politicians are actually on the payroll of the criminals who control the slaves. The national government won't provide guidance or resources. The other major force in Japanese cities, the *yakuza,* the organized crime network, has an enormous vested interest in keeping the flow of trafficked women high and the slaves in the brothels invisible and unheard. These thugs will threaten or attack social workers, charities, politicians, or anyone else who might disrupt their profits.

There is little notion in Japanese culture of public charity; support for charities tends to come directly from government. As a result, shelters for freed slaves have to do things such as running a coffee shop or passing the hat to generate funds. For the most part, the handful of dedicated women who set up the shelters are paying the running costs, including the expenses for medical treatments needed by freed slaves, out of their own pockets. When I met with the brave NGO workers in Japan, their desperation was palpable. They truly felt that they were fighting not just the criminals but also the entire structure of government and culture. That they did so with such unflagging grace made me feel awe and more than a little anger at the double standards that make their work so difficult.

COMPENSATED DATING

In the late 1990s, a scandal rocked Japan. The sexual exploitation of young girls by Japanese men burst into the media and the story was played and replayed. The stink it raised brought in new rules, education campaigns in schools, and a vast collection of disparaging editorials. Laws were passed in a number of cities. The country was in an uproar over the fact that girls were being used sexually, but the furor had nothing to do with forced prostitution or the enslavement of foreigners. The focus of this scandal was *enjo kosai* or "compensated dating," a practice that was apparently devised by Japanese high school girls and carried them through thrill seeking and moneymaking into prostitution. Using their cell phones, girls would log on to a Web site where they could register to receive a call directly from a man. A "date" would be arranged that could be as innocent as sharing a snack or could include sex. Girls as young as twelve, with most in the fifteen to seventeen age group, were taking part. Surveys of high school girls suggested as many as one in five had engaged in compensated dating. The girls almost universally explained that they wanted the compensation to buy designer clothing and pay cell phone bills. Some girls developed long-standing clients and received fixed monthly payments. The controversy exploded when a girl, always referred to as "Girl X" in the media, was beaten, sodomized, and infected with a sexually transmitted disease on a compensated date. When the Japanese public woke up to the situation, much of the shock came from the fact that nice, middle-class schoolgirls were involved.

Perhaps the surprise should not have been so profound given that Japanese men have a deep and widely held sexual obsession with school-girls. It is not just that some Japanese prostitutes do very well dressing in school uniforms and working in special brothels equipped as school-rooms. Intensely pornographic comic books about sex with schoolgirls are also sold everywhere and read openly. There is even a trade in the "used" underwear of schoolgirls that is so brisk that men buy sealed packets of panties from vending machines and corner shops. It was when this sexual obsession with schoolgirls both went fully public and, espe-cially, began to draw in middle-class Japanese children willing to be "compensated" for sexual abuse that even the look-the-other-way cul-ture of Japan was upset. The willing victims of compensated dating may have gone home to their parents and to school the next morning, but their plight brought about public outrage and immediate legislation. Of course, under international law, no child can consent to being sexually abused, and for similar activity in the United States a businessman or politician can end up in prison.

FROM "COMFORT" TO "ENTERTAINMENT"

I point to the scandal of compensated dating to dramatize the double standard that Japan holds toward the sexual abuse of children, one that can be briefly stated as "Japanese children, no; foreign girls, whatever." Sadly, there is more to the problem than just this double standard. Japanese men have expressed their concoction of racism and sexism for many decades in the sexual exploitation of foreign women. During World War II, the Japanese military enslaved as forced prostitutes thou-sands of civilian noncombatant Philippine, Korean, Thai, Vietnamese, and Chinese women and children. Large "comfort stations" were estab-lished in all the territories occupied by the Japanese army. Somewhere between eighty thousand and two hundred thousand women were enslaved in this way. In addition to the serial rape they suffered, many were tortured, and some were murdered. Collectively known as "comfort women," the massive scale of their degradation and abuse is staggering. Chong Ok Sun, a survivor of the comfort stations, described the treatment of comfort women in her testimony for the United Nations:

> One day in June, at the age of 13, I had to prepare lunch for my parents who were working in the field and so I went to the village well to fetch water. A Japanese garrison soldier surprised me there and took me away, so that my parents never knew what had happened to their daughter. I was taken to the police station in a truck, where I was raped by several policemen. When I shouted, they put socks in my mouth and continued to rape me. The head of the police station hit me in my left eye because I was crying. That day I lost my eyesight in the left eye.
>
> After ten days or so, I was taken to the Japanese army garrison barracks in Heysan City. There were around 400 other Korean young girls with me and we had to serve over 5,000 Japanese soldiers as sex slaves everyday— up to forty men per day. Each time I protested, they hit me or stuffed rags in my mouth. One held a matchstick to my private parts until I obeyed him. My private parts were oozing with blood.
>
> One Korean girl who was with us once demanded why we had to serve so many, up to 40, men per day. To punish her for her questioning, the Japanese company commander Yamamoto ordered her to be beaten with a sword. While we were watching, they took off her clothes, tied her legs and hands and rolled her over a board with nails until the nails were covered with blood and pieces of her flesh. In the end, they cut off her head. Another Japanese, Yamamoto, told us that, "it's easy to kill you all, easier than killing dogs."
>
> One Korean girl caught a venereal disease from being raped so often and, as a result, over fifty Japanese soldiers were infected. In order to stop the disease from spreading and to "sterilize" the Korean girl, they stuck a hot iron bar in her private parts. Once they took forty of us on a truck far away to a pool filled with water and snakes. The soldiers beat several of the girls, shoved them into the water, heaped earth into the pool and buried them alive.
>
> I think over half of the girls who were at the garrison barracks were killed. Twice I tried to run away, but both times we were caught after a few days. We were tortured even more and I was hit on my head so many times that all the scars still remain. They also tattooed me on the inside of my lips, my chest, my stomach and my body. I fainted. When I woke up, I was on a mountainside, presumably left for dead. Of the two girls with me, only Kuk Hae and I survived. A 50-year-old man who lived in the mountains found us, gave us clothes and something to eat. He also helped us to travel back to Korea, where I returned, scarred, barren and with difficulties in speaking, at the age of 18, after five years of serving as a sex slave for the Japanese.[15]

As the Japanese economy recovered after the war, the fundamental assumption that foreign women were fair game for sexual abuse came back as big business. Sex tourism from Japan to other Asian countries increased rapidly from the 1970s through the 1990s. Beginning on the Chinese island of Taipei, packaged sex tours expanded to Korea and the Philippines, and then Thailand. In the Japanese fashion, these tours were highly organized and shielded the tourists from contact with the outside culture; the price of sex with local women and girls was included in the overall price. By the early 1990s, twelve million Japanese men were going abroad each year, and one in five reported buying sex while abroad.[16] From the 1980s the demand for foreign women began to increase inside Japan as well, in large part due to the experience of sex tourism. After attacks on tourists in some parts of Asia, and with the fear of terrorism after 2001, Japanese men increasingly chose to stay home and have the foreign women brought to them. The result was the roaring sex business, the importation of "entertainment workers," and soaring profits for organized crime. Japan clearly has a serious problem with slavery, and it is a problem that is being insistently ignored. I'll explore how a country can overcome such problems at the end of this chapter, but first let's look at one country that is already working aggressively to end slavery, not to promote it.

LULA LEADS THE WAY

Brazil possesses few of the advantages of Japan when it comes to policing. It is a vast country with a wild frontier in the west and in the Amazon basin. On the frontier the rule of law is stretched so thinly as to disappear altogether at times. All along that frontier, slaves are used to cut down the trees of the great Amazonian forest, to hack away at sugar cane, to dig iron ore and smelt it, to clear brush for cattle farms, to burn timber to produce charcoal, and to do any other dirty and dangerous work that slaveholders can make a profit from. In official reports the government admits that there are some 25,000 slaves in Brazil, though the top antislavery official in the capital concedes the number is probably closer to 50,000. Even though there is no *koban*-style policing system, and even with the wild and unpoliceable frontier, Brazil freed 4,789 slaves in 2003 and another 2,745 slaves in 2004. Compare that to the 6 slaves Japan rescued in 2003 and 24 in 2004. In 2005, Brazil freed another 4,113 slaves. How can a poorer and wilder country like Brazil make such remarkable progress against slavery while a rich and well-policed country like Japan languishes in an antislavery coma?

POLITICAL WILL = ACTION ON THE GROUND

In the late 1990s I traveled to the far west of Brazil to study slavery in the charcoal camps. It was an amazing journey and one of stark contrasts. In lush forests, where flocks of brightly colored parrots flew through the tree tops, were wretched camps where slaves chopped wood, stacked it in hive-shaped ovens the height of a man, and slowly burned it into charcoal. All around the camps, for a mile or so, the land had been stripped and gouged. The exposed earth was red and eroded. The tree stumps, the great patches of burned over grass and wood, the trenches and holes, and the ever-present pall of smoke turned it into an ecological battleground. The wreckage of the forest was everywhere. Covered with black soot and gray ash and shiny with sweat the workers moved like ghosts in and out of the smoke around the ovens. The workers I saw were just muscle, bone, and scars, every bit of fat burned off by the heat and effort. The overpowering, choking smoke colored and flavored everything. The eucalyptus smoke, full of the sharp oil, was acrid and burned the eyes, nose, and throat. All of the charcoal workers coughed constantly, hacking and spitting and trying to clear lungs that were always clogged with smoke, ash, heat, and charcoal dust. If they lived long enough, they suffered from black lung disease.

Most of the ovens were oozing and belching smoke, and the heat was tremendous. As soon as I entered a *batteria* the heat pressed down. This part of Brazil was already hot and humid; take away any protection from the sun that the trees might offer and add the heat of thirty ovens, and you are working in a baking inferno. For the workers who had to climb inside the still-burning ovens to empty charcoal, the heat was unimaginable. When I got inside an oven with a man shoveling the charcoal, the pressure of the heat had my head spinning in minutes, sweat drenched my clothes, and the floor of hot coals burned my feet through my heavy boots. The pointed roof concentrated the heat, and in a few moments I was addled, panicky, and limp. The workers hovered on the edge of heat stroke and dehydration. When we spoke to them, they were often confused, as if their brains had been baked. The workers who emptied the ovens stayed almost naked, but this exposed their skin to burns. Sometimes, standing on the piles of charcoal, they stumbled, and if the charcoal gave way, they fell into red-hot coals. All of the charcoal workers I met had hands, arms, and legs crisscrossed with ugly burn scars, some still swollen and festering.

The charcoal workers were just one type of slave in Brazil, and the problem was well known. At that time, however, the government did little beyond practicing a vigorous system of denial and obfuscation. Labor inspectors and police were told to search out the camps where slaves were held, but when I visited the inspectors' office in the prime charcoal region, I found that they had not been given a telephone or a vehicle. Far from the camps in the countryside, they were effectively trapped in the city. The government had no real intention of dealing with slavery; the influence of rich landowners was too strong, and the slaves themselves were seen as irrelevant and disposable. Wherever profits could be made from human sweat, slavery grew like a cancer. In agriculture, land clearances, mining, charcoal production, and prostitution, men, women, and children lost their free will and sometimes their lives to the slaveholders.

Brazil also has a history of slavery in which a huge number of slaves, as many as ten times the number sent to North America, were brought into the country from Africa. From the beginning of colonization until late in the nineteenth century, some ten million people were transported and enslaved. But because the death rate on sugar plantations was so high, the slave population of Brazil was never more than half that of the United States. It also took much longer to bring legal slavery to an end, and when full emancipation came in May 1888, Brazil was the last country in the Americas to abolish legal slavery.

Denouncing slavery at the United Nations, condemning it in the European press, assuring the U.S. government of their earnest efforts, the Brazilian government dodged its responsibilities at home until 2002, its protests and assurances just a smokescreen. The small police unit called the Special Group for the Suppression of Forced Labor (GERTRAF) had its resources slightly increased to fund four poorly equipped squads. But if the whole neighborhood is full of cockroaches, four cans of insecticide won't go very far. Four squads in a country the size of Brazil, with many thousands in slavery, simply weren't enough.

LULA AND THE FIGHT AGAINST SLAVERY

Dramatic changes began to occur in Brazil after the election of Luiz Inácio Lula da Silva, known as "Lula," as president in October 2002. Lula had a background in organized labor that predisposed him to taking real action against slavery. He was also a person who understood poverty, having grown up in a poor family. Lula left school after the fourth grade, went to work in a copper smelter at age fourteen, lost a finger in an automobile factory accident at nineteen, and then worked his way up in trade union politics. President Lula has made it clear that he believes that Brazil's history of slavery is still hampering its development today. In October 2006 he stated, "This [slavery] system channeled wealth to a powerful elite and dug a social abyss that still marks the life of the nation."[17]

Within four months of entering office, Lula set up a National Commission for the Eradication of Slave Labor as a permanent part of the government and announced the National Plan for the Eradication of Slavery. Perhaps for the first time in history, a government proceeded in the right way, making sure that everything was in place *before* taking action. The commission brought together all relevant government agencies, the police and national law enforcement, and the antislavery and human rights organizations that had been doing most of the work up to that time. It was the right team to attack the problem.

The national plan included some excellent ideas. The law against slavery would be tightened and the penalties increased. One of the strongest new proposals was also very radical: the expropriation, without compensation, of land belonging to slaveholders. If approved, expropriation would provide a significant sanction against those using slaves. It was also suggested that expropriated land could be distributed to poor landless farmers, which could also help prevent reenslavement. According to the Brazilian Department for Labor Inspections, up to 40 percent of people freed from slave labor had been freed more than once, pointing to a cycle of poverty, economic crisis, and enslavement; providing access to land and a better chance at employment would prevent workers from falling back into slavery. The plan also established a "dirty list" of any people or companies that used slave labor. Those on the list would be excluded from receiving any sort of government funds, grants, or credits. Since much of the process of opening and developing land relies on government tax credits or support, slave-using companies and individuals would be driven out of that business. Most important in the short run was the expansion of the Special Mobile Inspection Groups, the antislavery squads that had been starved of funds and equipment by the previous administration. These teams were increased in number, given good four-wheel-drive trucks, and, crucially, linked to new "mobile courts." These mobile courts could impose immediate fines, freeze bank accounts, and seize assets, making it much easier to force farm owners to pay workers the money they were owed within hours of their rescue.

The Action Plan achieved immediate and dramatic results. In 2003 the number of slaves freed more than doubled, to 4,879, and people began to think that the government might actually hit its target of eradicating slavery by 2006. Sadly, the number of liberated slaves fell in 2004 to 2,745. The fall in numbers was due in part to slaveholders realizing that they could no longer operate without risk of arrest and that they needed to hide their slaves better. Slaveholders also began to fight back against the government's campaign, and in late 2003 violence and intimidation suffered by those working to stop slave labor rose, especially in the rural states of Pará and Tocantins. Antislavery activists in Tocantins had to flee after receiving repeated death threats. State officials were also targeted. In October 2003 a labor judge had to leave his city after receiving repeated death threats, and in February 2004 his deputy was killed. Also in Tocantins, a prosecutor fled after receiving threats. On January 28, 2004, three officials from the labor ministry and their driver were murdered while investigating farms in the state of Minas Gerais.

In February 2006 a federal deputy, the equivalent of a U.S. congressional representative, was convicted of having fifty-three enslaved workers on land he owned. He was fined more than $240,000 but is still fighting the conviction as I write this in April 2007. His case showed both the progress of the antislavery campaign and the resistance to it. Brother Xavier Plassat is the Catholic friar who heads up the antislavery work of the Pastoral Land Commission, the main social action and human rights organization in Brazil. He called the conviction of the deputy "a courageous step by the Labor Court system, following up on what inspectors caught in the act when they visited his properties." Plassat noted that in the past it was hard to get law enforcement to even look at such cases, and the arrest of a deputy would have been unthinkable, but he also explained that "We have a hard time getting the courts to deal effectively with these violators. Nobody has ever been sent to jail for the crime of slavery, despite the fact that more than 18,000 workers have been rescued in the past ten years. Over 500 individuals responsible for abuses should have been convicted."[18]

The most disappointing thing about the Brazilian government's campaign against slavery is the lack of convictions and the low fines given out to those who are caught. True, even with the slaveholders trying harder to hide their slaves, the number freed shot up in 2005 to 4,133, the dirty list began to cause government money to be denied to violators, and companies on the list began to look to antislavery groups, like the U.N. International Labor Organization, for advice about cleaning up their supply chains. But even these positive achievements leave critical steps untaken.

BRAZIL'S REPORT CARD

There may not be a country in the whole world doing as good a job of fighting slavery as Brazil, but I can't give the country an A-plus; probably the best grade I can assign the country's antislavery campaign is a B-minus. More than six hundred rural landlords have been caught with slaves during this period, but none of them are in prison, none have had property confiscated, and many continue the practice despite the implementation of innovative financial sanctions through labor lawsuits and the government's dirty list. The legislature is still debating whether it is constitutional to confiscate the property of slaveholders. More than $3 million was paid to freed slaves in 2005, but reported cases can still take up to forty days to be investigated, and many freed slaves are being reenslaved. There are now seven active mobile squads, but is that enough for 3.3 million square miles of territory? Brazil is absolutely on the right course, and compared with virtually every other country in the world is far advanced in the fight against slavery. What is needed now is a final push. A government that can free four thousand to five thousand slaves a year can eradicate slavery within its borders if it has the will and devotes the resources to the job. If it does the job right, Brazil's success can be an example for many other countries.

In order to end slavery, the government of Brazil needs to do several things. It can start by increasing the number of mobile squads to at least twenty and giving them funds and equipment appropriate to Brazilian conditions, particularly transport such as helicopters. The aim should be to free a minimum of ten thousand slaves a year and to lock up the perpetrators. In many countries this effort would be hampered by an inability to find people in slavery, but finding people in Brazil is not a problem. In 2006 more than eight thousand enslaved or escaped slave workers brought their cases to the Pastoral Land Commission. The organization manages to reach and deal with about 70 percent of these, finding slavery on about 250 farms a year, then helping ex-slaves to build new lives. According to Xavier Plassat, the cases are coming from all over and are straining the government's capacity to deal with them. The Pastoral Land Commission plays a vital role and provides a model of nongovernmental work against slavery that needs to be studied and replicated around the world. The Brazilian government's report card is much better than it would otherwise be because of the help of the Pastoral Land Commission.

The government needs to assign criminal prosecutors to the mobile squads. At the moment labor prosecutors travel with the squads, but the labor prosecutors cannot order the arrest and detention of slaveholders. The federal police on the squads can arrest people, but they usually do not because they cannot clearly identify who is responsible for the crime. Often the arrests they do make are for other charges such as illegal weapons possession. Clearly, the police need more training on how to identify the crime and the criminal. Perhaps more important is the need to straighten out the underlying structure of law.

The Brazilian government needs to pass laws that put slavery clearly under federal jurisdiction and that give criminal and labor prosecutors the legal tools required to bring criminal cases against slaveholders. The government also needs to begin expropriating property from those who use slave labor. There are plenty of precedents for expropriation in the many countries that confiscate the property of drug dealers and other criminals.

The tax authorities need to be authorized to claim back any money, grant, or credit paid to anyone caught using slaves. In 2006 there were about 230 farms and businesses on the list, most of these farmers or business owners who had exhausted all appeals against investigation and prosecution. Some of the accused are removed from the list through judicial appeal, but there are currently no guidelines for what should constitute grounds for removal. Fines are levied against offenders, but no one pays them because there is no enforcement mechanism for their collection. These basic laws are in place; it is simply a matter of building the enforcement mechanism.

Another easy change would be to increase the present two-to-eight-year sentence for slaveholding in the criminal code to an absolute minimum of four to eight years. One reason no slaveholder has ever gone to jail is the existing minimum two-year sentence. In Brazilian legal practice a two-year sentence is nearly always commuted to community service and probation. Brazil simply needs to make the felony of slavery an offense that allows immediate arrest and incarceration. For comparison, sentences for slaveholders in U.S. courts have been as high as thirty years and include orders for very large amounts of money to be paid in restitution to the victims.

The government needs to give the dirty list its own administration to ensure strict and immediate enforcement. The dirty list is a good idea, but it has little or no effect because the relevant agencies of the government do not use it as a guide to restrict or refuse grants to the offenders, nor does the Development Bank, which is crucial to most Brazilian businesses, use it. One of the spinoffs of the dirty list has been the group formed by some large corporations called the "Pact against Slavery." When slavery is discovered feeding into the supply chain of a large company, the company is presented with a choice: be linked to these slave-using suppliers from the dirty list or join the Pact against Slavery and help solve the problem. Strong government support for this group would move more companies into the pact and drive more slave-using suppliers out of business. This is a solution that could be copied with great benefit in many other countries.

The Brazilian government also needs to make public the number of prosecutions, convictions, and punishments relating to slavery. Transparency would help the public understand the tremendous task and the potential for historic achievement. The United Nations has been critical about this lack of transparency and has pointed to the serious discrepancy between the large number of people released from slavery and the small number of convictions.

To prevent the significant amount of reenslavement—up to 40 percent of people freed from slavery in Brazil can end up reenslaved—the government needs to build a parallel agency to the antislavery squads that will give freed slaves the tools, training, and funds they need to become economically autonomous citizens and stay out of slavery in the future. This agency could start with programs in the most affected states—such as Mato Grosso, Maranhao, Piauí, Pará, and Tocantins—to prevent workers from being reenslaved. The U.S. Department of Labor is funding a project in Brazil called "Trail to Liberty" that is trying to stabilize freed workers and establish a rehabilitation and reintegration sequence, but apart from this initiative few such projects are in place.

Agrarian reform is a big job and one that will take some time, but Lula, after his reelection in 2006, is the most likely person to attempt it. Like many other Latin American countries, Brazil has evolved from a state where vast tracts of land were controlled by the wealthiest 1 percent and sharecropping or tenant farming was the rule. With a burgeoning population, the demand for land and livelihood is growing rapidly and must be addressed. Freed slaves should have priority in land grants, and the main regions for reform and land grants should be areas where there is recruitment into enslavement. This step would deter migration driven by desperation and hunger, a journey that carries the migrant too often into the hands of the slaveholder. The proposed constitutional amendment for expropriation of slaveholder land would help, but expropriation is not always necessary for agrarian reform, since the expropriated land may not be useful or appropriate for small farmers. These actions are doable and affordable, especially when countries benefiting from slavery in Brazil could help fund the needed changes. First among these is the United States, the prime destination of Brazilian slave-produced commodities.

SO THIS IS OUR FAULT?

Slavery in Brazil feeds American and European markets. Almost every product of slavery in Brazil is aimed at the export market. Iron and steel are the third-largest export of Brazil; most of it comes to the United States, with a significant amount going to Europe. The iron and steel is produced with slave-made charcoal. There is no debate: slaves in charcoal production have been seen and documented by the Brazilian government, the United Nations, independent journalists and investigators, and me personally. In the United States the iron and steel goes into cars and trucks, furniture, buildings, and toys. In addition, mahogany (used in musical instruments as well as furniture), other timber, and beef come from slave labor in Brazil to American markets. Altogether the importation represents millions, if not billions, of dollars in sales. The farms, mines, and companies on the dirty list (and those that should be on the list) feed a supply chain that flows from Brazilian exporters to big U.S. importers and then to their customers, the U.S. companies that use the steel or wood or beef to make their own products.

A product chain doesn't end at the mall or in the retail shop; it ends when the consumer takes that car, bookcase, guitar, toy, or beefsteak home. Although some readers might feel that I am pointing a finger away from slavery on the ground, we need to face up to the fact that we play a part in this process, and we need to use our consumer power to ask companies to examine their supply chains and make sure they keep slavery from flowing into our homes. We can also ask our government to enforce its own laws and keep slave-made goods out of our economy, but that is harder to do since the slave-made goods get mixed in with goods made without slavery. The most effective way to stop slavery reaching into our homes, however, is to attack slavery not at the shopping mall, but where it occurs. Cutting the demand for slave-made goods in our own economy is important, since that would push some slaveholders out of the market, but there are a lot of steps in the supply chain between the shopping mall and the charcoal camp in rural Brazil. It is much more effective to make sure the Brazilian Special Mobile Inspection Groups, the antislavery squads, have the equipment and money they need to get the job done.

There is a clear model for providing this support. The United States hands out billions of dollars in funds and equipment each year to other countries as part of the War on Drugs. Helicopters, aircraft, four-wheelers, training, salaries—you name it, the U.S. government will supply all these things when they are to be used against drug producers and traffickers. A small expansion of this program to include antislavery police, like the Special Mobile Inspection Groups, could make a huge difference. There is also a relatively painless way to pay for this. Brazil, like many countries in the developing world, is carrying a significant amount of external or foreign debt to international banks. Some of that debt is "overhang," loans contracted by the military dictatorship that controlled the country from 1964 to 1985. This money went primarily to line the pockets of corrupt generals and their cronies. In 2006 Brazil's foreign debt equaled about $200 billion. Meanwhile, European countries have made tremendous progress in debt forgiveness, removing the old debts whose servicing costs were bleeding poor countries dry. Since 1996 the Heavily Indebted Poor Countries (HIPC) initiative, under which rich countries agreed to cancel $110 billion in debt, has removed about $31 billion of debt in twenty-seven countries. This debt relief releases funds for real development. Tanzania, for example, used about $80 million a year that otherwise would have gone to service its debt to increase spending on schools and public education, and some 1.6 million children are reported to have returned to school because of the debt relief.

The debt that Brazil services every year accounts for millions of dollars that could be spent on important programs like education and antislavery work that would stimulate the economy. Here is a simple first step: the United States and the international banks need to agree with the Brazilian government on a portion of the debt to forgive with the condition that some portion, say 50 percent, of the money that would have gone to debt service be applied to eradicating slavery in Brazil. The cancellation of just $500 million to $1 billion in debt would free up significant funds for antislavery and other important work. Given that the U.S. economy is benefiting from slavery in Brazil, it seems only fair to give some back in the form of debt forgiveness that gets people out of slavery. If this seems like a fanciful idea, note that the United States cancelled $4 billion in bilateral debt with other countries in 2005 and supported a program by the richest countries to forgive another $60 billion. In the same year, the U.S. Treasury secretary, John Snow, called for a 100 percent reduction in a number of debts owed by African countries. We already know that debt cancellation can save lives; it can also free slaves.

MAKING IT HAPPEN

When slavery ends, it will do so because people have made a conscious collective decision to end it, including the decision someone makes as a citizen of a country. The role of national governments is absolutely central to the eradication of slavery. No one questions whether governments should take on the job of ending slavery. Slavery is a crime in every country; governments have *already* taken the collective decision to stop it. Now it is just a matter of bringing political will and resources to bear. Admittedly, sometimes a country has a hard time facing up to slavery. No government, no society, likes to admit that slaves live inside its borders, feed its economy, and suffer terrible violations of their rights. Around the world nations display split personalities when it comes to slavery: denouncing it to the world, they are unable to look it in the face at home. Too many political leaders are in denial, and if the majority of those in power practice that denial, it is deadly.

Nearly every country will need to build its own unique set of responses to slavery. These responses will have many common elements, but the precise mix will vary from country to country. Japan, for example, has the resources it needs to eradicate slavery quickly but has little of the political will necessary to get the job done. A poor country like Ghana may have the will, but it does not have enough money to take on the slaveholders. Burma has almost no resources to fight slavery, but its problem lies elsewhere: the military dictatorship is the main slaveholder and perpetrator of vicious and terrible crimes against its own people.[19] A democratically elected government exists in Burma—locked away in jail by the dictatorship—and when the heroes of the legitimate government finally come to power and the corrupt dictatorship falls, slavery in Burma will be on the way out.

In the rich countries of the developed world, slavery can be defeated quickly; it is primarily a matter of priorities and resources. But in the United States, as long as the government is willing to accept a national clear-up rate (the percentage of all violations that are solved) for the crime of slavery of less than 1 percent, then little is going to change. On the other hand, most American citizens are not willing to accept that failure to address this crime. When Americans finally realize there are tens of thousands of people in slavery in the United States today and next to nothing is being done about it, an outcry will be heard. The same sound is going to be heard in Germany and France, in Canada and Great Britain. Spain and Portugal will have to face up to their daily importation of slaves from South America. And Italy, which may have some of the best laws on the books to protect people who have been rescued from slavery, will finally have to address the huge demand for enslaved prostitutes that Italian men are either purposely oblivious to or positively engaged in.

In Eastern Europe, the Middle East, South America, and many of the countries of Southeast Asia, governments will face a tough struggle with the corruption that feeds on slavery and fuels it in turn. Slavery and corruption go hand in hand and will need to be attacked together. Certainly, many people throw up their hands and say that corruption can never be stopped, but that is simply not true. As mentioned earlier, a hundred years ago the United States was extremely corrupt, and it is no coincidence that a key political, social, and moral issue at the beginning of the twentieth century in the United States was the "white slavery" problem. At that time corrupt politicians and police in many (if not most) major cities were actively engaged in the enslavement of mainly foreign-born women. The reforms of the Progressive movement did not come about overnight, and the last pockets of corruption weren't cleaned out till the 1950s. Today there is still some corruption in many U.S. cities, but it is the exception, not the rule.

The same process of cleaning up corruption can be achieved in most countries. In corrupt countries I have visited, the average citizen is fed up with it, understands that corruption is crippling the society, and will do almost anything to be rid of it. The United Nations has assembled an anticorruption team that, though doing a good job, gets very little publicity, probably because ending corruption is a long process not characterized by dramatic events of the sort that the media like to cover. The team's system for reducing and then eliminating corruption has been tested and found successful in a number of countries. Antonio Maria Costa, who heads up the U.N. crime office, notes that "Corruption not only distorts economic decision-making, it also deters investment, undermines competitiveness and, ultimately, weakens economic growth. Indeed, there is evidence that the social, legal, political and economic aspects of development are all linked, and that corruption in any one sector impedes development in them all."[20] In chapter 1, I showed the clear link between poverty, corruption, and slavery. This is one of the toughest jobs we face in ending slavery, but the payoff will go beyond the freedom brought to slaves. Rooting out slavery and the corruption that enables it will dramatically improve lives for almost all citizens in many countries and should be supported by the countries of the developed world.

Because they know they must stop corruption to end slavery, antislavery groups are often at the leading edge of the fight against corruption. A wonderful example occurred in Nepal in early 2006 when a women's group was working to rescue women who had been trafficked into prostitution. The workers were having reasonable success in finding and liberating women but were failing to get traffickers and slaveholders locked up. Again and again the judges and prosecutors were paid off and the perpetrators walked free. One day an antislavery worker witnessed an amazingly blatant bribe. While she was standing in the courtroom, an accused trafficker handed over a kilogram of gold to the judge and prosecutor. Not surprisingly, the antislavery worker began to shout at the judge, who then threatened to send her to jail for contempt of court. After leaving the courtroom, the antislavery worker and her group quickly mobilized other women and returned with a large crowd and a big padlock. As a crowd gathered and journalists took notes, they announced they were locking the courtroom and closing down the dishonest court. The judge backed down, returned the gold, and sentenced the trafficker to five years.[21]

Although each country will need to assemble a unique set of strategies to end the slavery within its borders, is there anything that can be said that applies to all of them? In a word, yes. There are fundamental components that need to be in place to eradicate slavery. For many countries it will be a matter of seeing which of these components are already working and then enacting or strengthening the others. Free the Slaves has published a separate policy paper for U.S. legislators, business leaders, and citizens that proposes detailed actions that the United States must take if it wants to end slavery at home and abroad.[22] For all other countries, there are the key foundation blocks (discussed in the following sections) that must be in place for governments to play their part in eradicating slavery.

STOP LOOKING FOR THE QUICK FIX

Every politician and government official (and concerned citizen) needs to understand that slavery and human trafficking are multidimensional and that a constellation of government responses and strategies are required to address the many facets of the problem. Slavery is obviously a legal problem, but it is, to a greater or lesser extent in every country, also a problem of economic development, migration, gender discrimination, ethnic prejudice, corruption, and political will. And each of these categories can also be subdivided into many parts. Well-meaning politicians in many countries have become aware of one facet of slavery or trafficking and then rushed new laws or regulations into place. For example, under pressure Japan cut the number of entertainer visas while leaving a vast system of discrimination and exploitation untouched. Whether this is a well-meant action, a thinly veiled public relations exercise, or something else, the result can be a sense of frustration when the larger problem continues to grow. No quick fix—whether it is busting up brothels, buying people out of slavery, or passing laws (without making sure they get enforced)—will eliminate slavery. Although devising a strategy is not easy, any country that can build a highway or a health service or an education system can assemble the minds needed to think through the mix of factors that support and enable slavery inside its borders. If advice is what people need, that is available. At both the governmental and the personal levels, we simply must think deeply and carefully about every factor that has to be nailed down to build a slaveproof world.

FOCUS ON OUTCOMES

To mobilize a nation, all the players must focus both on the outcomes of slavery and the actions needed to end slavery. The outcome of human trafficking is to place people into slavery. The outcome of slavery is that people come under the complete, violent control of a slaveholder, who has control over the type of work they do, their work environment and the conditions of this work, and their freedom of movement. Any situation that leads to this lack of freedom needs to be covered in national law. Many countries adopt laws that—because of a partial understanding or in response to a particularly sensational case—focus on only one segment of enslavement such as forced prostitution. Likewise, the players must focus on the outcomes of eradication, specifically freeing people from slavery and reintegrating them into normal life. More than one country has equated passing laws with getting the job done, and neglected the enforcement that is needed for them to have an effect.

Focusing on outcomes means measuring them as well. It is true that measuring slavery is difficult because of the often-hidden nature of the crime, but it is critical to centralize every scrap of information available in order to build the benchmarks that can determine what progress, if any, is occurring. All the possible players—elected representatives, government officials, NGOs, the electorate, law enforcement—need to agree on the benchmarks they will use to measure their progress in actually eradicating slavery.

BUILD A ROBUST LEGAL RESPONSE

Once a clear picture of trafficking and enslavement is available, a country can build a legal response that deals with the crime. Clearly, appropriate legislation punishes slaveholders and traffickers and does not punish their victims. In too many countries, freed slaves are treated as illegal aliens, second-class citizens, or worse. Some countries and languages have a special name for ex-slaves and an informal apartheid system that keeps them poor and powerless. The law that decriminalizes victims also needs to be explicit on one key point: the consent of the victim is irrelevant. If a person was enticed into slavery on the promise of a job or a trip to a richer country, that does not constitute complicity. International law is clear that people cannot legally hand themselves over to slavery, and national laws must be equally clear that slaves will never be blamed for the crime. When there is a law against slavery, it must be enforced, and slaveholders must face prosecution. It is clearly a failing of the generally admirable Brazilian response that while hundreds of slaveholders have been arrested, none have gone to prison. To attain prosecutions and convictions, police and prosecutors must be trained to get the job done. (Training should not be an obstacle; it is offered by the United Nations and several other international bodies.) Because trafficking into slavery is a crime that often crosses international borders, a diplomatic step is needed. Bilateral legal agreements between countries that are linked by the slave trade are essential to avoid loopholes slave traders can exploit. These ideas merely outline what needs to be included in a robust legal response; other ideas about trade law will be developed in chapter 7. That said, most countries became committed to establishing a good set of antislavery laws when they signed the U.N. convention that includes the protocol on trafficking in persons.

BUILD A DEDICATED LAW ENFORCEMENT TEAM

A small but crucial extension of the legal response is to assemble dedicated antislavery enforcement teams. Labor inspectors should have the right to look at all industries, no matter how informal, for evidence of forced labor. Every law enforcement agency in the world operates specialized units, whether for homicide, counterfeiting, drugs, child exploitation, or dozens of other crimes. Brazil is showing how dedicated antislavery teams can radically increase the number of people coming to freedom, even with its teams that are ill equipped, underpowered, undertrained, and relatively unsupported by the legal system.

PROTECT AND SUPPORT FREED SLAVES

In addition to decriminalizing the victims of slavery and trafficking, governments need to provide for victims' rehabilitation and support. Being enslaved can be terribly damaging, and because slavery is the theft of work and life, it leaves the victim destitute as well. Government clearly has a role in helping provide physical security, basic material assistance, medical care, legal assistance, and counseling to survivors of slavery. Governments don't have to take on all these jobs alone. In the United States most of the support given to freed slaves is through experienced service providers who receive some government funds to run their programs. Freed slaves need help to get back on their feet and to build the strength and confidence to testify against slaveholders. This help should be given no matter where the freed slave has come from. Trafficking victims may have been brought into a country illegally, but they must be treated as crime victims, not criminals.

RAISE AWARENESS AND PROMOTE PREVENTION

In many parts of the world, slavery can be hidden in plain sight. Where slaveholders operate with impunity, as in rural Pakistan, slavery can be discovered by simply walking up to a laborer in the field and asking "who is your master?" In countries like the United States where awareness is low, slaves can be out in the open, but shielded by our ignorance. Governments can increase public awareness of slavery and trafficking in the same way they confront a public health crisis: with advertising and education campaigns. Governments have a duty to work with other groups to produce public awareness materials that focus on the crime of slavery and that discourage the demand that leads to slavery, whether it is for prostitution, child domestics, or farmworkers. Governments should also mount public awareness campaigns aimed at potential victims of enslavement, raising awareness of the enticements and recruitment methods used by slaveholders. Campaigns aimed at potential victims would reflect local cultures and be transmitted in appropriate languages. Such campaigns have been mounted in many countries with success. One of the strongest chains that hold slaves in bondage is lack of knowledge. Nepali kamaiyas, Ghanaian fishing slaves, and Indian bonded workers have all said that they never knew that their enslavement was illegal until they learned it from their liberators. The message that everyone has the right to freedom is a powerful impulse for liberation—if slaves hear it.

USE DIPLOMACY, TRADE, AND AID TO END SLAVERY

In the spring of 2000, I had a call from a staffer in the Clinton White House asking about slavery in Mauritania. Mauritania is a country with extensive slavery, much of it old-style hereditary chattel slavery. In the late 1990s, as cases of this slavery became increasingly visible, the United States placed economic sanctions on the country to urge it to enforce its own laws. By 2000 nothing had changed in Mauritania, but the rest of the world was changing. The rise of violent forms of Islamic fundamentalism meant that good relations with a Muslim country like Mauritania could be useful to the United States in many ways. The White House staffer wanted me to say that slavery was decreasing in Mauritania as part of a justification for lifting the sanctions. I couldn't say it; it just wasn't true.

At the same time, I knew that slaves always come last in considerations of foreign policy, so I reached for a realistic answer. I suggested that since the sanctions would be lifted anyway, the lifting should be linked to antislavery provisions. That linkage didn't happen either, but a story from Bangladesh points to how easy it would be for countries, especially the rich countries, to use diplomacy to help end slavery.

In the spring of 2004 a contact from Bangladesh came to me with shocking photographs. They showed children enslaved in the fishing industry on an island off the coast of Bangladesh. With tremendous bravery my contact had infiltrated the island and recorded the brutal eighteen-hour workdays, the beatings, the sexual abuse, and the deaths of children as young as eight. Approaching law enforcement on the mainland, this antislavery worker had been threatened with violence that would include his whole family if he did anything to expose this crime. Finding no cooperation in Bangladesh, he brought the photographs and report to me. Talking it over we decided that diplomacy might be the answer, and I took the materials to Ambassador John Miller, the head of the Office to Monitor and Combat Trafficking in Persons in the U.S.

Department of State. His reaction was immediate and positive. Armed with our materials, he went straight to the top in the Bangladeshi government, and within days a military raid, bypassing the corrupt local police, liberated the enslaved children.

Such diplomatic efforts can span several areas of diplomacy. John Miller's work as a diplomat clearly demonstrates this. In addition to success in Bangladesh, he pushed to have Japan placed on the Tier 2 Watch List and then traveled there for full and frank discussions with the Japanese government. His globe hopping and quiet talks with a host of foreign officials paid off in 2005 and 2006, his last two years heading up the antitrafficking office, when eighty countries brought in new antislavery and antitrafficking laws. Foreign aid could also be thought through with an antislavery focus, some of it targeting the underlying economic desperation that engenders slavery. Trade policies could make slave-made goods taboo on the world market. Trade financing could be linked to demonstrable efforts to remove slavery from local as well as international markets. From the Peace Corps to Fulbright scholarships to the exchange of orchestras and operas, our cultural outreach could shine a light on this fundamental shared belief—slavery must end. All of these ideas will be explored in more depth in the following chapters.

CALL OUT THE ARMY (AND NAVY AND AIR FORCE)!

The U.S. military, and to a lesser extent the militaries of other rich countries, has a truly global reach, and could play a role in ending slavery in many ways. One way is reflected in a remarkable step taken in 2006 by the American armed forces. Recognizing that trafficked and enslaved women were being forced into prostitution to serve soldiers, the top brass banned all U.S. soldiers, no matter where they were, from patronizing brothels or prostitutes. Given the age-old link between soldiers and prostitution, a link that was thought to be normal for young soldiers a few years ago, this was a profound breakthrough. And if the soldiers were trained to recognize the signs of human trafficking in the cultures around them, their sharp eyes could help increase the number of rescues and liberations.

A second way governments, through their militaries, could dramatically influence global antislavery work is through direct engagement. There is a clear precedent for this. From 1811 to 1867 the British navy's antislavery squadron, operating off the Atlantic coast of Africa, liberated 160,000 slaves. Freed from captured slave ships, the slaves were returned to areas under British protection on the African coast, particularly Sierra

Leone. This operation was not cheap, and many sailors lost their lives, mainly to disease, on this duty, but the superpower of the day had determined that the slave trade must end and that it was willing to do what was necessary to make that happen. Today every country has agreed to an international law prohibiting the use of their ships or planes in human trafficking. At sea and in the air, national militaries could be interdicting the slave trade at a much higher rate. The tragedy that happened in Nepal, described at the beginning of this chapter, could have been prevented by the presence of a small contingent of blue-helmeted U.N. peacekeeping troops. Remember that those peacekeepers are soldiers supplied by governments around the world, and with diplomatic agreement those troops could easily be deployed to free and protect slaves.

If a candidate running for president or prime minister wanted to make the end of slavery a goal, that person might build the recommendations in this section into proposed policy and make a promise as well to incorporate an antislavery focus in all of the government's work. An antislavery focus would include making slavery a priority in all international visits, high-level meetings, and diplomatic efforts. In every country that I know of, a *low-level* government official or diplomat is charged with responsibility for this issue, and slavery is discussed in the side meeting of the side meeting to the top-level conference. When the president, prime minister, secretary of state, and any other cabinet-level official of any country travels and meets with another head of state or top official, that person needs to be asking how the two countries are going to work together to bring slavery to an end. Talking about slavery is not controversial. No head of state (aside from the Burmese dictators and a few others) will be offended by being asked to join a global consensus to end slavery. Of course, politicians are much more likely to give slavery a high priority if the voters ask for it first. Each of us needs to be ready to ask candidates where they stand and how high they are going to put ending slavery on their list of priorities.

Finally, all of the rich countries of the developed world are grappling with the issue of immigration, and many of them are paralyzed on this issue because it polarizes the electorate. Most wealthy countries need workers, but they also fear changes that large numbers of immigrants will bring. Real leadership and a deeper understanding of the impact of immigration are desperately needed. One area of confusion is the way that human trafficking and slavery fit into questions of immigration. Restrictive immigration policies, in combination with the struggle confronting those who are desperate to improve their lives, can leave the poor vulnerable to human trafficking. We can address the illegal flow of slaves into the rich countries by dealing with the reasons life is not livable in their home countries, as well as by facing up to the economic demand for people to fill jobs in richer countries. Often the driving force behind immigration and the lure of the human trafficker is not absolute poverty and deprivation but the realization of income inequality. Although some people are trafficked from the very poorest countries, many come from countries on the middle of the world economic ladder. For the young educated person living in the former Soviet Union, the problem is more about thwarted ambition than starvation. With a college degree but unable to get any sort of job, and watching as the family declines along with the national economy, the materialist nirvana of Western Europe or the United States has a powerful appeal. High-level diplomatic conversations between origin and destination countries are needed so that both can help solve this problem by registering and regulating agencies that help people find work overseas, acting to protect citizens traveling for work, and making sure that migrant workers have a clear understanding of both the realities of working abroad and the risks of human trafficking.

We know that collective conscious commitments to end slavery work when a village decides for freedom, and we also know they work when a country like Brazil puts forward a plan and a commitment, however tight resources might be. Governments alone cannot end slavery in the world, but they represent the concentration of power and resources linked to the largest collective and popular agreement. National governments have the legal responsibility to protect their citizens from slavery, and they have the legitimate power to do so. The problem in both rich and poor countries is one of governance. All political leaders denounce slavery, but the numbers in slavery continue to increase, the perpetrators go uncaught and unpunished, and the minimal resources needed to rehabilitate freed slaves are not available. Of course, political leaders must face many pressing problems, and they are most likely to respond to the problems brought to their attention loudly and repeatedly. I have met political leaders whose commitment to ending slavery is deep, but they tell me that it is not something their constituents are pressing for, or are even aware of. These political leaders need our support. All of our leaders need to hear clearly that ending slavery is the legacy we want to leave to our children. A democracy is the physical expression of how its citizens want the world to be. Is there any electorate on earth that wouldn't vote for freedom for others?

WHAT GOVERNMENTS CAN DO AND WHAT WE CAN DO AS CITIZENS TO FREE MORE SLAVES

This chapter is about the potential of national governments to liberate slaves and to help them achieve lives in dignity. All governments have pledged to end slavery, but how can we make sure this promise is kept? Here are eight things our governments can do to end slavery and one thing that we as citizens can do to help our government make it a top priority. Every government should:

1. Build a national plan to end slavery within its borders, bringing together all relevant government agencies to achieve this end and appointing an antislavery ambassador charged with coordinating the government's efforts. Such a plan works through everything that will be required (and what help will be needed from other countries and groups) to stop all forms of slavery. National leaders must initiate and own this plan if it is to be effective.

2. Make the law fit the crime. Revise ineffective laws so they will work as they should. Antislavery laws must address all forms of slavery, punish the slaveholders, compensate the slaves for their stolen labor, decriminalize slaves who are undocumented or who have been forced to work in illicit activities, and provide for rehabilitation and reintegration. Most of all the law must be prioritized for enforcement.

3. Task and train law enforcement officials to detect slavery, help survivors to safety, and punish the slaveholders; ensure that there is one person in each police precinct who is tasked with leading antislavery efforts.

4. Task and train enough labor inspectors to effectively monitor workplaces and locations known to be prone to slavery. In North America and Europe, slavery is most prevalent in domestic servitude, prostitution, farmwork, restaurant work, and sweatshop labor. In the developing world slavery is more widespread and is often found in farmwork, mining, domestic servitude, prostitution, work in shops and street markets, and labor in small factories and in production areas like brick kilns, forest clearance, and fishing.

5. Close the loopholes. Nearly every country has legal loopholes that are being exploited by human traffickers and slaveholders. Countries should examine immigration, labor, commercial, licensing, procurement, and other laws from a slavery perspective and close those gaps.

6. Register and regulate agencies that help people find work overseas and educate migrants about the potential risks.

7. Ensure that every newborn receives a birth certificate and that the birth is registered. Children who do not legally exist are more easily captured and enslaved. Poor countries will need help to establish a birth registry.

8. Use diplomacy, trade, and foreign aid to target slavery. Require trading partners to take antislavery actions. Give debt relief on the condition that savings are used for antislavery efforts. Countries that are linked by the slave trade should enact bilateral antislavery agreements.

9. Voters and ctizens: Ask your elected officials what they are doing to end slavery. Make it clear that this is a priority for you.

6

Global Problem, Global Reach

S lavery is global. As we think through how to end it, we need to find ways to use those organizations that are global in scope. Three of these groups—the United Nations (U.N.), the World Bank, and the World Trade Organization (WTO)—offer tremendous opportunities for bringing the end of slavery closer. Some skeptics might disagree, not surprisingly since these same organizations have been roundly criticized for lagging far behind their potential. In the same way that the actions of national governments have sometimes increased vulnerability to slavery, international groups have, at times, created situations conducive to slavery. But I am convinced that drawing the U.N., the World Bank, and the WTO into the abolitionist camp will pay large dividends.

In a time marked by the diminishing but still immense power of the nation state, a lot is happening at the often-uneasy boundary between local and global. Wherever we live, ideas and groups that transcend borders touch us. Some of these groups, like international crime syndicates or al-Qaeda, are dangerous. Others, like the World Health Organization or the global antislavery movement, point the way to increasing our common human dignity. Globalization is a verb, an active process, and it offers the chance for the world to reach a truly universal consensus on human rights, a consensus that includes an end to slavery.

The first formal expressions of this universal consensus arrived with the United Nations, especially in its Universal Declaration of Human Rights in 1948. In this chapter I explore how groups like the U.N., the WTO, and World Bank can help end slavery. The global reach of these organizations is well suited to this job, and each can play an important role in abolition, but each also has to overcome a gross overestimation of its power. The U.N., the WTO, and World Bank have all been described as great powers, manipulating the affairs of the world, but in reality the one thing they all have in common is a difficulty in living up to their own reputations.

HOW THE UNITED NATIONS CAN BECOME AN ANTISLAVERY POWERHOUSE

The United Nations suffers terribly from the distance between dream and reality. That distance is seen over and over when something bad happens in the world and people ask, "Why isn't the U.N. *doing* something about that!?"—not realizing that the U.N. isn't *allowed* to do much of anything. The U.N. suffers from a problem not shared by many public institutions: its reputation is too good. If the U.N. candidly admits how little power it really has, then it loses much of the little power it does possess. When it comes to global slavery, the U.N. is trying hard, but in ways that are hamstrung by national governments, stymied by bureaucrats in its own ranks, and scattered and disorganized across a range of its own agencies. At the same time, the U.N., its ancestor the League of Nations, and its older cousin the International Labour Organization (ILO) are important repositories of our global thinking about slavery, and have been for years. This thinking is a little irrational at times, but it reflects what the world has been able to agree on: that slavery must end. To understand the current state of the U.N.'s work on slavery, we need to look back over the twists and turns of its past efforts to bring eradication to the world stage.

The history of the U.N. and its antislavery work is a hodgepodge of contradictions. World War I destroyed the economies of Europe, killed millions, and brought many governments and institutions crashing down. The survivors were mad with grief, bitterness, and cynicism. Morally, physically, and economically exhausted, they set out to build mechanisms to make that war the last. Remembering the insane and ineluctable descent into the conflagration of 1914, they wanted an organization that would safeguard collective security and provide a place where differences could be worked out diplomatically. From that desire the League of Nations was born. But it was born with a defect, for no nation would cede power to the League—so while it could be a place to talk, it could never enforce a decision.

In spite of the League's impotence, the tiny Anti-Slavery Society, one of the few nongovernmental organizations in existence in 1919, seized it as an important tool. The director of the Anti-Slavery Society felt that the League was a platform that might allow the voices of slaves to be heard, if only through the mouths of campaigners. Concerns about slavery exploded just after the war, when investigators and journalists rediscovered the extensive slave trade centering on the city of Mecca in what is now Saudi Arabia. Many Muslims of the time financed their pilgrimage, or hajj, to the holy city by bringing along a slave to sell in its busy market. Since the faithful came from all over the Muslim world, Mecca was known, sadly, as a place to buy exotic slaves. The situation came to the notice of the League of Nations when a power struggle began just across the Red Sea in the kingdom of Ethiopia. Rather than allowing their opponents to take control of the population, members of the Ethiopian ruling family decided to simply enslave and sell their subjects. District governors and members of the royal family began to round up large numbers of people and sell them in the Mecca market.[1]

The exposure of the slave trade around the Red Sea focused public attention. Since nearly all the members of the League of Nations had enacted laws and signed treaties banning slavery, the League might have been expected to take a role in its eradication. Sadly, a constant theme in international affairs is that the national aims, policies, and economic interests of rich countries always overwhelm any attempt to eradicate slavery. As a silent and powerless constituency, slaves are easily ignored. Little was actually done to stop the slave trade, but the Anti-Slavery Society saw its chance and pressed the League to investigate the large-scale enslavement in Ethiopia as well as to set up a Temporary Slavery Commission to investigate "all forms" of slavery around the world.

This inquiry was a quiet bureaucratic decision with great historical resonance. For the first time, a global investigation of slavery, including the debt-bondage slavery in South Asia and the millions of colonial subjects in Africa being enslaved through systems of forced labor, was undertaken. When the Temporary Slavery Commission gathered testimony, countries lined up to deny the existence of slavery in their own territories and to denounce the slavery of their neighbors. Anyone who might speak from experience, or from the point of view of slaves, was carefully excluded. Yet despite the manipulation and obfuscation, the commission's report recommended that a new treaty be negotiated, one that addressed and condemned slavery in all its forms and in all places.

GIVING PRACTICAL EFFECT THROUGHOUT THE WORLD

After a tricky period of negotiation, tweaked and pushed along by the Anti-Slavery Society, the League of Nations put forward the Convention on Slavery, Servitude, Forced Labor and Similar Institutions and Practices, known today as the "1926 Slavery Convention." A convention expresses what countries generally agree are some good ideas. It's an agreement on principles with some vague and some specific recommendations for action. Many countries might sign a convention, but it has no effect until they write the principles into their own laws and then enforce them. This convention is important because it was the first time the world officially agreed that slavery must end and even tried to define what needed ending. In it slavery was defined as "the status or condition of a person over whom any or all of the powers attaching to the right of ownership are exercised."[2] The convention also prohibited all acts of capture, force, selling, buying, exchanging, trading, or transporting any persons in order to enslave them. The definition used the idea of the "powers" of ownership to represent the complete control over the slave exercised by slaveholders. The convention was a breakthrough, but it suffered from being the product of a committee of competing interests.

The final text of the convention reflected the fact that in international affairs, slaves tend to take second place to national and economic interests. In retrospect, the hypocrisy in the roll call of exceptions and omissions requested by governments is sickening. The British presented themselves as the global leaders in antislavery work but wanted to make sure that slavery in what is now India, Pakistan, and Burma went unmolested. The Spanish excluded their colonies in Morocco. The United States, though not a formal member of the League, signed the convention but excluded "forced labor for private purposes" to protect the Southern states that were practicing slavery through the arbitrary arrest and imprisonment of African Americans who were then leased to private companies.

Still, the convention was important in three ways: it set the moral position, it was the first global treaty to ban slavery and the slave trade, and it addressed slavery "in all its forms." But as the preeminent historian of the U.N. and slavery, Suzanne Miers, explains, "As a practical instrument for ending even the slave trade, it left much to be desired. . . .

No time limit was set for the eradication of slavery. Worst of all, no mechanisms were established for enforcement or even for monitoring the results. They were rejected as infringements of national sovereignty. . . . The Convention was, and remained, a paper tiger."[3]

The events surrounding the 1926 Slavery Convention set a pattern for the work of the United Nations right up to the present day. Other conventions on forced labor and human trafficking, and most recently on organized crime and trafficking in persons, were later enacted, but each iteration was like the remake of an old movie: the characters and settings changed, but the plot remained the same. At each step exclusions protected slaveholders both private and public, and no mechanism for enforcement was included. But we cannot blame this on the United Nations. That body has to submit to the will of the powerful countries that run it, and they were the ones who were willing to let other interests overrule the true eradication of slavery.

The U.N. itself went into zombielike paralysis throughout much of the Cold War. It kept up the appearance of doing something, but it was frozen and deadlocked by the polarized great powers. When it came to the problem of slavery, the communist countries insisted that slavery could exist only under capitalism, while the capitalist countries retorted that anyone living under communism was a slave. When a permanent working group on slavery was finally appointed in 1975, after years of work by the Anti-Slavery Society, it quickly descended into charade. The working group's members denied slavery in their own countries and sniped at one another from their Cold War bunkers. The group's investigations were so ineffectual that its reports were rarely included in the business of the larger U.N. In 2000 the working group was asked to simply endorse a detailed report by the International Labour Organization that exposed the enslavement of its own citizens by the military dictatorship in Burma.[4] Fearful of offending anyone, the working group refused. After promulgating the (watered-down) conventions that condemned global slavery, the U.N. had met the challenge with a remarkable lack of action.

MEANWHILE, DOWN ON THE MEKONG DELTA

Although the system is flawed, individuals and groups have emerged within the U.N. and done excellent antislavery work.[5] In Vienna, the Global Programme against Trafficking in Human Beings, part of the U.N. Office for Drug Control and Crime Prevention, struggles along with few resources. In spite of that, it has had an impact, improving the slavery and trafficking laws in Africa, bringing antitrafficking groups together so that they can learn from one another, educating law enforcement and launching a global initiative to fight human trafficking. In Southeast Asia, the United Nations Inter-Agency Project on Human Trafficking in the Greater Mekong Sub-region (UNIAP) has stitched together an amazing collection of people and has achieved cooperation between countries that are normally at one another's throats. The winners are the people, mostly women and children, who would be trafficked into slavery. In just one example, this group helped to expose the theft of Cambodian babies who were being adopted by unknowing American couples for a $20,000 fee.

The U.N. Inter-Agency Project, however, demonstrates the need to streamline U.N. operations. Because different parts of the U.N. have developed their own responses to slavery and trafficking, UNIAP faces the daunting challenge of coordinating, just in this one region, thirteen different U.N. organizations, not to mention six governments plus eight more international nongovernmental organizations. In classic U.N. style, UNIAP met this challenge by setting up yet another group in 2003, an intergovernmental antitrafficking initiative known as COMMIT (Coordinated Mekong Ministerial Initiative against Trafficking). COMMIT brought the governments into direct action against slavery, which is difficult and sometimes expensive to accomplish with any single government, much less six. If duplication of effort is going on, then careful evaluation is needed on ways to increase efficiency. Each group or government needs to keep the issue of slavery fully integrated into what it does, and the challenge is to keep the focus on freeing and reintegrating slaves. I would bet that streamlining through reducing redundant administration could lead to much more money going to liberate slaves and help them build new lives.

TRY NOT TO USE THE "S" WORD

The International Labour Organization was established in 1919, at the same time as the League of Nations, but unlike the League, it has survived. In its constitution the ILO set forth its aims: to bring dignity to all workers and promote safe working conditions, reasonable hours, adequate wages, no child labor, and social security in old age. It seeks to accomplish these by bringing together three key actors: governments, workers (often represented by labor unions), and employers (likewise represented by employer or business associations). When the U.N. was created in 1946, the ILO became its first specialized agency. Like the U.N., the ILO was caught in the Cold War crossfire, but since the early 1990s, it has blossomed as more attention has been directed to ending child labor and slavery. Indeed, the ILO has been a leader in exposing the modern enslavement of children and adults, though for historical reasons it uses the term *forced labor* instead of *slavery*, which serves to keep the public confused. For most of its existence, the ILO was a species of lame duck. Its work on forced labor (slavery) was limited to receiving reports submitted by governments describing how well the governments were doing in keeping the promises they made when signing ILO conventions. Not surprisingly, the reports all seemed to say that things were going very well indeed. Occasionally, the ILO would go out on a limb and investigate a government that was clearly lying or refusing to answer any questions.

In spite of having little power, the ILO has been the seat of two significant advances in the past twenty years. One grew from a campaign against child labor that culminated with child workers from around the world marching into the ILO annual conference in Geneva and exuberantly pressing their case to the normally stuffy bureaucrats.[6] The result was the Convention on the Worst Forms of Child Labour, a convention that clearly targeted child slavery and helped to dramatically expand, with crucial support from President Bill Clinton, an international program to eliminate child labor. This program has been spending more than $50 million a year for the past five years, and the results show that when resources are adequate, significant progress can be made. A 2006 major report on child labor by the ILO made a bold assertion considering that it came from cautious bureaucrats who are known to never promise more than they can deliver.[7] The title of the report was "The End of Child Labor: Within Reach"—which seems pretty far-fetched when you think about the pervasive and historically unceasing reality of children working all over the world. But the ILO workers had watched the resources and expertise go in and the results come out. From 2000 to 2005, damaging child labor (we're not talking about kids with paper routes, lemonade stands, or Saturday jobs here, but dangerous, dirty, demeaning work that no child should ever do) fell by 11 percent, and the number of children in the most dangerous kinds of work fell 33 percent in the five-to-fourteen age group. In a world focused on a "war on terror," this astounding change went unnoticed, but for literally millions of children, it meant the beginning of a new life. The ILO led this transformation while handicapped in ways that are explained below. The important thing is how relatively inexpensive the outcomes were and how the lessons of this work can be carried over to the eradication of slavery.

The role as a passive recipient of reports also began to shift in 1998 when the ILO issued its Declaration on the Fundamental Principles and Rights at Work. One of the four fundamental principles of the declaration was "no slavery," and this opened the door to lobbying by Anti-Slavery International (previously known as the Anti-Slavery Society) for a seemingly innocuous but radical proposal that a team should be created to take *positive action* against slavery. This idea was taken up, and the ILO Special Action Program to Combat Forced Labor was created in 2001, with Roger Plant heading it. Plant was an inspired choice because he was not a career diplomat but someone who knew the reality on the ground after researching slavery in sugar production in the Dominican Republic and exploring human rights violations around the world. While capable of diplomatic niceties, Plant is not a man who likes to wait, and his commitment and grueling work ethic brought about the second key advance in the ILO's work against slavery. Under Plant's direction an in-depth investigation of slavery worldwide was undertaken, backed up by action projects that tested ways to bring slavery to an end. The result was a 2005 global report on forced labor that helped to bring the subject to the notice of governments.[8] Like the report on child labor, this remarkable report passed by the public relatively unnoticed, but it forms the basis for Plant's hard-nosed advocacy with recalcitrant governments. Most important, the research is so clearly documented that it can be repeated in a few years and will give us our first chance to see what changes are occurring, for better or worse, in global slavery. Incredibly, no one knows whether slavery is growing or shrinking or how many of the world's slaves are men or women or children. People make guesses, some of them educated guesses, but that is the limit of it. The Special Action Program is one of the most effective activities of the U.N. system, yet it runs on a tiny budget of about $16 million a year, the largest part of which, some $11 million, is spent on direct support to the victims of slavery. It is an indication of where slavery ranks in the current priorities of the U.N. that the program receives less than .0008 percent of the U.N.'s budget.

Positive things can also be said about another U.N. agency, UNICEF, and the work it is doing against child labor. In many parts of the world, UNICEF has built a slavery lens into its work with children. Building on a deep understanding of the needs of poor and vulnerable children, the organization has prepared some of the best materials on the rehabilitation needs of child slaves. From the broadest levels of the U.N.'s initiatives down to individual local projects, UNICEF has taken aim at child slavery. The amount of resources allocated to child slavery within the UNICEF budget is not clear. About $200 million of the $2 billion budget goes to "child protection," but that category includes other areas as well. Brought into closer coordination and provided with more resources, UNICEF could be making significant inroads into child slavery.

The successes of the child labor program and UNICEF and the breakthroughs of the Special Action Program on Forced Labor raise some questions.[9] If these programs can do so well, what is holding up the U.N. and its agencies from making a real dent in global slavery? Of course, there are many important jobs the U.N. must do, but where is the call to the world's governments to use the tools of the U.N. to break up and then bury slavery? Where is the special global reach of the U.N. in addressing slavery?

CAN YOU CROSS THE OCEAN WITHOUT ROCKING THE BOAT?

Over time bureaucracies almost always grow and almost never shrink. One of the reasons why the U.N. and the ILO cannot make headway against slavery has to do with their cultures. The U.N. is an institution that is very nervous about doing anything that will upset the status quo, offend its funders, or lead to an accusation of playing politics. The culture can stifle risk taking, creativity, and energy. At the grassroots there are amazing U.N. workers—real heroes delivering food to the starving, giving medical care in epidemics, and diverting the catastrophic collisions of war-bent dictators—but at its core, in the halls of New York, Geneva, and Vienna, things are different. In those halls are still some heroes, but the wrangling over undependable budgets, and the ease of pushing paper instead of creating change, means the U.N. often moves at glacial speed on even the most desperate issues. Then there is the fact that the U.N., and the ILO especially, are simply out-of-date in the way they are organized.

In 1919 it was a radical step to combine workers, employers, and governments into the ruling body of the ILO, but times have changed. The second half of the twentieth century may well be remembered as the revolution of the nongovernmental organizations. Since the first groups like the original Anti-Slavery Society (the very first human rights organization in human history, founded in 1787) and the early Red Cross, the number of groups representing our beliefs, hopes, and aims—whether to protect animals, the rainforests, or the lives of slaves—has exploded. Few remember how recent all of this growth has been. Amnesty International only got started in 1961, Greenpeace in 1971, and the United Way didn't take off until after World War II. Almost all the major charitable and advocacy groups in the world had their beginnings in the 1950s and 1960s. Today far more people find expression for their interests in nongovernmental groups than they do in political parties or labor unions. Notice that in Great Britain the ruling Labour Party has about 250,000 members, while the Royal Society for the Protection of Birds (made up mainly of birdwatchers) has over a million members. That pattern is repeated over and over in all the wealthy countries and many poor ones as well. The U.N. and the ILO actually rely on these nongovernmental human rights and development groups to help them assemble their policies and write their conventions. What they will not do is let them sit at the table. The tripartite system at the ILO of employer organizations, trade unions, and governments excludes groups, like human rights organizations, that represent much larger constituencies. At the same time, this three-way ruling group is desperately dependent on the NGOs for innovation and follow-through. When asked, each of these three explain that bringing in the nongovernmental organizations would never work, but their reasons are hard to follow, except for the elephant in the room—the necessity to share their power. If human rights groups were included in the decision making of the ILO, I would expect to see things both speed up and become more efficient.

This is no way to run the organization that we all look to for disaster relief, world health programs, and conflict resolution. The root cause of any erratic pattern of decision making by the U.N., however, is that the institution itself is completely dependent on its member nations for funding and power. And here we discover that the core of the problem is not the U.N. at all, but the nations that are jerking the strings from above the stage.

AN OFFER YOU CAN'T REFUSE

Despite being born out of a war that was waged to guarantee democratic freedoms, the U.N. is anything but democratic. The General Assembly puts on a good show and can meet and debate and vote. But when it adjourns, little of substance has happened because the General Assembly is allowed neither power nor democracy. The United Nations is an oligarchy with one primary body exercising the most control: the Security Council. The Security Council has five permanent members—Great Britain, France, Russia, China, and the United States—and ten other members that are elected on a rolling basis by the General Assembly, allowed to participate for two years but not allowed to be reelected. According to the rules, the General Assembly can recommend, but only the Security Council can decide. In the Security Council, the five permanent members have a stranglehold on decision making, since each holds the power of veto.

The result is that the U.N. looks democratic from the outside but is basically run by the Security Council with the applause of some members of the General Assembly, the surly cooperation of other members, and the shouts of protest from many of the other countries of the world. Since 2000 the attitude of the United States toward the United Nations chilled, and its control has become more arbitrary and imperious. At this point it becomes hard to see a way forward. (And, to be fair, France, China, Russia, and Great Britain also put their own interests ahead of global concerns at times.) The ideal of democracy is that people are represented in ways that are inclusive and protective of the minority. The United Nations is charged with supporting this ideal and all of the other fundamental human rights around the world, but according to its own rules, it cannot live by what it preaches. This problem is aggravated since the most prominent member of the U.N., the United States, often fails to provide democratic leadership. The United States' refusal to support some of the most basic human rights proposals demonstrates this.

Consider the U.N. Convention on the Rights of the Child, debated and passed by the General Assembly in 1989. This convention sets out the basic protections that every child should have, exactly the sort of guarantees that all parents would want for their children. Not surprisingly, nearly every country in the world rapidly ratified it; after all, who is going to vote to deny children safety and care? In terms of global democracy, this was a landslide, but it was not quite unanimous. Two countries failed to vote for children. One country, Somalia, didn't actually have a functioning government that could vote on anything. The other country, the United States, argued, in part, that the convention would ban seventeen-year-olds from military service.

Then there is the International Criminal Court (ICC), an idea first explored when the U.N. was set up back in 1946. The idea was to have a court that would allow individuals to bring cases that concerned fundamental violations of human rights when their own national courts were unwilling or unable to give them a hearing. This court would close the loophole in international law that left individuals out in the cold and allow them to bring cases on genocide, war crimes, and slavery. In many countries women and children are systematically excluded from the legal system, so the ICC gives them a place to seek justice.

The United States, though it once supported the idea of the court, is now its most vigorous enemy. After trying everything to abort the court before it could be born, it joined with six other countries,[10] some of them known for torturing and abusing the rights of their own citizens, to vote against it. As countries began to ratify the convention that would establish the court, the United States bullied them shamelessly, threatening to pull foreign aid, trade credits, education grants, you name it, unless they promised the United States a special exemption from the court's jurisdiction.[11] Small, poor countries were given a stark choice: they could abandon their principles about equality before the law or they could be punished economically. It was like watching a Mafia don making offers that couldn't be refused. When the most influential member of the U.N. devotes substantial energies to subverting the democratic process and defeating equal justice, we should not be surprised that an issue like slavery gets pushed to the background.

For the antislavery movement, this ongoing sabotage of the ICC is a grave disappointment, since the court's founding documents specify that slavery is a crime that comes under its jurisdiction. For the first time in history we have a global court prepared to give a hearing to slaves who are denied justice in their home countries. The role of government corruption in supporting slavery is well known; finally here is a chance for slaves and ex-slaves to get their day in court. It was not an accident that the very first arrest warrants issued by the court in 2005 were for the leaders of the Lord's Resistance Army in northern Uganda, a group infamous for abducting thousands of children and using them as expendable soldiers and sex slaves.

USING THE TOOLS WE'VE GOT

We need to find a way for the United Nations to play a meaningful role in eradicating slavery. But with the present power structure designed to maintain the status quo, we need to do that without expecting major changes in the way the U.N. is organized. If we wait for real democracy to blossom at the U.N., we could be waiting for decades before we start addressing slavery. Slaves shouldn't have to wait either; we should use the

U.N. now because fighting slavery needs the organization's global reach. Fortunately, a number of mechanisms are already at work in the U.N. that can be applied to slavery. The U.N. can play a role that no other organization or government can perform, but the cooperation of the Security Council will be needed to make that happen. Taking on slavery will have several positive outcomes for the permanent members of the Security Council. Although there is contention in many areas, slavery is an issue on which strong consensus can be built. And since the greatest numbers of the world's slaves are concentrated in the poorest countries, the superpower nations would show leadership and support for *all* countries by taking the lead against this crime. Fortunately, getting the Security Council to take leadership on slavery need not be a complex or even difficult task, and it can be broken down into clear and easy steps.

The first step would be the appointment of a special representative of the secretary-general on slavery. A special representative is a fairly rare bird, an expert in a certain field who acts independently of his or her own government. After appointment, the special representative speaks with secretary-general's authority on a particular topic. One of the special representative's main products is an in-depth report that assesses a problem and gives specific recommendations for addressing it. The last special representative to the secretary-general was appointed to take up the issue of children in armed conflict, the vexing and increasing use of child soldiers. Appointing a special representative on slavery would not be revolutionary. A rapporteur (a lower rank of investigator) was appointed in 1969, for example, during the formation of the working group on contemporary forms of slavery. Currently, there is a special rapporteur on human trafficking, working hard on a limited budget. Given more power than a rapporteur, a special representative can also act as a diplomat when visiting countries in order to study the problem. As the voice of the U.N. secretary-general, the special representative has to be treated respectfully by governments and can use that opportunity to speak privately with high-ranking officials. We need a special representative on slavery for at least two reasons. The first is that the work of the U.N. against slavery is piecemeal and uncoordinated; a special representative could recommend ways to bring those disparate parts together. A special representative could also resolve the various antislavery conventions dating back to 1926 into a coherent single statement. By unifying and coordinating the definitions and conventions by which the U.N. operates, the special representative could help achieve a much-needed clarity.

If worrying about definitions seems too academic, remember that slavery is a crime. In fact, slavery is one of the few crimes to have achieved *jus cogens* (compelling law) status. This means that all countries agree that it is illegal everywhere and all the time and no country is allowed to make it legal. The International Law Commission explains that the "prohibition against slavery is one of the oldest and best settled rules of *Jus Cogens*."[12] But how can you investigate and prosecute a crime that lacks a clear definition? Every state and nation has to occasionally stop and clean up outdated or confusing laws (it is still illegal for a British member of Parliament to come to work wearing armor, for example). Slavery laws need this cleanup as well to deal with new ways criminals find to enslave people. Who in 1926 would have dreamed that criminal gangs would have an electronic global Internet to help them traffic slaves?

The second key reason the secretary-general needs a special representative on slavery is to plan for a much more robust U.N. response to slavery. A main job for the special representative would be to organize a Security Council meeting devoted to slavery (a job not allowed to a rapporteur). In recent times, the Security Council has addressed slavery only once, and then in a very restricted way. In 2005, it passed Resolution 1612 on children and armed conflict, which condemned the forced recruitment, abuse, rape, and exploitation of child soldiers. This resolution was a good first step, but it called for no action beyond "monitoring and reporting." If we really want to eradicate slavery, the Security Council has to take slavery as seriously as it does a threat like nuclear proliferation and go beyond just observing and reporting on the problem.

The Security Council meeting prepared by the special representative would have four objectives. None of these are radical ideas, and they respect the U.N.'s preference for taking things slowly and carefully. The first objective would be to make it clear that the U.N. is serious about global slavery and is ready to move ahead. In many ways simply having a meeting of the Security Council devoted to global slavery accomplishes this, but this commitment should be recorded in a resolution. The second objective would be for the Security Council to demonstrate that it supports the work of the secretary-general and the special representative. The permanent members of the Security Council could show this by making matched contributions toward the special representative's budget. The third objective would be for the Security Council to set up a small group of experts to review all of the existing U.N. conventions related to slavery, recommend how to unify and improve these conventions, recommend how to coordinate what each U.N. agency does about slavery, and keep track of what each government accomplishes with their help. That work would flow from and take direction from the special representative's report. Finally, the fourth objective, a crucial positive action, would be for the Security Council to establish a commission to determine how the existing U.N. inspection mandate could be extended to slavery. Both the committee of experts and the commission would need strict deadlines and be staffed with real go-getters. Bringing in the inspection mandate may not sound terribly frightening, but it would put teeth in the antislavery movement.

We can more easily understand the inspection mandate by looking at the recent history of Iraq. After the first Gulf War in 1991, Iraq became subject to U.N. weapons inspections as well as a number of other diplomatic and economic sanctions. Weapons inspections were ordered by the Security Council based on two U.N. conventions, one on chemical weapons and one on biological weapons. The chemical weapons convention was the first disarmament treaty to mandate the elimination of an entire category of weapons by a global inspectorate. Under these international laws, the U.N. could send inspectors to Iraq for two reasons: to see if Iraq was keeping the promise it made when it ratified the biological weapons convention and to enforce the internationally agreed upon elimination of chemical weapons.

When countries ratify a U.N. convention, they are promising to fulfill the provisions of that convention, unless they have specifically excluded some part of it before ratification. If a country seems to be failing to keep that promise, the U.N. can send inspectors to discover the truth and recommend changes. Saddam Hussein embarked on a merry dance with the U.N. inspectors lasting five years, misleading them, expelling them, readmitting them, and rejecting several U.N. resolutions that admonished him to cooperate. (It is also true that the inspectors successfully danced around Hussein, ultimately collecting the evidence showing that his "weapons program" was mostly bluff.) Hussein's refusal to cooperate with the inspectors was one of the reasons given by the United States when it finally attacked and occupied Iraq in 2003. This military action occurred without the approval of the U.N. The United States tried a last-ditch effort to get a resolution through the Security Council allowing military action against Iraq, but the Security Council *rejected* this resolution in part because the inspectors were convinced that Hussein was not an international threat at that time.

SEVERE PENALTIES

From this dramatic case, cast with a larger-than-life villain in Saddam Hussein and an American president willing to break with global consensus and go to war, one thing is clear: countries are accountable for the promises they make when they ratify U.N. conventions, and the U.N. has the power to press countries to keep those promises. When the sanctions began, because Iraq failed to keep its promises, they decimated the country's economy.[13] If it seems far-fetched to compare Iraq under Saddam Hussein to any country that is failing to keep its promises under the slavery conventions, remember that the human cost of slavery, though hidden, is vast and monstrous. True, Hussein was a proactive tyrant who would seek out new ways to torture and kill his "enemies," but what of rulers who actively ignore slavery in their own countries, or even support and participate in slavery? What of the dictators of Burma or Sudan who enslave their own citizens by the thousands with deadly result? Should there be a higher level of enforcement for some international treaties and little or no enforcement when it comes to the universally ratified conventions against slavery? That is a question that must ultimately be answered by the global citizenry, not the U.N.

If we look around the world, we see many countries failing to keep the promises they made about slavery. For example, look at Article 3 of the most important of the U.N. antislavery conventions, the Supplementary Convention on the Abolition of Slavery, the Slave Trade, and Institutions and Practices Similar to Slavery:

> 1. The act of conveying or attempting to convey slaves from one country to another by whatever means of transport, or of being accessory thereto, shall be a criminal offence under the laws of the States Parties to this Convention [countries that ratified the convention] and persons convicted thereof shall be liable to very severe penalties.
>
> 2. (a) The States Parties shall take all effective measures to prevent ships and aircraft authorized to fly their flags from conveying slaves and to punish persons guilty of such acts or of using national flags for that purpose. (b) The States Parties shall take all effective measures to ensure that their ports, airfields and coasts are not used for the conveyance of slaves.
>
> 3. The States Parties to this Convention shall exchange information in order to ensure the practical co-ordination of the measures taken by them in combating the slave trade and shall inform each other of every case of the slave trade, and of every attempt to commit this criminal offence, which comes to their notice.

According to one U.N. estimate, up to 800,000 people are trafficked into slavery each year, transported from one country to another, or within countries. A significant proportion must be flying or traveling by ship. They flow into the United States alone at the rate of 14,500 to 17,500 a year.[14] Are governments really taking "all effective measures" to stop this trade in slaves? Brazil has been doing better than most countries in freeing slaves, but even there no slave traffickers have gone to jail. Is the normal sentence for slaveholders in Brazil of two years' community service really thought of as a "very severe penalty?" Thousands of women have been brought into Japan for enslavement in prostitution. Many if not most of those women can identify the men who trafficked them, yet Japan arrests a handful of perpetrators each year. This list of countries could go on and on. Even the simple point to which all countries have agreed, "to inform each other of every case of the slave trade," has never been acted upon. Given the reality of global electronic data collection, what could be the excuse for that failure? It can't be lack of time to make this work; this convention became international law in 1957.

A handful of countries might be hiding chemical and biological weapons, and they should be inspected and pushed to keep their promises under the conventions they've signed. At the same time, nearly every country in the world has failed to keep its promises, to a greater or lesser extent, under the antislavery conventions. This is where the U.N. inspectors come in. The commission established by the Security Council, in its meeting devoted to slavery, will deploy independent and objective inspectors to countries to assess their performance against their promises. To show true leadership, the five permanent members of the Security Council should ask that their countries be inspected first. These inspections will identify and make constructive suggestions about closing any loopholes that exist within laws and enforcement, providing help to victims, and improving international cooperation. Obviously, the inspection program should not be backed up with threats of armed force; we know that armed conflict only increases the incidence of slavery. But many other motivators are available in the international arena, and I suspect that most countries will welcome, rather than resist, the help and guidance offered them. A few countries may want to play Saddam Hussein's game of hide and seek with the antislavery inspectors, but they would pay a high cost. As the flow of trafficked people starts to be choked off at borders, ports, and airports, there will be less money to be made that way. When sanctions are brought to bear, the real pain starts, and most governments will not think the pain is worth the relatively small returns that slaves represent.

The cost of this inspectorate and the support for the technical assistance it provides to governments will not be cheap, but it will not be particularly costly either. This work will not be about shipping tons of food or disaster relief; it is about talk, advice, building cooperation, and training. Given the high human cost of slavery, the profits it generates for criminals, and the economic payoff generated when freed slaves take an active role in the economy, any expenditure should be thought of as pump priming. Weapons inspections in Iraq cost the U.N. several hundred million dollars over the years, but the hundreds of billions that economic sanctions cost Iraq is not a cost most countries would wish to pay to preserve slavery. With the inspectorate at the core of the U.N.'s work against slavery, many of its other agencies can be coordinated into the task as well. Some of these may seem surprising, but nearly all have a role to play.

BREAD AND PILLS AND GUNS AND ROSES AND SATELLITES

Coordinating the different parts of the U.N. to address global slavery shouldn't be restricted just to those agencies that currently work on the issue. Many of the forces that push people into slavery are the focus of U.N. activity. When other parts of the U.N. begin to build slavery into the framework of their work and coordinate their antislavery efforts, big things can happen.

BREAD

A perfect example of an agency that could be part of the antislavery effort is the U.N. World Food Programme (WFP). In 2005, the WFP fed ninety-seven million people in eighty-two countries. It provides emergency food aid as well as supporting food self-sufficiency in the poorest parts of the world. There is more than enough food in the world to feed everyone, but the poorest people can't afford to buy it, or they have nowhere to raise their own food. The link between hunger and slavery is clear. The poorest countries, which tend to be the hungriest as well, are also the countries most likely to have high levels of slavery. Many of the slaves I have met, especially those in India, Pakistan, and Nepal, were driven into slavery by hunger. When the alternative is starvation for parents and their children, even slavery becomes an option. It is no coincidence that some of the WFP's current hunger hotspots—Mali, Haiti,

Sudan, and Niger—are also countries with long-term, deeply entrenched slavery. Some serious questions have been raised about how the WFP has been used by the United States to disperse its own subsidized agricultural surpluses around the world. Although this food is sometimes the difference between life and death, dropping large amounts of free food into a weak economy can sometimes threaten the viability of local agriculture, increasing poverty and vulnerability to exploitation.

Although the effect of U.S. agricultural giving needs to be looked at carefully, there is a place for food subsidies, particularly when the food is locally grown and thus supports the local economy. One thing that we know for certain is that a food subsidy, even for a relatively short period, can be the wedge that breaks open slavery. In Bihar state in India, when local vigilance committees ensure that free lunches are cooked at the local school, children are prevented from falling into the hands of traffickers. A big pot of rice and lentils works on several levels. It quells the hunger that pushes many parents to the desperate act of giving a child up to a dubious promise of work and food in another city, it draws children into the school where they get education that helps them to crawl out of the hole of poverty, and it means that the teachers are much more likely to come every day—both because of the free lunch and because if they didn't show up the parents would chase them down. The total cost of the daily lunch for the whole school is around $6 a day, an amazing bargain if it kept even one child out of slavery.

When slaves reach for freedom, two extremely critical and decisive moments can be expected. The first occurs when the slaveholder realizes what is happening and, since all slavery has violence at its core, makes a last-ditch violent attack to hold on to the slave. The second occurs two or three days following escape when, without aid and protection, a slave can be dragged back or starved into submission. These critical moments are addressed by the antislavery laws in both India and the United States. When they work properly, the laws provide immediate payments for food and shelter for a newly freed slave and family. Because many slaves have to flee with only the shirts on their backs, this grant is all that stands between them and hunger. By removing this immediate fear, the freed slave can concentrate on recovery and the next steps on the path to stable freedom and a new life.

The U.N. food program already knows how to get food to the people who need it; only two steps are needed to turn it into an antislavery machine as well. The first step is to build an awareness of slavery into its planning; the second is to see that it has the resources to assemble a special unit that searches out and attacks slavery through food aid, giving slaves the food security they need to make the break for freedom. This type of special unit would work best in places like Niger or Nepal where large-scale liberations are planned; indeed it could have been critical to preventing the botched liberation of the Nepali kamaiya. There are smart people in the WFP with deep experience in the very countries with the largest amounts of slavery in the world, and adding slavery to their mission would be a natural and fruitful extension of their work.

PILLS

Operating alongside the World Food Program is the World Health Organization (WHO). These two U.N. agencies are about the same size and spend about the same amount, $3 billion a year. The achievements of the WHO are impressive, particularly in the eradication of diseases like smallpox and polio, both now reduced by some 99 percent. Health programs reduce slavery for many of the same reasons that food programs do. From sleeping sickness to HIV, disease can debilitate entire populations, wasting what productive capacity people have and pushing them into vulnerability. Slaves regularly suffer from untreated diseases and wounds; they rarely receive medical attention. When slaves come to freedom, one of the first things they want to organize is access to medical care for themselves and especially for their children. They know all too well the heartbreak of a high infant and child mortality rate.

If WHO strategies are refocused to incorporate slavery, important things will happen. Health workers, because they come into contact with whole populations, are likely to encounter slaves. If they are trained to recognize them, liberation can be hastened. Medical care for freed slaves will improve their chances for autonomous and productive lives. I am not calling for any alteration in the basic work of the WHO, only that sensitivity to slavery be added in the same way that, in the past, an increased sensitivity to gender became part of U.N. policies, with great benefit. Expertise in slavery-related injuries and illnesses is needed, and who would be better at building that expertise than those most experienced in providing medical care in the world's poorest countries?

GUNS

The peacekeeping forces of the U.N. often face a difficult job. Inserted between warring groups, these soldiers have to be a kind of reverse-military, *not* reacting to threats, *not* taking military action, *not* planning offensive operations. Yet their presence can be crucial in saving lives and protecting noncombatants from the horrors of modern small-scale conflicts. Since the end of the Cold War, more than one hundred ethnic, sectarian, and religious conflicts have erupted across much of the developing world. In the past decade this total is twice that of the previous decade. Two experts explain:

> These wars have killed more than five million people, devastated entire
> geographic regions, and left tens of millions of refugees and orphans. Little
> of the destruction was inflicted by the tanks, artillery or aircraft usually
> associated with modern warfare; rather most was carried out with pistols,
> machine guns and grenades. However beneficial the end of the Cold
> War has been in other respects, it has let loose a global deluge of surplus
> weapons into a setting in which the risk of local conflict appears to have
> grown markedly.[15]

These small arms have tremendous killing power and are light enough to be used by children as young as nine or ten. They are also ridiculously cheap; fully automatic assault rifles often sell for $15 or less. In the hands of untrained, irregular combatants, the result is the use of civilian massacre as a tactic and a ratcheting up of the risk for peacekeepers. An increase in the numbers of fatalities of U.N. peacekeepers, Red Cross workers, and other humanitarian workers has kept pace with the dispersion of small arms. Of course, the ethnic and sectarian conflicts fueled by the increasing availability of small arms also foster a rapid emergence of slavery. Most countries that have suffered these destructive conflicts (Liberia, Sierra Leone, Sudan, and Bosnia are good examples) have seen a marked increase in slavery of child soldiers, women enslaved for sexual exploitation, and slavery in industries, such as gold and diamond mining, that fund the warlords.

The soldiers who make up the U.N. force are some of the best that their countries have to offer, but this is not necessarily saying a great deal. For the poorest countries, sending a detachment to be peacekeepers is a moneymaker supporting their overall military budget. There are about eighty-one thousand troops and police wearing the blue helmets of the U.N. peacekeepers. India, Pakistan, and Bangladesh supply nearly thirty thousand of that number; Jordan, Nepal, Ethiopia, Ghana, and France also contribute numerous troops, but altogether more than one hundred countries send personnel. Since the peacekeeping force was set up in 1948, more than two thousand U.N. soldiers have been killed, three-quarters of them since the end of the Cold War.

In 2007 the peacekeepers were maintaining eighteen different operations and are at the highest levels of deployment in their history. Active conflict in Liberia, Ivory Coast, Haiti, Burundi, and Sudan require large numbers of troops. In 2006 the U.N. force was expanded in the Democratic Republic of the Congo, troops were sent to East Timor, and peacekeepers were sent to Lebanon to calm tensions after the invasion by Israel. In early 2007 a new force prepared to enter the Darfur region of Sudan as well. The cost of the forces runs about $5 billion a year, set to increase to $7 billion if Timor, and especially Darfur, are sent large numbers of troops. This money is raised through a complicated formula. The United States contributes the most, about 27 percent of the total, followed by Japan, Germany, the United Kingdom, France, and a number of other countries.[16] (This list includes some of the world's largest dealers in small arms, countries that are supplying, directly or indirectly, the very conflicts that the U.N. is sent to police.) The funding almost always runs in arrears, as countries drag their feet about making their contributions.

Although some readers may question my judgment, I believe there is an antislavery role for the U.N. peacekeepers. Doubters can point to the fact that some peacekeepers have actually been implicated in human trafficking and prostitution. In the late 1980s, U.N. troops deployed to Mozambique were caught in the commercial sexual exploitation of local women and girls. In the recent past, a rapid increase in prostitution was noted when U.N. troops arrived in Bosnia, Kosovo, and Cambodia. Some U.N. personnel were reported to be involved in recruiting young women for a brothel in Bosnia. More than 150 cases of sexual abuse of local women and girls by U.N. forces in the Congo were reported, most involving the purchase of sex with small amounts of food or money, and allegations were made of rape and the requirement of sex for jobs by civilian employees of the U.N. force. Some U.N. troops in Haiti were accused of sexually exploiting underage girls.[17]

Sadly, the U.N. was slow to respond to such reports, which first gained global attention in Bosnia in the 1990s. David Lamb, a former police officer from Philadelphia and U.N. human rights investigator in Bosnia, described his investigation of sex trafficking in Bosnia: "There were credible witnesses, but I found a real reluctance on the part of the United Nations . . . leadership to investigate these allegations."[18] At the same time, employees of DynCorp, a company hired by the U.S. government to supply police officers to Bosnia, were also accused of buying sex slaves and patronizing brothels. In many conflicts, commanders and political bosses of U.N. peacekeeping forces failed to recognize how their forces were acting as a spur to human traffickers. One former commander in Bosnia apologized for this after the fact, but clearly something has been rotten in the U.N. peacekeeping force. Other national armies have also been corrupted, but we should be able to expect more from a peacekeeping force.

In 2004, the U.N. began to clean up the force, a welcome step but much too late to save women and children from abuse in the Congo and other countries. Over 300 people were investigated, resulting in the firing of 18 civilians, 17 police, and 144 military personnel. Most were simply sent home. What, if any, punishment they received on arrival home is not clear, though a U.N. representative stated, "The U.N. is working with the Member States that contribute troops to ensure that follow-up action is taken and that those guilty of misconduct are disciplined."[19] Obviously, troops sent in to protect innocent citizens in a time of conflict cannot be allowed to abuse them, nor is the use of prostitutes by soldiers, no matter how ancient this practice, acceptable for U.N. or any other troops. The U.S. Department of Defense has put in place rules banning the use of prostitutes by any U.S. military personnel; the U.N. forces could easily adopt these rules. Though most of the U.N. troops are decent and professional, any cover-up diminishes the trustworthiness of all the soldiers. The deployment of an all-female unit of peacekeepers to Liberia in early 2007 is also a step in the right direction, one likely to dramatically reduce concerns about sexual exploitation.

It is not only possible that the U.N. peacekeeping force be cleaned up; it *must* be. The U.N. needs to make it clear that troops will be monitored closely and punished for any such violations. Countries with the best-trained and best-disciplined troops, like Norway and Canada, may have to consider increasing their contingents. All the countries that write checks for the peacekeepers will have to understand that training them properly and cleaning up this mess will cost money, but it is something that must be done. The U.N. must have a peacekeeping force above reproach, simply because it is the only legitimate *global* force we have. There is today, and will be in the future, a clear need for a military or police force to protect slaves in the process of liberation. The chaos, failure, and terrible human cost of the botched emancipation in Nepal could have been avoided by the deployment of a small U.N. force to the rural areas where debt-bondage slavery was prevalent. Preventing the horrific death toll and enslavement that took place in Sudan, Liberia, Sierra

Leone, Congo, and other collapsing states would have been well worth the cost of the peacekeepers, and such intervention is not the appropriate action of any individual country. From Brazil to West Africa, from Southeast Asia to rural Peru, the judicious use of U.N. peacekeepers could speed the safe and sustainable global eradication of slavery. The Security Council needs to provide a clear mandate for the force and the resources to back it up. A small force could be assembled with a specific antislavery mandate. Such a specialized group would be more likely to receive permission from national governments to enter their territory. A force that was trained in the process of liberation; knowledgeable about the right moment to intervene; and prepared to offer food, shelter, and medical support in addition to security would be invaluable in achieving large-scale liberation. Remember that small-scale landowners or businesspeople hold most of the world's slaves. They can bribe or threaten the local police, but they would be cowed by an independent and well-trained U.N. force. With the local government providing interpreters and access to communications and supplies, a U.N. force, often simply by its presence, would do the heavy lifting.

Some caveats must be added, however. The first decade of the twenty-first century has taught us that democracy cannot be installed through military intervention. By the same token, true abolition and the establishment of full citizenship for ex-slaves does not arrive at the barrel of a gun. Force can break the back of slavery, but it does not create the context of ongoing stability and security needed for true liberation. If the judicious use of a specialized U.N. force can open the door, other U.N. agencies can bring the food, education, and medical care that must follow to ensure lasting freedom. Anytime an armed force arrives there is cause for concern; most countries see the arrival of U.N. peacekeepers as an admission that they have lost control over their own territory. A specialized force must never be seen as a quick fix, and it can never be allowed to short-circuit the building up of a nation's own capacity to liberate and protect slaves. Nor should a specialized force take independent lethal action against traffickers and slaveholders; that should be reserved for national law enforcement. The goal should be the creation of a secure context in which slaves can more readily come to freedom and build new lives in safety. Perhaps the best model would be such a specialized force working closely with a country's existing antislavery efforts. Brazil, with the expansion of the antislavery squads under President Lula, demonstrates that more boots on the ground lead to dramatic increases in slaves coming to freedom.

ROSES

If the peacekeepers are the guns of the U.N., then the United Nations Educational, Scientific, and Cultural Organization (UNESCO) is the roses. UNESCO emphasizes sharing ideas, building knowledge, helping children to learn about global rights, and promoting cultural ways of celebrating our common humanity. The UNESCO budget runs around $600 million a year and funds everything from archaeology, books, and ballets to conferences, studentships, and Web-based learning.

In the 1980s and 1990s the organization went through a rough patch. UNESCO's management structure had become the most top-heavy in all the U.N., and that is saying something. The situation became so flagrant that the United States, the United Kingdom, and Singapore all pulled out, creating a hole in the budget that you could march an orchestra through. Reform took time, but the number of bureaucrats was cut in half, programs were made more efficient, and eventually the United States, the United Kingdom, and Singapore came back on board.

UNESCO has the kind of global reach that is needed for the campaign to end slavery. Its programs filter into schools, and it supports the creative work of artists, writers, and filmmakers all over the planet. In 2004 UNESCO mounted a campaign commemorating the transatlantic slave trade. Educational materials were produced and sent out to thousands of schools, film and archaeology projects were supported, and reports were made on modern slavery as well. The global eradication of slavery will need coordination of all parts of the U.N. The aim for UNESCO will be to use its creative skills to help children and adults move from the past to the present, to imagine a future without slavery.

SATELLITES

Few people realize that the U.N. has its own space program. It is called the U.N. Office for Outer Space Affairs, or UNOOSA, which is such a silly sounding acronym that most people just call the organization "Unispace." Aiming to promote peaceful uses of space technology, Unispace is the discussion center for issues of space law. Where Unispace really comes into its own is in coordinating the application of satellite imaging in situations of environmental destruction or disaster or in using satellite photos to monitor conflict or to plan relief operations. Working with groups like the World Health Organization, it has used satellite images to generate both maps of malaria-afflicted areas and good directions to reach the almost inaccessible rural areas where treatment is needed. A project using communications satellites in West Africa led to quick eradication of the larvae that spread the river blindness disease— the leading cause of preventable blindness in the world. In this project 100,000 people were saved from going blind, 1.25 million were cured, and millions more were protected from infection. The people were saved by the medicine that was given, but the satellite images helped to effectively target the work.

Proper and efficient targeting is what space technology can bring to the fight against slavery. Slavery is often hidden away in remote, unmapped areas, but it is hard to hide from satellites. Slaves are used to destroy the environment—through logging and strip-mining especially— and the scars of this destruction are visible from space. In Brazil, India, West Africa, and other parts of South America, South Asia, and Africa, the telltale signs of slavery can be seen from above.[20] Obviously, you can't tell an enslaved worker from a free worker from space, but you can see where illegal, potentially slave-based work is occurring and respond appropriately. Refugee groups, many of them vulnerable to enslavement, can also be tracked from space, and locating and monitoring these groups can be critical to their safety. Space technology won't take the place of liberators on the ground, but it can help them to do their job more effectively.

Most of the agencies I've been discussing that could be mobilized against slavery come under the U.N. Economic and Social Council (ECOSOC). Several of the specific actions to be taken by the Security Council would be carried through by the ECOSOC, since it is charged with finding solutions to such problems and promoting economic and social progress. If there is one place to locate the coordination of the U.N.'s work against slavery, it is most likely within ECOSOC.

GETTING THE BANK ON BOARD

Operating in parallel with the United Nations are two organizations with an equally global reach: the World Bank and the World Trade Organization (WTO). Much of what needs to be done to end slavery, and demolish the poverty and corruption that support it, can be achieved more easily with the support of these international financial institutions. But at the moment international finance sometimes helps, sometimes does not, and sometimes works against freedom for slaves.

Money flows around the world in a vast stream, much of it channeled through the Internet from rich country to rich country and from business to business. Some of the money finds its way to Africa, South Asia, or South America, but instead of remaining there it is sucked up and delivered back to the North America and Europe. The international financial institutions aim at human and economic development, but the process is flawed and sadly help does not always reach those who need it most. The antislavery movement has to navigate a financial and development system that can sometimes erect barriers to freedom but that also has the potential to create new avenues to liberation.

A good place to start is the World Bank. Set up in 1944 to foster the reconstruction of Europe, the World Bank later branched out into helping developing countries get the financing they needed for economic and social development. By its own description, the World Bank focuses on ending poverty: "Our mission is global poverty reduction and the improvement of living standards." Certainly money from the World Bank flows to projects in developing countries. At the same time, funds in the form of repayments, interest charges, and so forth also flow from developing countries to the World Bank.

A good deal of the controversy surrounding the loans and grants made by the World Bank rests on two similar-sounding concepts: conditions and conditionalities. *Conditions* are placed on World Bank loans in the same way that we agree to certain conditions when we borrow money to buy a car or a house. Loans to poor countries have conditions like a fixed interest rate, often 1 percent, a grace period before repayments are due, and a final repayment date, usually forty years after the loan is given. *Conditionalities*, on the other hand, are actions required of a particular government in order to get funding, whether a loan or a grant, for a specific project. The idea is to link cash to political change that improves lives. The policy change can be almost anything—free legal services for the poor, implementation or improvement of a pension system, or even the appointment of a children's ombudsman—as long as it has a sound economic basis. A government that agrees to the conditionalities and can provide proof that the requirements are met is awarded ongoing funding. Some conditionalities have come under withering criticism in the past, and the World Bank itself admits that some of them have had a negative impact on efforts to reduce poverty and protect the environment.[21] World Bank staff have worked for years to promote funding linked to conditionalities that would support human rights and a healthy environment, but they complain of internal struggles holding them back.

For the antislavery movement, the glittering possibility on the horizon is the potentially profound impact of grants and loans linked to anti-slavery conditionalities. The World Bank gives large grants in addition to loaning money. A good deal of HIV/AIDS work in Africa is funded by World Bank grants that can be as high as $100 million. No grant for anti-slavery work, from any source, has ever come near that level. We know that government policies can make or break antislavery efforts, and the carrot of large-scale grants and loans could be instrumental in spurring new laws that would liberate and protect slaves. World Bank officials could choose antislavery measures, such as those listed in this book, and require that they be implemented as a conditionality of a grant or loan. Conditionalities for governments might include the formation of anti-slavery task forces, provision of grants to freed slaves to help them begin their new lives, and even the appointment of an ombudsman for freed slaves—all suggested government action in chapter 5. These require-ments mean extra work for the World Bank, but the goals are wholly in line with the bank's mission of global poverty reduction and improve-ment of living standards.

If the World Bank reviews each of its grants and loans through an antislavery lens, it will ensure that no projects would increase a local population's vulnerability to slavery. The World Bank's board of direc-tors has announced that the bank would not approve any loan that undermines human rights, but the bank needs to go further and be more specific. One step in the right direction is new rules that have been cre-ated for the bank's International Finance Corporation (IFC). The IFC is the part of the World Bank that lends to the private sector and that has financed projects for more than 3,300 companies in 140 countries. Although currently hard to enforce, the new lending rules call for greater guarantees for labor and environmental protection. The bank intends to extend these rules to all funding that it provides; it should take this step immediately and should dedicate funds to the rules' enforcement. For the rules to be effective, protections for whistleblowers would be needed. World Bank employees, as well as staffs of companies receiving funds, can do their part by blowing the whistle when labor and environmental abuses happen, especially when such abuses increase the local popula-tion's vulnerability to slavery. The bank has also set new rules for its own purchases based on the ILO's core labor standards. But as beneficial as these rules are, the role for the World Bank in ending slavery should go further.

As we saw in chapter 1, the links between vicious and self-reinforcing cycles of poverty, high debt loads, corruption, and slavery are a fact of life. We have also seen that in freedom, ex-slaves tend to become productive members of their local economy; this strengthens the local economy helps build a stronger national economy. The World Bank took a positive step when its board of directors announced that the Bank would not approve any loan that undermines human rights. But the World Bank needs to go further and build a specific program aimed at slavery, as it has done for corruption. The good news is that the World Bank has the economists, sociologists, anthropologists, political scientists, and global reach needed to develop a large-scale strategy for slavery eradication, and it has the resources to test that strategy. But even after the World Bank adopts a slavery lens, a great deal more can be done through trade, by helping the poor earn more in the global economy. Unfortunately, the world trade system often works against the poor as well.

IS TRADE MORE IMPORTANT THAN SLAVERY?

At about the same time as the World Bank was set up, the United States and Britain made plans to start an international trade organization that would set trade rules. Although President Truman and Congress abandoned that idea, the United States and seven other countries did agree to liberalize trade through the General Agreement on Tariffs and Trade (GATT). GATT dealt only with commercial policies like tariffs and quotas, setting rules covering trade barriers and allowing policy makers to negotiate ways to reduce obstacles to trade. Every few years a round of talks was held aimed at easing restrictions on international trade.

The eighth round of talks began in 1986 and is known as the "Uruguay Round." This was a critical time in trade, as many countries had dropped their currency controls, allowing the free flow of money around the world. Before the late 1980s, "export of capital" was a crime in many nations. As barriers to trade and finance fell, the resulting globalization of the world economy raised a whole new set of challenges and problems. The issues were so complicated that the Uruguay Round didn't finish until 1994.

During the Uruguay Round the terms for the World Trade Organization (WTO) were negotiated, and in January 1995 the WTO was formally established with the aim of regulating trade. The WTO does this by building agreements about how and when countries can use trade barriers like tariffs, quotas, and other standards. In general, if countries have trade disputes, they rely on the WTO's system of binding dispute settlement, and the WTO's power lies in this system. A country can choose not to take a case to settlement, or not to answer a case brought against it, but it still has to pay for lost trade or accept retaliation if a judgment goes against it. Any country that wants to join the WTO and take part in the decision making is expected to sign and ratify all of the WTO agreements and treaties, and by 2007 the WTO had 150 member countries.

Although the idea of facilitating trade is good, the members of the WTO don't always work in ways that help poorer countries develop. This occurs in a number of ways, and almost all of them reflect the power of the rich countries to control trade negotiations and get the rules they want. Although developing countries get special privileges and exceptions and more time to comply with WTO rules, they still have a serious problem gaining access to the markets of Europe and North America. The raw goods and commodities produced in developing countries often have to compete with commodities that are heavily subsidized in North America and Europe, even within their own internal markets.[22] These subsidies border on the obscene. The average cow in North America and Europe, for example, receives a subsidy of $2 a day, more than what a billion people in the developing world have to live on.[23] When big, efficient cotton farmers in a country like Brazil have trouble competing against subsidized cotton from the United States, farmers in a dirt-poor country like Chad don't have a chance. Subsidies drive down the market price for such goods and mean that raw cotton, rice, and sugar from the developing world will earn little on the global or domestic market. And what's more, once exported, cotton and sugar are turned into clothes and food products in factories in richer countries and sold back to the poor countries at a profit. If a poor country tries to block these imports in order to develop its own industry, it can be denounced for erecting a trade barrier and brought to mediation. Of course, a poorer country can also use the system to denounce subsidies as unfair. In 2004, Brazil won a case against American subsidies in which it complained that the subsidies depressed world cotton prices and gave American farmers an edge over less-developed countries. It was the first time that a country's farm subsidies have been challenged, and may prompt more cases. The United States has appealed the decision and continues to pay subsidies.

The issue of subsidies and their link to slavery was brought home to me in May 2007 when I met with three long-serving antislavery workers, one from Ghana and two from Haiti. I asked them what they felt was the one thing the U.S. government could do to support the end of slavery in their countries. Remarkably, though they had never met and lived thousands of miles apart, they all answered without hesitation: "End the rice subsidy." They explained that in their countries U.S. rice was so cheap it forced local farmers out of the market. The result was increased poverty in the countryside and a growing dependence on an imported staple. Admittedly, these three were not economists, but their grassroots experience gave real weight to their concerns about subsidies.

HOW DO WE TAKE SLAVERY OUT OF WORLD TRADE?

I have been pointing out the failings of the WTO since it aims to regulate global trade, but I probably shouldn't. The WTO can't tell a government what to do. The United States regularly ignores WTO rules, failing, for example, to bring its tax system or its antidumping regulations into compliance. The United States gets away with this because it can. Any country that chooses to ignore the rules can do so; it just has to put up with being punished by other countries through their trade laws. But in general countries are reluctant to punish the United States or China, which are just too big to take on or make angry. Small countries can also ignore the rules, but if they do and they are sanctioned, the punishments tend to hurt them more.

At the present time, under Article XX of the GATT treaty, a country should be able to stop importing goods made by slave labor. This article says that a country can block trade to protect "public morals." Slavery is clearly a violation of public morals, but the trick is in the enforcement. There have been disputes concerning dolphin-friendly tuna, shrimp, and endangered sea turtles, disputes all concerned with environmental protection but with a parallel to potential disputes about protecting human rights. Rulings in these disputes point to at least three obstacles to banning slave-made goods from trade. First, in order to comply with WTO norms of nondiscrimination and national treatment, a country instituting a ban would have to show that the trade restriction has been imposed against *all* countries exporting slave-made products. Given the hidden nature of slavery, demonstrating this would be extremely difficult and could easily be called into question. Second, to ban slave-made goods a country would have to show that it first exhausted all other possible remedies within the trade rules. If it hasn't, then it might be accused of committing an "arbitrary or unjustified discrimination." Finally, WTO mediation rulings are undecided whether Country A is even allowed to ban slave-made goods in order to get Country B to reduce slavery within its borders. In spite of those hurdles, a country could ban slave-made goods and take the case to mediation, and then simply take the consequences of any rulings. Sometimes it seems that WTO rules will not allow a ban on slave-made goods; at other times it appears the WTO doesn't have the authority to address the issue. Clearly this confusion needs to be talked through by member countries and cleared up. Meanwhile, countries like Brazil and Ivory Coast don't want to have their products banned just when they are trying to clean up the situation, and they will reasonably argue that time is needed to resolve the issue before any trade bans are launched.

At the same time, we see some trade interventions that can have a direct impact on human rights. Possibly the most dramatic example is that of South Africa. A white-controlled government of South Africa imposed an extreme form of racial segregation, apartheid, in 1948. A boycott of South African goods was begun in 1959 as a protest against this segregation. In the 1980s universities, mutual funds, and pension funds began to sell stock they held in South African companies. This divestment put serious pressure on the apartheid government, and by the late 1980s twenty-five governments had enacted trade sanctions with U.N. support. It is widely thought that this divestment campaign, sucking capital from the South African economy, pushed the apartheid government over the edge. The new multiracial democracy in South Africa was born in 1994.[24]

A more sobering lesson is to be learned from the trade sanctions levied against the military dictatorship in Burma. Both the United States and the European Union have enacted sanctions, but the Burmese junta has chosen to let its population suffer rather than take the United States and the EU to trade mediation. As in Iraq under Saddam Hussein, in Burma the dictators intend to hold out against trade pressure aimed at protecting human rights.

If there is a third model, it is the Kimberley Process. Under pressure from human rights groups and governments, the diamond industry was compelled to find a way to stem the flow of "conflict diamonds," or "blood diamonds." These are the illegally mined raw diamonds used to finance rebel movements and fuel conflict in Africa. The Kimberley Process set up a plan for inspecting and certifying batches of diamonds in order to reject those being put into the market by armed gangs. Forty-five countries take part in the Kimberley Process, and it seems to be slowing the entry of blood diamonds into the global market. However, unlike the Cocoa Protocol (explained in chapter 7), it does not provide for an independent, credible, and verifiable system of certification. Note the importance of this process for slave-produced commodities. Rather than imposing a sanction, these WTO member countries, with support from the U.N., waived the normal trade rules and set up the diamond inspection system. With adjustments, a similar system could likely be applied, at least to slave-mined minerals like gold and building stone.

How do we proceed? On the one hand, we have our desire to reject slave-made goods and the national laws that enforce this desire; on the other hand, we have overarching rules of trade that seem to be clear on paper but are ambiguous when it comes to enforcement. While the debate and negotiations drag on, countries are both exporting and importing (as well as transshipping) slave-made goods every day. What can be done to fix this?

I suggest that at least three things need to be done, one soon and the other two over the next few years. The first step would be to insert into the working of the WTO recognition of slavery and its *jus cogens* status in international law. Article XX of GATT permits trade restrictions on grounds of public morals and public health. The United States or any other country could move this along by bringing a trade dispute for the WTO to rule on, a dispute that would then clarify how Article XX could be used against slavery. Alternatively, Article XX could be considered in the current Doha Round of WTO negotiations. But since the Doha Round seems to be stalled and the issue has not been raised, we might have to wait until the next round of talks, making this a long-term tactic.

The second step would be to take a case into mediation by "disputing trade"; in other words Country A states that it will not accept goods under the normal trade rules from Country B because slavery has entered the product chain. Disputing trade would seem to be simple, but remember that Country B does not have to answer this charge and can choose to simply forfeit the disputed trade. If the case is not answered, the mediators do not make a ruling, and no precedent is set. This is exactly what has happened with the United States and Burma. The United States has stopped imports from Burma because of that country's woeful human rights record, yet Burma has not challenged this at the WTO. Burma's laundry stinks enough already; the dictators don't want to hang it up for an airing in the WTO as well. But without a challenge, no ruling comes from the WTO. Because of that I would make a radical proposal: that two countries cooperate to bring a trade dispute over slavery to mediation *in order* to clarify rules and establish precedent. The reality is that the United States and some European countries, as well as many developing countries, are producing slave-made goods. There is a fear that if all goods tainted with slavery were suddenly banned, the result would be the mutually assured destruction of trade. Given that many commodities, like cocoa, cotton, or sugar, are stained by a tiny fraction of slave-made product that cannot be separated from the whole, this fear is reasonable. No one wants to throw out the whole cotton harvest because a few bales are contaminated with slavery. Two countries that have said they are committed to ending slavery, such as Brazil and the United States, could orchestrate a trade dispute with the aim of resolving how the rules could be put to work against slavery. The need is for mediation that would lead to a more nuanced approach, one that can separate the blatant perpetrators like Burma from countries that are trying to address slavery in their products like Brazil.

The third step in this process would be for member countries to insert into the structure of the WTO bureaucracy an independent department concerned with slavery and other labor issues.[25] A member country could initiate this process by asking the WTO secretariat to set up a study group to look into these issues. Careful work needs to be done on the agreements regulating trade so that they ban the worst abuses without disadvantaging developing countries. To build the rules of world trade without protections for the workers who actually make trade possible is simply unfair and potentially cruel. Today the structure of the WTO determines that most of the weight is given to trade interests at the expense of the workers. That imbalance needs to be corrected within the organization itself. Human rights groups will never be able to fix the problem from the outside. Creating a department, in and of itself, would not solve the problem, but it would create an impetus for change.

Such an internal and independent department would also take on the task of reconciling the trade treaties and regulations with the existing international law and U.N. conventions on slavery. Although many of the fundamental human rights agreements are vague, they can still be discussed, worked through, and then defined in a way that they could be legally enforced in international trade.[26] The WTO does not have to become a human rights organization, but its members should build human rights into the global trade regime. The payoff is that slavery is a drag on trade and national economies, so its eradication *should* be a key element of trade law. Freed slaves increase both production and consumption; they are an untapped market and a source of economic growth. Making more money from ex-slaves is, by itself, not the most important reason to eradicate slavery, but it does fit within the goals of poverty reduction and increased trade of both the World Bank and the WTO.

Although these adjustments to the WTO would be helpful, we need to recognize the real power in this situation. The WTO is subject to the will of its members; its bureaucracy cannot act without their specific authority. The director general of the WTO can't even suggest ideas for negotiation without exceeding his power. Slavery occurs within countries, and it is first and foremost the responsibility of national governments to root it out. The WTO could help to interdict products of slavery once they start crossing borders, but the protection of citizens from slavery rests with governments. Obviously, many national governments are not up to that task, and that is where the WTO could be one of the tools helping to end slavery.

These systems for regulating trade are both recent and malleable; they are still in the process of design and implementation. It is late, but not *too* late, to enlist the World Bank and the WTO in the fight against slavery. To do that we need to make sure our governments take action. In the United States, Congress decides trade policy. The executive branch may do the negotiating, but Congress authorizes and approves. Citizens of all countries need to ask their politicians to make a place at the negotiation table for the enslaved. The cost of building a slavery lens for the WTO and World Bank would be small, and if done with care it should not limit any fair and legitimate trade.

MAKING IT HAPPEN

There are no perfect organizations, governments, or businesses—or people for that matter. Whatever their histories, the U.N., the World Bank, and the WTO are global organizations that can be aimed at slavery. The U.N. needs reform, and it needs to be more efficient, but if we wait for that to happen, another fifty years may pass and more people will have been born, suffered, and died in slavery. Slaves can't wait for bureaucratic reform, and neither should we. Fortunately, most U.N. (and World Bank and WTO) workers agree and are willing to get moving against global slavery now. They are a brainy and experienced bunch; what they are lacking is leadership. Whatever the new U.N. secretary-general, Ban Ki-moon, has in mind, and however a brilliant leader he might turn out to be, that leadership has to come from the Security Council. This can happen quickly, because the power of the five permanent members is such that they don't have to ask permission to move ahead. On a noncontroversial issue like slavery, they can act decisively and in concert once they make up their minds. The steps they can take are discussed above, but it is worth repeating them briefly, and worth repeating that every one of these steps has been taken before on other issues. In a nutshell, the Security Council of the U.N. needs to do five things:

Appoint a special representative of the secretary-general on slavery. This special representative should be given the mandate to review and report on the state of global slavery, and to prepare plans, materials, and proposals for a Security Council meeting devoted to contemporary slavery.

Hold a meeting of the Security Council devoted to slavery. This meeting would have clear-cut goals and would constitute the first step in making the U.N. a global leader in ending slavery. With the materials and plans for the meeting prepared by the special representative, and talked over in advance with the permanent members, the meeting would confirm the U.N.'s commitment to ending slavery. The Security Council would then back up that commitment in easy, noncontroversial ways.

Make significant public contributions to the special representative's budget. The work of the special representative ultimately has to come from national governments. If the permanent members of the Security Council make matching contributions to the special representative's budget, they would show that they are taking the problem seriously.

On the recommendation of the special representative, appoint a committee of experts to review the existing conventions on slavery and recommend how to unify and clarify these conventions, as well as coordinate and improve the U.N.'s programmatic response to slavery. This group would be given a year to compile a report and return with precise new definitions of slavery and human trafficking that could be put to the General Assembly, along with an action plan to bring the eradication of slavery into the work of all the departments of the U.N., from the food program to the space program.

Establish a commission to determine how the existing U.N. inspection mandate could be applied to slavery. When that commission came back with a resolution to form an inspectorate for the slavery and human trafficking conventions, there would, at long last, be teeth in the U.N.'s work on slavery.

We can be glad that the United Nations and international bodies like the World Bank and WTO already have a pretty clear idea, more than most governments, about how to end slavery. The U.N., the World Bank, and the WTO are complex and inevitably bureaucratic organizations, but they are capable of amazing accomplishments (like eradicating polio and smallpox) when their resolve and expertise are brought to bear on a problem. Often hostage to the fortunes of the richest countries, they are always fighting both the right issues and to maintain their own funding and status. Sometimes these organizations don't quite measure up to their reputations or the ideals they represent. But what is important is not their reputation. What is crucial to ending slavery on our planet is what the U.N., World Bank, and WTO can actually do. Warts and all, they know how to feed people, cure their illnesses, shelter refugees, finance change, and modulate trade. They know how to make things happen across the same borders that slavery so easily transcends. Human traffickers and slaveholders scoff at national borders; their crime is as pervasive and ubiquitous as the air. The reach of our liberators cannot stop at the borders; it has to be long, strong, and global.

WHAT THE UNITED NATIONS, WORLD BANK, AND WORLD TRADE ORGANIZATION CAN DO TO FREE MORE SLAVES

This chapter is about the potential of international organizations to liberate slaves and to help them achieve lives of dignity. Although they often seem far away from our daily lives, these institutions are ultimately answerable to our governments and to us as citizens. The United Nations and its members have pledged themselves to end slavery; how can we make sure that this promise is kept? The World Bank aims to use its power to end poverty and protect human rights. Here are four things these international bodies can do to end slavery, things that our governments should press as top priorities:

1. The United Nations should appoint a special representative of the secretary-general for slavery and human trafficking. The special representative would be charged with preparing for a meeting of the Security Council on contemporary slavery.

    When the Security Council meets to address slavery, it should pass a resolution making clear that ending slavery is a priority of the United Nations. It should follow that commitment with three concrete actions:

    a. The permanent members, and any other members who choose to, should make a contribution to the budget of the special representative as a sign of their commitment.

    b. On the recommendation of the special representative, the Security Council should appoint a committee of experts to review the existing conventions on slavery and recommend how to unify and clarify these conventions as well as how to coordinate and improve the U.N.'s programmatic response to slavery.

    c. The Security Council should establish a commission to determine how the existing U.N. inspection mandate could be applied to slavery. When that commission comes back with a resolution to form an inspectorate for the slavery and human trafficking conventions, the U.N.'s policies on slavery will, at long last, have teeth.

2. The World Bank should guard against funding projects that increase vulnerability to slavery, and it should require antislavery measures be included in funded projects as a conditionality of loans and grants.

3. Member countries should insert into the workings of the WTO a recognition of slavery and its *jus cogens* status in international law, and they should create an independent department concerned with slavery and other labor issues. Any member country could start this process by asking the WTO secretariat to set up a study group to look into it.

4. Two member countries should cooperate to bring a trade dispute over slavery to WTO mediation *in order to* clarify trade rules regarding slavery, to resolve how the rules could be put to work against slavery, and to establish precedent.

7

Ending the (Product) Chain

One crisp September day in 2000 Brian Woods and I climbed the steps of a beautiful eighteenth-century house just off Red Lion Square in central London. As we waited at the big black door with its polished brass knocker, we thought about the angry men waiting for us inside, important and busy men whose lives and work we had disrupted in a very painful way. They were senior executives, and their businesses, their products, and in many ways their lives focused on that bittersweet miracle—chocolate. Their anger was focused on us, for that day we were the messengers delivering the news they would prefer to be silenced. We had discovered that their chocolate was polluted with slavery.

Earlier that year Brian, Kate Blewitt, and I had made a film, transforming my book *Disposable People* into a full-length documentary.[1] Actually Brian and Kate were the filmmakers. I was mainly along to supply facts about modern slavery. Their earlier film about Chinese orphanages and the widespread neglect of baby girls and resulting deaths had reduced Oprah Winfrey to tears, won many prizes, and spurred a huge increase in the adoption of Chinese baby girls by European and North American couples. How many filmmakers can point to literally thousands of saved lives from just one film? I was lucky to be working with them.

We filmed in India, Washington, D.C., Brazil, London, and the Ivory Coast, looking for stories that would tie slavery to the lives of people who live in Europe and North America. It wasn't hard. The crew went to the Ivory Coast because we had found a U.N. report that talked about children being forced to work on farms growing cotton. The hope was to track down this story and film it; the image of enslaved Africans in cotton fields had too much resonance to pass up. But when the crew reached the Ivory Coast, a local worker announced that nineteen teenagers had just been liberated from slavery on a cocoa farm.

The boys had all come to the Ivory Coast from the neighboring country of Mali looking for work. Once in Korhogo, in the Ivory Coast, unable to understand the local language, they were "befriended" by labor recruiters who promptly sold them into slavery. Believing they were going to good jobs, they were taken to an isolated farm, where they were enslaved. More than three hundred miles from home, far from any settlement and with no idea where they were, the teenagers were trapped. When one boy tried to run away, he was savagely beaten. At night they were locked in a small room, with only a tin can as a toilet.

On the farm the work was hard. In oppressive heat, with biting flies around their heads and snakes in the undergrowth, the boys worked from dawn till dusk tending and collecting the cocoa pods and doing other farm work. Often given only braised banana to eat for months at a time, they developed vitamin deficiencies. Weak from hunger, they staggered under great sacks of cocoa pods. If they slowed in their work, they were beaten. You can see the scarred back of one boy, a teenager named Drissa, in the photos in this book.

The farmer who held the teenagers captive controlled them with simple brutality and with a more subtle psychological terror. The farmer told them that he had put a spell on them and that if they tried to run away, they would be paralyzed and easily recaptured. If they dared to break the spell and escape, worse was in store when they were captured (as they almost always were). Runaway slaves were beaten as an example to the others. Stripped of their clothes, with their hands tied behind their backs, they were viciously whipped. The beatings continued twice a day for several days—the farmer repeatedly demanding an answer to the impossible question "How did you break my spell?" Some boys didn't survive. Those who did were sent back to work as soon as they could walk. When their wounds became infected, they had to rely on maggots feeding on their flesh to clean the wounds and save them from gangrene. The brutality, the isolation, the hunger, and exhaustion—all combined to break the spirit and will of the boys, locking them into years of slavery.

Finally, one boy managed to escape and reach a nearby town; from there he was able to contact the local representative of the government of Mali, a man named Abdul Makho. With the help of local police, Makho led a raid on the farm and freed the nineteen teenagers. What he discovered shocked him: "They were unrecognizable when we found them," Makho said, "like from another world."[2] Taking them back to his home, he gave them basic medical care, food, haircuts, and new clothes to replace the rags they were wearing. Anything else they owned had been left behind in the rush of the raid on the farm. It was at this point that the film crew caught up with them.

The footage of these newly freed slaves is harrowing. Although some are clearly relishing their freedom, others are gaunt and blank-eyed. They move slowly, in pain, like stick figures, and when they lift their shirts, scars and open wounds lace their backs and shoulders. The teenager Drissa seemed to be in shock, and the other boys explained that he was a new slave who had been on the farm only six months. This, they said, was the most dangerous time, the "breaking-in" period of regular whippings and cruelty designed to crush any will to escape. Others who had been enslaved longer were able to speak more clearly about their experiences. "Our master used us as slaves," one said. "He took us there and never paid us a penny. He said that if anyone escaped, they would be caught and killed." The boys were very frank about their situation and about how they had been resigned to the terror they suffered. Another explained that "no one dared challenge him [the master]; he was too powerful. We were terrified of him; no one dared escape. If you ran away, he would catch you, tie you up, beat you, and then lock you in a hut. They would tie your hands behind your back. Then one person would beat your front, and someone else your back." Stripped naked and bound, any boy who resisted was viciously beaten in front of the others as a warning. The teenagers reported that one boy had been beaten till he stopped moving, at which point the farmer took him off the farm and into the forest. They assumed he was dead.

A moving exchange came as Kate asked a young man named Amadou how he felt about his five and a half years in slavery. Amadou replied with remarkable sensitivity: "When I think of all that suffering, it hurts my heart deeply. I want to say so much, but I just can't find the words." Kate then explained to him that cocoa was used to make chocolate, a sweet food that people love, but Amadou said he never knew this and had never tasted it. When he was then asked if he had anything to say to the millions of people who eat chocolate every day, Amadou replied, "If I had to say something to them, it would not be nice words. They enjoy something I suffered to make; I worked hard for them, but saw no benefit. They are eating my flesh."

Amadou's powerful words set off shock waves when the film was broadcast on national television in the United Kingdom. The United Kingdom is a country of chocolate lovers, with each British citizen munching through an average of two hundred chocolate bars a year. Moreover, the country is proud of its history of chocolate making. From the early eighteenth century, chocolate houses rivaled coffee houses as the place to socialize and do business in English cities. In the nineteenth century, a number of Quaker families took up chocolate making in a big way and at the same time led campaigns against legal slavery. In the 1840s one Quaker firm figured out how to reduce chocolate to a paste that could be pressed and molded into shape, thus creating the chocolate bar. These chocolate companies also have a history of being advanced and humane in the treatment of their workers and sensitive to the environment. When the film showed young slaves, scarred from their ordeal, speaking of lives sacrificed to grow cocoa, the public reaction was one of shock and outrage. A rash of newspaper stories followed the broadcast, and a hurried disclaimer came from the chocolate companies.

As Brian and I entered the meeting room, we could feel the chocolate company executives' rage, anxiety, fear, and confusion. They had suddenly found themselves converted from good corporate citizens into villains. I knew they were going to have to blow off a lot of steam, but before they could start, I tried to explain that it was simply chance that had drawn our attention to cocoa, that we had gone to the Ivory Coast in search of slaves growing cotton. I wanted them to know that chocolate was only one of several commodities in which cases of slave labor could have turned up. This did nothing to calm them. As they responded they fought to hold their emotions in check, swinging from anger to a sense of persecution to righteous indignation. They had a right to all of these feelings; most of them had spent a life building businesses based on providing a high-quality, noncontroversial product, one that was loved by and linked to children through everything from chocolate Easter bunnies to Christmas treats. One man spluttered that he had been to the Ivory Coast many times and had never seen workers in chains; another implied that we must have come out of some loony antiglobalization sect. All were suspicious, yet they knew that something had to be done.

Their shock resulted from a very public and dramatic naming and shaming, but we should not feel any sort of moral superiority. Imagine turning on your television to see your company, school, office, or charity being damned for profiting from the work of slaves. Impossible? That's exactly what these executives assumed. I feel certain that these executives had no idea that slaves were growing some of the cocoa they turned into chocolate bars. But we have to ask, should they have known? The answer to that question is one that reaches out to every single one of us. Yes, they should have known, but then so should every one of us enjoying our chocolate and the many other foods and products that are laced with slavery. For the chocolate companies a day of reckoning had come, and in time their response was to do something truly historic. But first it is important to examine how slavery flows into our shops and homes.

BITTERSWEET

The truth is that all of us have a hand in slavery through the things we buy. The basic reality that we have to grapple with as consumers and businesses is that a *lot* of commodities and products have a *little* bit of slavery in them. The small proportion of any product tainted with slavery today contrasts strongly with the situation in the nineteenth century, when the majority of American-grown cotton, and nearly all of the rubber from the Congo, had slave input. Today slavery creeps into products like a poison, tainting and polluting them in a way that is difficult to see. The list of slave-touched products is long, so long that all of us are likely buying, eating, or wearing something that has slavery in it. We can point to documented cases of slavery in the production of cocoa, cotton, sugar, timber, beef, tomatoes, lettuce, apples and other fruit, shrimp and other fish products, coffee, iron, steel, gold, tin, diamonds and other gemstones, jewelry and bangles, shoes, sporting goods, clothing, fireworks, rope, rugs and carpets, rice, bricks, and on and on. For consumers, the idea of using slave-made goods, even feeding slave-produced food to our kids, is revolting. That knowledge certainly spurs all of us as consumers to action, but how do we get slavery out of our homes?

This question runs smack into the challenging fact that whatever the total volume of any good or commodity that enters the global market, normally only a small percentage of it is produced using slavery. For example, only a tiny fraction of the world's cotton or cocoa or steel has slave input. Our problem is that it is almost impossible to know which shirt or chocolate bar or car part actually carries slavery into our life and home. When slave-using cotton farmers in India, West Africa, or Uzbekistan sell their crops, they get the same price as their neighbors who do not have slaves. The price for their crops is set in markets that reach from the tiny farm in India or Africa to the commodity markets of New York, Chicago, and London and ultimately to the local shop or mall where our purchasing helps to determine global demand and thus global prices. The shirts on our backs are the end of a long chain that may begin in slavery.

Let's take a moment to follow the path of a shirt tainted with slave-grown cotton. The cotton grown and harvested with slave labor is picked up from the farm and unloaded for processing at the cotton gin and mixed with cotton from all the other local farms. It is at this point, when the product is just a giant bag or basket filled with loose cotton bolls with the cottonseeds still tangled in the fibers, that the farmers normally get paid for their crops. All farmers tend to get the same market price, whether they are using slaves or not. Loose cotton bolls are then pressed into frames until they are ready to run through the gin, where the seeds, leaves, and dirt are removed and the raw, cleaned cotton is made ready for the next step. Once ginned, the cotton is packed into bales. At this point each large bale is a mixture of "free" and "slave" cotton, with no way to tell which is which. From the gin the cotton moves to a factory, which may be in another country or even on another continent, for carding, spinning into thread, and weaving into cloth or making some other cotton product. The product chain stretches out and crosses over borders: spun thread will go to another mill to be made into cloth, then perhaps to another factory for dying or printing, then to another factory for cutting and sewing into a shirt (though these days some factories only cut and others only sew), then to a distribution center for packaging and shipping (a trip that usually crosses the line between poor and rich countries). Finally, the shirt reaches a wholesaler, who sends it to the retail shop, where you find it on the rack. In addition to all the mills, factories, and warehouses, a long line of people have been involved with your new shirt: truck drivers and salespeople, sailors on cargo ships, dockworkers, seamstresses, cotton buyers, mill and factory hands, gin workers, and the transport workers who drive the raw cotton to the gin. At the beginning of the chain are lots of farmers and a handful of slaves. Along this chain, some of the workers are being paid well, some are being exploited, and some aren't being paid at all.

Although our first reaction may be to boycott the shirt or any other product tainted with slavery, a boycott can hurt all the workers along the process, including the farmers who grew their cotton without slaves. Back at the cotton gin, the slaveholder pockets the money for his slave-made goods—a price set in a market that is based on the presence of free workers, the global demand for cotton, taxes and tariffs, and the subsidies the rich countries give their farmers. Slaveholders are feeding on our purchases, but if we just stop buying any goods that may be tainted with slavery, we may be doing exactly the wrong thing.

For all of us, the initial reaction is to push that crime away, to distance ourselves. The last thing we want to do is support slaveholders in their crimes. Yet for every criminal using slaves to grow cotton or cocoa or sugar, hundreds or thousands of farmers are producing the same crops without using slaves. Cotton producers can be large agribusinesses, individuals farming a few acres, and every size of farm in between. Small farmers in the developing world already have serious problems competing against the vast subsidies given to U.S. and European agribusinesses. Cotton farmers in the United States receive something like $4 billion a year to help them grow a crop that is valued on the global market at around $3 billion. The cotton farmers in India, Benin, Mali, Burkina Faso, and Togo (all countries with high levels of slavery) find it difficult to compete with such subsidies, even though they can raise cotton at a lower cost than American farmers can. European countries also pump money into the pockets of their own farmers, creating an unfair advantage on the world market. Obviously, in a truly free market the farmers who could sell their crops at a lower price would win out. But the current "free market" is clobbering the poor farmers in the developing world by giving their competition vast subsidies funded from our taxes. Subsidies don't cause slavery; they just help stack the deck against farmers in countries where slavery is already a problem.

Poor farmers also have to face competition from the handful of their neighbors who can grow cotton more cheaply because they are using slave labor. If consumers in the rich countries also turn against the farmers who don't use slaves, by mounting a boycott that destroys what little market they do have, the result can be destitution and potentially enslavement. So while our disgust says "boycott," the truth is that a boycott can hurt the innocent more than the guilty. We think of ourselves as consumers. We want to vote with our dollars (or pounds or euros) in the marketplace for the things we believe in. But this is a problem that can't normally be fixed by the consumer at the point of purchase.

The place to stop slavery is not at the cash register but where it happens—on the farm, in the quarry, or in the sweatshop. The $30 you don't spend boycotting the purchase of a shirt is worth little or nothing to the fight against slavery. The slaveholder has already received his profit, and if a boycott leads to a collapse in cotton prices, the slaveholder just moves his slaves to another job or dumps them or worse. Meanwhile, boycott-driven unemployment puts the poorest farmers, mill hands, and other workers at risk of enslavement. A boycott is a blunt instrument that sometimes is exactly the right tool but often runs the risk of creating more suffering than it cures. Sometimes what seems to be the immediate and obvious answer isn't the best one.

SETTLE DOWN WITH A CUP OF COCOA

Fortunately, there is another, more effective, way to stop slavery, but a cup of cocoa might be in order, because this is something of a long story. If companies and consumers work with antislavery groups and we all take responsibility for the product chain of the things we make, sell, and buy, then the slavery can be removed from the product at its source. Slavery enters a commodity or product on the farm or in the factory, and it is on that farm or in that factory that the slavery must be stopped. To take the slavery out of cotton or cocoa or any other product, we have to set slaves free and arrest the criminals who enslave them. We also have to crack the system feeding slavery into the product chain; otherwise, criminals will just suck more people into slavery.

Stopping the slavery where it starts makes sense, but doing so can be harder than it sounds. To understand the challenge of scrubbing slavery from just one product chain, let's follow some cocoa beans from tree (in West Africa) to tummy (yours and mine). Back in the Ivory Coast, more than 600,000 small farms together produce nearly half the world's cocoa. These farms are rarely more than ten acres in size, and despite people in francophone Ivory Coast calling them *plantations*, they have nothing to do with *Gone with the Wind* except for the fact that slaves might be present. As in most countries, the farms that are farthest from police stations, regular inspections, and roads and transport are more likely to use slaves. The farm where the nineteen teenagers from Mali were held was carved out of the forest and is a three-day walk from the nearest police station. Harvested cocoa needs to move from the farm to the coast for export. Under the laws of the Ivory Coast, which are designed to protect brokers, a foreign chocolate company cannot buy cocoa directly from a farmer. Brokers buy up cocoa crops in rural areas, and then take large shipments to cities, or directly to the coastal port, where they are mixed with other shipments. The broker comes right to the farm, even in remote areas. Of course, the broker is going to take a cut, and that lowers the price paid to the farmer for the cocoa.

Some farmers try to increase their income by forming small cooperatives in their villages. Members of these groups bring all their cocoa together and then sell it, getting a slightly better price because they have already brought the cocoa to a place where further transport is easier. The idea of farmer cooperatives is an old and established one in developed countries, but it is fairly new in the Ivory Coast, and although cooperatives can increase their income, many farmers just don't trust the idea. A good farmer cooperative does three things: First, it helps the farmers get the best price by combining all the crops in the area and giving the sellers more power in the exchange. Second, a good cooperative also buys supplies in bulk, so that all the farmers order their fertilizer, tools, and other goods through the cooperative, and the order will be so large that it gets a volume discount. Third, a strong cooperative will often serve as a savings and loan institution, advancing credit when necessary to tide farmers over until they sell their next harvest. The farmer cooperatives, however weak they are now, are important because they are one of the few places that immediate antislavery and child labor work can be done.

Unfortunately, very few of the farmer cooperatives in the Ivory Coast have attained this level of sophistication; most serve only as a selling club. Members tend to demand that the income from sales be distributed immediately out of fear that someone in the cooperative will abscond with the funds. The advantage of buying fertilizer or other goods in bulk is lost, as is the chance to hold back funds for the annual payment of school fees for the farmers' children or some other planned expenditure. Paying school fees is an expense often cited by the farmers as a difficult challenge, and when they can't afford the school fees, the children stuck at home are more likely to be caught up in dirty and dangerous work.

Clearly, the situation is not just about dashing in and busting slaveholders. Many farm families are stuck at the bottom of the economic ladder, and when they fall off the bottom rung, bad things begin to happen, both to foreign workers and to their own children. The farmers themselves tend to have little or no idea if their neighbors are paying their foreign workers or enslaving them. At the moment most would not want to know because this information would just bring problems from buyers and the government. The cooperatives know about the volume and the quality of the cocoa beans that arrive at the depot, but how the beans were produced isn't obvious; again, that is the kind of information that could be harmful for the cooperative, potentially making everyone's crops impossible to sell (except quietly and at a steep discount).

FOLLOW THE BEAN

The cocoa goes through other hands as well. The brokers sell to wholesalers, who sell to bigger wholesalers, who are licensed to sell to the foreign companies that buy most of the crop. The licensing of the wholesalers is critically important to the government of the Ivory Coast because cocoa is by far its biggest money earner, accounting for 90 percent of its foreign exchange earnings. Over the years the rulers of the country have pocketed billions by skimming the flow of cocoa profits. Félix Houphouët-Boigny, who held power from 1960 to 1993, put millions of dollars in Swiss bank accounts and spent an estimated $1 billion to build the world's largest Catholic cathedral (bigger even than St. Paul's in Rome and so big that it is visible from space) in the small rural town of his birth. It sits there today, a vast, empty palace of marble and crystal, gawked at by the occasional backpacker.

In the past the flow of cocoa meant that even with deep corruption the Ivory Coast avoided the extreme poverty of neighboring countries. For many years the Ivory Coast was seen as an oasis of stability in a region racked by conflict. Although the literacy rate and life expectancy remained low because public funds were flowing into pockets and not services, there still seemed to be enough to go around. All this changed after 1999 when a coup deposed Houphouët-Boigny's successor, and a subsequent election was rigged and rife with violence. The resulting struggle led to the emergence of Laurent Gbagbo as president, but repressed problems had been aired, and tensions quickly increased.

These problems centered on two issues that directly influence slavery in the Ivory Coast: control of land and citizenship. When the French ran the country as a colony, they practiced widespread use of forced labor that amounted to state-sponsored slavery and resulted in high profits. When Houphouët-Boigny took over as president after the country gained its independence in 1960, he had already made his name by organizing the non-French cocoa growers to import foreign migrant workers to cultivate their farms. By the twenty-first century, many of these migrant worker families had been in the country for several generations but were still being systematically denied citizenship, social protections, and the right to own land. The northern, more rural part of the country was also the home of tribal groups different from those that controlled the coast and the government. Northern groups were more likely to be Muslim, while southern tribes were more likely to be Christian. Membership in a northern tribe was a barrier to advancement in a corrupt system run by the Christian south. The southern tribes maintained their control over the country in part by strictly limiting citizenship and land ownership; "foreigners" (meaning the descendants of immigrants) and northerners were denied citizenship and land. Northerners found it hard to build any wealth when they could serve only as sharecroppers to wealthy landowners. A mutiny by some troops in 2002 led to dismemberment of the country. In the north opponents of President Gbagbo seized territory while in the south Gbagbo began brutal ethnic cleansing of "foreigners" in some areas. On the western borders, armed gangs from Sierra Leone and Liberia took advantage of the crisis to seize land. Low-level fighting broke out for control of the cocoa-growing regions, the economic prize everyone was after. The conflict was not as violent as it might have been because no one wanted to damage the cocoa crops or disrupt the flow of cocoa to market. Today a significant part of the crop is smuggled out of the country to the north, while rebel militias extort "taxes" on cocoa flowing down to the coast for export.

When the cocoa does reach the coast, some of it is processed on the spot and turned into cocoa powder and cocoa butter. The world's largest cocoa processing plant was built there in 2000 by the American food giant Cargill. The rest of the cocoa is cleaned, graded, dried, and then packed for shipment by a number of export firms. Over the past ten years, the buying power of these firms has been concentrated as some seventy companies have been reduced to fewer than a dozen, with huge food conglomerates like Cargill and Archer Daniels Midland taking the lion's share. Placed on ships, a cargo of cocoa might be destined for the chocolate factories of Switzerland, Belgium, the United Kingdom, the United States, or even Russia and the Far East. While still at sea the cocoa may be bought and sold many times as part of the trade in cocoa futures on the New York or London market. As much as $2 billion changes hands every month on the London market alone. Part of this buying and selling occurs when companies that use a lot of cocoa try to stabilize what they spend on cocoa by buying up shipments for future delivery, and the other part is due to speculators who play the ups and downs of the market (some of which they cause) to make a profit.

Ultimately, whether it becomes a part of the futures market or is simply bought and sold in the warehouse, the cocoa reaches its destination. Once the cocoa is off-loaded in Antwerp or New York, it moves to a factory for processing into one of the thousands of things we buy that include cocoa: chocolate candy, cakes, cookies, puddings, breakfast cereals, and drinks. The cosmetics industry also uses a lot of cocoa, especially cocoa butter, in makeup, lipsticks, and skin lotions. Although the United States consumes the greatest volume of cocoa, the British, Germans, and French actually eat 50 percent more chocolate per person than Americans do.

From the little farm in rural Ivory Coast, behind rebel lines, worked by migrant teenagers, it is a long way to the local grocery store where we buy our cocoa cereals, chocolate chip ice creams, and nutty chocolate bars. I wanted to take that trip to show how the product chain is tangled and complex. You might think the chain is too complicated to fix, that slavery embedded in that tangle will be impossible to dislodge. But sometimes we have to dig deep, study, and think hard to get to the solutions. That's fine, it is worth the effort, because when we get it right, slaves are freed. And there are experts we can call on for help. While it looks confusing and complicated to us, some people make their living by knowing all about the cocoa supply chain; these people follow that chain everywhere it goes, walking up and down it literally and figuratively almost daily. If you are in the chocolate business or your job is to supply cocoa to major food producers, you need to know that product chain like the back of your hand or you are out of business.

SO, MR. CHOCOLATE COMPANY, WHEN DID YOU STOP USING SLAVES?

After the shock of finding that they had slavery in the product chain of their cocoa, the chocolate companies scrambled for answers. Forward movement was slowed, however, by the fact that the biggest of these companies, Hershey, Mars, and Nestle, are fiercely competitive. Because they control so much of the market, they are also nervous about ever being accused of price-fixing or violating antitrust laws. Some of these companies actually had rules that none of their employees should ever be in a room alone with a person from another company. The tainted cocoa from the Ivory Coast went to all the companies, so they all shared the same problem, but none of them were accustomed to sharing anything beyond Christmas cards with their competitors.

Because they were trying to find the best way to communicate, and because determining the extent of the slavery problem was difficult, at first there was a good deal of commotion without getting much traction. Something was needed to focus their attention, and this came suddenly in 2001 when Congressman Eliot Engel of New York introduced an amendment to the agriculture appropriations bill to give the Food and Drug Administration funding to require a "no child slavery label" for chocolate products. This amendment passed the House of Representatives with a substantial margin in a 291 to 115 vote. This legislation was the cat among the pigeons, and the fluttering was furious.

If this amendment had become law, the chocolate companies would have been forced to put a label on every chocolate bar that read something like "No child or slave labor went into this chocolate bar." With this label in the wings, the companies faced a great problem: how to show that there was no slavery in their cocoa. Many bought their cocoa on the New York exchange, nowhere near West Africa. And since the Ivory Coast government controlled access to the cocoa farms, how could the chocolate companies suddenly mount an inspection of the 600,000 possible locations of slave labor? Cocoa from different countries was getting mixed up in the processing plants of Europe and United States, creating another barrier to tracing any that might have been touched by slavery. Plus, the chocolate companies pointed out that the government of Ivory Coast should be rooting out slavery in its own country, and asked how enforcing the laws of the Ivory Coast had suddenly become *their* responsibility.

History repeats itself. All these thoughts and many others ran through the minds of the chocolate executives, just as they had done for other businesspeople for the last couple of hundred years. In the 1850s, British businessmen rode a booming industry based on American slave cotton and repeated, like a mantra, the three reasons why they couldn't just stop: first, both their business and slavery were legal (not a valid argument today); second, they did not have the responsibility to make rules or act like the police in a foreign country; third, if they didn't use the cheaper slave cotton, their competitors would, and they would be driven out of business.

When Engel, followed by Tom Harkin in the U.S. Senate, spurred the companies with the threat of a legally required slave-free label, it was a powerful (and scary) motivator for the chocolate companies. Their alarm was increased by the fact that no one—including the companies, child labor experts, product-chain specialists, and antislavery groups—could figure out an effective way to actually prove that cocoa was "slave-free." Some cocoa on the world market was known to be clean since it came from "fair trade" farmer cooperatives in Ghana or Central America that policed their members, or from places where government checks were sound. But so little fair trade cocoa was on the world market that there would be very little chocolate for anyone to enjoy if that were the only source, and the companies (and farmers) could have been pushed toward bankruptcy. Much worse might have happened in the Ivory Coast. Since cocoa is the main support of the country's economy, cutting the Ivory Coast off from the U.S. market could have brought on tremendous hardship and social unrest. Luckily, and in part by accident, this sort of crisis was avoided.

In many ways it was a fortunate accident that our film investigated slavery in cocoa (unless you were a chocolate company executive) rather than another product. Three reasons explain this: First, for chocolate a small number of companies control most of the market, so there were fewer decision makers who had to be gathered and motivated. Second, this was a product with a high level of public recognition and appeal. This is a family food, a celebration food, a luxury feel-good food that people feel very strongly about. No one wanted a favorite comfort food spoiled with bad associations, so it was a lot easier to get people to care about slavery in cocoa production than it was to get them worked up about slavery in the brake linings in their cars (yes, it is there too). The third reason had to do with the nature of these companies, and we will look at Hershey and Mars as examples. Not many people know it, but the Hershey Company is primarily owned by a charity devoted to providing a home and school for orphaned and disabled children. In 1909, unable to have children of their own, Milton Hershey, the founder of the company, and his wife, Catherine, established a school for orphan boys. In 1918, three years after Catherine's premature death, Milton Hershey endowed the school with his entire fortune of Hershey Company stock. Today, the Milton Hershey School is still the largest shareholder in the Hershey Company. I'm guessing that when the trustees of this children's charity discovered that their primary source of income included the work of child slaves, their reaction was a conviction that immediate positive action was needed.

The Mars corporation came at the problem from a different angle. This company is one of the largest businesses in the world that is still owned by a single family. The current owners, Forrest, John, and Jacqueline Mars, are children of the man who invented M&Ms and grandchildren of the founder of the company, who invented the Mars Bar. (Each of the three is listed as having personal wealth exceeding $10 billion.) How the Mars family reacted to the news of slavery in cocoa production is not clear, but employees have stated that they were told that the company saw this as a moral issue, not one to be decided just in terms of dollars and cents. Beyond that, the motivations and concerns of the Mars family are opaque. In my opinion this is a rather secretive family and company, which spends millions to keep its affairs hidden and to lobby Congress on everything from the estate tax to trade regulations. It is my understanding that this is a company with a history of aggressively fighting trade unions, preferring a more familial approach to their employees. I feel that it is a shame that the Mars family wasn't more forthcoming about their views; if there was ever a time for them to speak out against slavery, this would have been it. Their previous reticence would have only added weight to their denunciation. Whatever their orientation, they moved resources to the problem, assigning personnel and significant amounts of money to move things along.

BREAKTHROUGH

With two of the largest and best-known chocolate companies in the world pushing for action, other companies lined up as well and moved quickly to defuse the catastrophe they saw looming with the slave-free label. Pushing this along, Engel and Harkin called the chocolate companies to Washington for a closed-door session of hard talk. The companies had already started lobbying, pointing to the impossibility of finding enough cocoa that could be guaranteed to be slave-free, but they knew they were facing potential disaster. Harkin and Engel understood that too and offered a compromise—if the companies would agree to work with labor and antislavery groups to get child labor and slavery out of their product chain, they would pull the amendment. The negotiations over this compromise were protracted and fierce, but the result was a breakthrough in the 250-year history of the antislavery movement.

Primarily the work of Harkin's and Engel's senior staffers, Bill Goold and Pete Leon, the agreement signed by the chocolate companies was titled the "Harkin-Engel Protocol." By this time the big companies had been joined by the trade associations representing all of the smaller chocolate companies as well, so nearly all the chocolate makers of the United States and Europe were included. The use of diplomatic language was deliberate, for this was a truly international agreement addressing a global problem. In the protocol, signed on September 19, 2001, the chocolate industry agreed to do several things, but three action points were crucial. First, it made the commitment that by May 1, 2002, a binding memorandum would be signed by all the stakeholders (this included the chocolate industry, antislavery groups, trade unions, child labor groups, consumer groups, and the governments) to agree on and set up a detailed plan for the way forward. Second, by July 1, 2002, it would create a joint international foundation paid for by the industry but run by a mixture of businesses, human rights groups, and unions. This foundation would do the research and run projects to take child labor and slavery out of cocoa production. Third, by July 1, 2005, it would put in place "credible, mutually acceptable, voluntary, industry-wide standards of public certification, consistent with federal law" that cocoa was not being grown with child and slave labor. The protocol was a historic document, the first "treaty" to be struck between an entire industry and the antislavery and anti–child labor movements in the more than two hundred years of their existence. Compared to most treaties, it was also remarkably clear and precise: there would be an agreed-upon plan of action, followed by the establishment of a jointly run organization to do the work, and then the creation of a credible and transparent system to make sure that the work got done—each step with its own deadline.

Not surprisingly for something that was being tried for the first time, not everything went according to plan. Early board meetings of the new foundation, now called the International Cocoa Initiative, were tense. The board operated by consensus and was evenly divided between industry and nonindustry representatives. There were two co-chairs and two co-vice-chairs so that no block or group could run things, an arrangement that was smart but also needed some getting used to. And the biggest hurdle was never an agenda item: trust. Chocolate company executives worried about anticorporate ideologues on the board spending the foundation's millions to sabotage their companies, and antislavery workers worried about executives putting profits before human rights. The executives, after years of fierce competition with one another, also had to get used to working together. Their task wasn't easy, but it was important. Their undertaking was a test to determine if businesses and human rights workers could get over their distrustful conflict and work together to forge common goals that would clean up the product chain and take people out of slavery. The game plan and the foundation were set up on time and began to work, but in two other areas the process crashed into reality.

A problem emerged with one of the first steps in the action plan: to survey the cocoa farms in Ghana and the Ivory Coast. The chocolate industry contracted with an organization that specialized in African agriculture to carry out the survey. This seemed a reasonable choice, but crop experts are not slavery experts, and different skills are needed to research human rights abuses. Input from antislavery workers failed to make it into the survey, and the result was a lost opportunity. The research report, released in 2002, was fine except for one thing: it didn't ask the right questions.[3] The report provided important information about how many children were using dangerous tools and chemicals on the farm, about the size of crops, and about the economic challenges of cocoa farming. It even included information about "nonrelatives" who worked on the farms, but whether these were neighbors or enslaved teenagers from Mali was not clear. The tragedy was that it did not resolve the question about the number of slaves in cocoa. One Malian agency chief in the Ivory Coast suggested that 90 percent of farms used slaves, while other estimates ranged all the way down to 1 percent. Today we still do not know the truth, not even a rough guess as to the actual extent of slave labor in cocoa. That is a shame, since to really address a problem you have to begin to understand it, and without that information, as of 2007, we are just feeling around in the dark.

The other catch in the plan was that everyone seriously underestimated what it would take to mount "credible, mutually acceptable, voluntary, industry-wide standards of public certification, consistent with federal law" by July 2005. The actual methods of this certification were not too complicated; inspectors just had to visit a large random sample of farms asking the right questions and looking for signs of labor abuses. But how do you ensure that this certification is "credible" and who, exactly, issues the "certificate" and what, exactly, does the certificate certify? Plus all this monitoring takes place within sovereign countries, so a crucial dimension that could make or break the inspection process was (and is) the viewpoint of the governments of Ivory Coast and Ghana.

Although we may think that taking slavery out of cocoa production is more important than any political consideration, imagine just for a moment the following scenario: After a film has been made about slavery in the tomato fields of southern Florida (an actual current problem), the government of Ivory Coast notifies the U.S. government that it is going to send inspectors to Florida to determine if American produce should be allowed to be exported. It tells the United States that it will be setting up an inspection system that will "certify" if American tomatoes are slave-free and can leave the country. The Ivorians also explain that since the U.S. government has a vested interest in exporting tomatoes, it can't oversee the inspection since that would threaten its credibility. If this scenario really happened, I doubt the Ivory Coast tomato inspectors would ever be allowed past border control, and the U.S. government might even slap sanctions on a country that attempted such an insult. Countries are touchy about sovereignty, especially countries that were once under the colonial thumb. Is it surprising that African governments would balk at being told how to police and manage their own economies? Clearly, they would have to be brought along and included in the process as well.

The work needed to bring the governments into agreement took a long time, especially in the Ivory Coast, where the attacks of rebel forces left the government with little time, attention, or resources to devote to the issue. At the end of the day, the governments of the Ivory Coast and Ghana insisted that they would be issuing the "certificate," though the inspection process would be done independently of the government and be double-checked by yet another independent body. It is hard to imagine the governments doing it any other way—can you imagine Americans letting the French inspect and approve all their cheese products or vice versa?

The certification deadline came and went without result; the system was still being worked out in July 2005, and the governments had yet to agree that the inspection could even take place. Both governments asked, reasonably, how did this protocol give anyone the authority to set deadlines for them? Eighteen months later a pilot program of inspection began, with the shape of the outside body that would certify the inspection still under debate. At the same time, who was paying for this inspection and certification was never specified in the protocol agreement, only that the chocolate industry, along with "other major stakeholders," would make it happen. Dividing up costs is always tricky. The local governments wondered why they should have to pay for something that was being forced on them from the outside, while others reminded them that unless the inspections were done, they might not be able to export their cocoa. Industry was willing to take on some of the cost but felt the governments had responsibility as well. In addition, a number of other businesses that use cocoa, like the cosmetics industry, had been getting a free ride on the protocol. Chocolate companies carried all the weight as cosmetics companies didn't take part or support the work to take child and slave labor out of the products they make. At the beginning of 2007, a handful of chocolate companies were paying out millions, while other businesses that make a profit from cocoa were freeloading. Under the protocol they can only be *asked* to join, but no regulation requires they pay their share. Meanwhile, as discussed in chapter 4, the International Cocoa Initiative continues to expand its work in West Africa, helping farm communities to recognize and renounce child and slave labor, and shelters are ready to take in anyone found in slavery on the farms.

Of course, not everyone is happy with the progress made by the protocol. Many groups that chose not to take part in the work condemned the protocol for not going far enough. The industry and the antislavery groups that are part of the process have been roundly attacked for not meeting the July 2005 deadline to set up certification. Many U.S.-based groups see any cooperation with business to be dubious at best and positively dangerous at worst. They say not enough is happening and point to the results of the 2002 study by the International Institute of Tropical Agriculture that estimated that 5,100 children were employed as full-time workers in cocoa farming, approximately 3,000 of whom had come from another country. But critics tended to ignore the fact that this research was done *before* any work was done to fix the situation. Some critics argue that the protocol is just a scam for the chocolate industry to privately regulate its own conduct and avoid government controls and that a broader-based approach is needed. I have to admit to being baffled by this viewpoint. More participants would be better, but this is the first time in history that governments, antislavery groups, anti–child labor groups, trade unions (both international and local), consumer groups, local farmers, and a whole industry have joined together to combat slavery and child labor, so who, exactly, is being left out? Of course, if all these different participants were just talking and not acting, it would be a scam. Talk is cheap, but even a cursory look shows words being backed up by money. The International Cocoa Initiative, setting up the programs on the ground to push slavery out of cocoa, received more than $5 million from the chocolate industry from 2002 to 2006, with another $4 million in the pipeline for 2007 and 2008. Another $1 million was handed over by the industry to the U.N.'s International Labour Organization to set up the West Africa Cocoa and Commercial Agriculture Project (WACAP), with thirty pilot projects reaching six thousand displaced children in the country (with some interruptions due to the civil war). At least another $1 million over three years has gone into work leading up to the pilot inspection and certification work in 2006. Altogether, this is more than $10 million that would have never been spent on antislavery work without the protocol bringing human rights groups and the chocolate industry together. Of course, there is more to be done and more money is needed. The cocoa-using industries, including cosmetics makers and general food producers in addition to chocolate companies, could use their market power to create incentives for more humane cocoa production. The incentives might include proactively creating a bigger market for cocoa that is grown by cooperatives or fair trade groups that ensure slavery doesn't come into it.

For all its failings and missed opportunities, the protocol represents an important new way for consumers and businesses to take part in eradicating slavery and cleaning up the products they buy or sell. In spite of many attempts to strangle this infant in the crib, it is beginning to grow up. It is, however, still in its childhood. I believe that the real verdict on this method of tackling slavery in the product chain won't be available until something like 2015. By then the inspection and certification system will have most of the kinks worked out, and we will have figured out the best ways to find the kids trapped in slave labor on farms, to get them out, and to help them to recover. By 2015 we will have checked all the other countries that grow cocoa and decided which of these need help and inspection as well. By that time consumers may even have a clear understanding of the role they play and be making thoughtful and active purchasing choices to end slavery. Already the Cocoa Protocol has shown that people and companies all along the supply chain can take responsibility (even if reluctantly at first) for addressing, monitoring, and working with governments to get child and slave labor out of the foods we love. Since the protocol was hammered out, both Ghana and the Ivory Coast have developed programs and asked for foreign help to address the child and slave labor problem. The protocol has also shown how two U.S. politicians could use the bully pulpit of their office to fight slavery around the world.

THERE'S MORE TO LIFE THAN CHOCOLATE

Almost all of us eat chocolate (and we tend to feel a little pity for those who can't), and everyone who eats chocolate wants that fudge brownie to be slave free. The protocol process is aimed at taking the taint of slavery out of a single commodity, cocoa; if this method turns out to be successful, we will have a tool that we can use on the other products that bring slavery into our homes.

From every step we take forward with the Cocoa Protocol, we learn lessons about what is needed to make this product chain work and be slave free. Every commodity has challenges, but some have advantages as well. Cocoa benefited from the fact that there were a relatively small number of companies that produced and sold the majority of chocolate. The fact that there are literally millions of farms growing cocoa worked against it, making it hard to build an inspection system that would oversee them all. It is important to test the idea of a protocol with other commodities touched by slavery and bring together consumers and businesses and antislavery workers. The short list for possible new protocols includes things that we touch, eat, or wear every day.

As the product chain of cocoa is dissected and explored and as some of its secrets are uncovered and ways of cleaning it up are worked out, other companies are getting a rude awakening of their own. An in-depth article in *Bloomberg Markets* in December 2006 told one such story, investigating possible slavery in the production of pig iron in Brazil. The reporters were astounded by what they found. "In my twenty-five years of reporting, I have never seen anything like this," one reporter told me. Another explained to me that he was "jaded after years in the trade. I thought I had seen it all, but this, it touched me deeply, I can't stop thinking about it." What they had seen were slaves in the charcoal camps of western Brazil, in the forests of Amazonia, and in the gold mines of eastern Peru, but what they brought to the story was a business focus that followed the products of slavery straight into the U.S. marketplace.

Using product-chain expertise most human rights workers lack, the reporters documented that:

> the products of Latin American slave labor end up in cars and trucks made in the United States by Ford Motor Corp., General Motors Corp., Nissan Motor Corp. and Toyota Motor Corp. Pig iron that goes into steel used by Whirlpool Corp., the world's largest appliance maker, and is used in foundries at Kohler Corp., which makes sinks and bathtubs, can be traced back to slaves in Brazil. Nucor Corp., the second-largest U.S. steel company, buys pig iron made with charcoal produced by slaves. In Peru, slaves mine gold that ends up at the world's biggest banks.[4]

To its credit Ford Motor Company suspended imports of Brazilian pig iron from the moment it was alerted to the problem, and the company mounted its own investigation. Ford's head of global purchasing said that if its supplier could not certify the pig iron was free of slave labor, Ford would move to alternative suppliers. A company the size of Ford might be able to go it alone and demand a clean supply chain, but the situation with pig iron is ripe for a combined effort by all the companies using pig iron and steel.

Pig iron is used to fabricate thousands of products and components and serves as the key ingredient in steel. Your car, your refrigerator, the bridge you drive over, all those tools and derricks used in the oil business and the refineries that make the gasoline you use, the steel in your desk and chair, light fixtures, bathtubs and sinks, bed frames, lawn mowers, dishwashers, ovens, air conditioners, patio furniture, the beams that hold up your office building, toys, tricycles and baby car seats—they all have iron or steel parts. Much of the iron and steel used in the United States comes from Brazil, and as the head of the antislavery police there explained, "Slavery is endemic to the charcoal camps that supply the pig iron industry. We see it time and time again."[5]

The steel industry could benefit from a unified effort to get slavery out of its supply chain for several reasons. Steel is pervasive in our lives, probably the one product of slavery that every single person in North America and Europe touches every day. But unlike cocoa, its production is not spread across hundreds of thousands of farms; there are just a few hundred charcoal camps. These charcoal camps are not something anyone can hide, even out in the boondocks. A camp is a great gash in the forest, with glowing welts that are the domed mud brick ovens, each pouring out smoke. They are remote, but they are not invisible.[6] Some of the camps are run without slavery, but that can be determined by on-site inspection. What's more, the Brazilian government, as we've already seen, is already trying to grapple with this slavery. So the steps along the chain where we can intervene are clear: inspect the camps, follow the charcoal to the smelters, follow the pig iron to the exporters and then to the companies in North America, Europe, and Asia, where it is turned into the products we use. If the companies using this iron and steel take some responsibility, and consumers do as well, then the cost of cleaning up the charcoal camps where the slavery enters the product chain can be spread across a number of actors. There are hurdles here, of course, and two are particularly high. First, even if the Brazilian government dramatically increases the funding for the antislavery squads, many camps exist, and new ones are appearing all the time. Still, Brazil would probably welcome financial help to police more of the camps. Second, much of this charcoal production is part of the informal or black market economy, and the people running the camps, as well as the people who control the land under the camps, have reason to keep their activities secret. In addition to practicing slavery, they are not paying taxes, are possibly cutting down trees on protected government land, are displacing indigenous people, and are bribing the local police.

Another commodity that could have its supply chain cleaned of slavery is timber. Logs are big, and they have to travel on trucks or barges that are easy to see. The forests of Brazil, Peru, and other South American countries are clearly visible on any of the satellite photo maps available now on the Internet, and so are the long lines that grow like ice crystals from roads that penetrate the forest. These lines are the tracks of the loggers, in search of the valuable trees, like mahogany, often destroying all the others in the process. Given the ability of the Northern Hemisphere to grow renewable timber crops, there is little reason to cut the Amazonian forests for uses as profligate and mundane as building timber and furniture or, worse, for burning them into charcoal. What might be considered legitimate uses, like the need of musical instrument makers for relatively small amounts of specific types of wood, can fit comfortably into a managed ecosystem.[7]

A good example of a musical instrument maker that does it right is C. F. Martin & Company, which is sometimes called the "arms dealer to the peace movement" since its guitars have been the weapon of choice for iconic musicians like Bob Dylan. For years Martin has been working with environmental groups to ensure that the mahogany it needs for its guitars is harvested safely and in a sustainable way. The difficult part for even a careful company like Martin is that in rural Peru where mahogany is harvested, the forests are deep, and some of the officials are corrupt. In 2005 the Peruvian government regulator found that the country's largest timber exporter had bought fifty-three shipments of mahogany with falsified paperwork in a six-month period. For that crime twenty-eight logging groups had their permits revoked, but we don't know if that stopped them cutting or just pushed them further onto the black market. There have also been suggestions of labor abuses in some of the camps harvesting mahogany. The Martin Company has been clear that it wants to do whatever it can to clean up its supply chain, and it understands that the cleanup must be done in the logging camp. The company is ready to act, but in some ways a more important question is the one to be answered by the seventy thousand people who buy Martin guitars every year and the hundreds of thousands who cherish these instruments. These guitars are played by some of the most famous musicians of our day (including Beck, Paul Simon, Merle Haggard, Tom Petty, Eric Clapton). A word from any one of these luminaries can make things happen, and these stars speaking in unison can mobilize formidable economic and consumer clout to work with them and antislavery groups to reach down into Peru and take the slave labor out of the music we all love. Is this community of musicians ready to speak out against slavery and mobilize consumers? Are Martin and other guitar companies brave enough to ask their customers to work with them to get slavery out of the instruments they love? If *brave* seems a strange word, I use it because too many businesses can't get past a paralyzing embarrassment when they discover something dirty in their product chain.

As strange as it may seem, the illiterate ex-slaves in northern India have something important to teach the executives of North America and Europe. As the antislavery movement has uncovered slavery in the product chains of more and more of the goods we buy, the reaction of executives, even the most well-meaning, has been pretty similar. Whether the product is cocoa, timber, steel, clothing, or toys, when the bad news of slavery comes, businesses tend to go into defensive mode, bring in the lawyers, zip their lips, and distance themselves as much as possible from the news. Admittedly, when a company's livelihood is threatened, this could be seen as a reasonable response. It is also a response that has a tincture of shame, of just wanting the problem to go away, and that doesn't really help anyone. Though they are not aware of it, in many ways these companies are playing out some of the psychological patterns that ex-slaves struggle with as they work through blame and guilt and shame in their effort to build a new life in freedom.

Many freed slaves feel deep shame about their enslavement. They know it was not their fault, rationally they understand that their suffering was caused by others, but they still feel dirty and embarrassed by what happened. Victims of sexual assault sometimes feel this way, somehow ashamed that they couldn't prevent or thwart the attack. The healthiest of the ex-slaves (and victims of sexual assault) are those who work this out and put the shame behind them, placing the responsibility on the perpetrator where it belongs.

Businesses often fail to understand that if they are honest about what they discover and are earnest and committed to cleaning up their supply chains, consumers will stay with them. Communicating this to the public can be a delicate matter. Some people may come away thinking, "Company A sells chairs made with slave steel, so I'll just buy from Company B," so the message has to be finely crafted. Every day, public knowledge of contemporary slavery is growing. Today voluntary labels on some products, like the RugMark label for carpets discussed later in this chapter, certify that no children or slaves had a hand in their making. Soon more products will bear these labels. The companies that get in front of this wave will build relationships with consumers by joining with their conscious decision that slavery is something they do not want in their lives. To describe one way to make this happen, I want to focus in depth on the little-used but extremely powerful antislavery laws of the U.S. legal system. Each country's legal system is unique, but the underlying concepts in the U.S. system could be brought to bear in other countries as well.

LAWS TO MAKE IT HAPPEN

Slavery in the product chains of the food we eat, the clothes we wear, and the cars we drive is an ugly blot on our lives. We think of it as well as an indictment of the businesses that sell these products. In fact, although it is a serious problem *for* business, it is really a problem *of* government. In the United States, we have laws and regulations that mandate the power of government to control any business that uses any slave-made products or commodities. These laws date back more than a hundred years and have tended to be forgotten in the rush to make new laws concerning crimes like human trafficking that focus on the victim, but these laws make it clear that any goods with slave input are contraband and forbidden in the United States. What's more, the Supreme Court has ruled that these laws do not stop at our borders or when noncitizens practice slavery in other countries.

THE THIRTEENTH AMENDMENT AND SLAVERY IN THE GLOBAL ECONOMY

The Thirteenth Amendment to the U.S. Constitution abolished slavery. Although the Thirteenth Amendment ended legal slavery, legal scholar Tobias Wolff shows how it has been applied to illegal forms of slavery since the Civil War.[8] Over time the Supreme Court has applied the amendment to changing industrial contexts, and Wolff argues that it can be applied equally to modern slavery in the global market.

After the end of legal slavery, bondage appeared in other guises, including the Chinese coolie system and a kind of debt-based slavery in the Deep South backed up by local police called "peonage." The Supreme Court ripped away these disguises. Rulings in the *Slaughter-House Cases* of 1872 ended peonage involving Mexican workers and the coolie system, and *Clyatt v. United States* in 1905 overturned the peonage system that continued to enslave African Americans in Southern states.[9] For Wolff these rulings lead to three key points about the antislavery law enshrined in the Constitution.

First, according to the Thirteenth Amendment, no United States citizen can own a slave, no matter where that slave is located, and no U.S. citizen can be either a master or a slave. Second, the law forbids any business activities that *support* slavery. No U.S. company can engage directly in any commerce that supports slavery, a rule that also applies to businesses operating outside the United States. In the *Slave Trade Cases* of 1864, the Supreme Court ruled on U.S. participation in the global slave trade outside national borders.[10] At that time, despite the fact that the slave trade was outlawed in the United States, some businesses in states like Rhode Island and New York were still building ships for the transatlantic slave trade. Though they built and outfitted the ships, these U.S. businesses were not involved in the actual transport of slaves, slave trading, or importing slaves into the country. The Supreme Court ruled, however, that they were profiting from and supporting slavery. According to the Court, the construction of slave ships was a component of the global slave trade unconstitutionally located in the United States.

Third, the Thirteenth Amendment also applies to industrial markets for slave labor. Wolff explains that the amendment recognizes that some industries are more likely to use slave labor than others. In Supreme Court rulings such as the *Slaughter-House Cases* (1872) and *Pollock v. Williams* (1944), the Court said that whatever new forms slavery might take, they are still unconstitutional under the Thirteenth Amendment.[11] Without boxing itself into a highly specific definition, the Court has consistently considered any form of labor abuse that includes a person who is controlled through violence or its threat, who cannot walk away or choose to change employers, to be tantamount to slavery.

Wolff shows that these three points also apply to the current global market in which U.S. corporations are increasingly employing workers, subcontracting workers or facilities, or buying up commodities or components that are touched by slavery in other countries. This conduct can happen in three ways: an American company can directly subject foreign workers to slavery; the company can hire someone else to subject the workers to slavery; or the company can profit from slavery that it had no part in creating, as with pig iron from Brazil or cocoa from the Ivory Coast. The Supreme Court has ruled that however it happens, if companies profit from slavery, they are in violation of the Thirteenth Amendment. And, as we know, the Thirteenth Amendment, along with every other statute condemning slavery, is regarded as *jus cogens* (compelling law) and for that reason overrides any commercial or economic interests.

PROHIBITING THE PROFITS AND PRODUCTS OF SLAVERY

The rulings of the Supreme Court concerning profiting from slavery are clear. The 1864 *Slave Trade Cases* held that it was illegal for an American company to profit from slavery, no matter where that slavery occurred. There is a strong historical logic to this; in many ways the slave trade was the first truly globalized market in human history. The slave trade of the past and human trafficking of today by their nature transcend borders.[12] Even in 1864 the Supreme Court recognized the fundamentally international nature of the crime and said that circumstantial evidence of slavery was sufficient to bring a charge. The Court said that since slavery was so repugnant, a trader or business owner, such as a shipbuilder or outfitter, should "keep his operations so clear and so distinct in their character, as to repel the imputation of prohibited purpose."[13] In other words, the business owners should avoid any possible activity that could tie them to the slave trade. Following the confiscation of the *Weather-gage*, a ship that had been fitted out in an American port to carry slaves, the Court explained, "Undoubtedly, it is the preparation of the vessel, and the purpose for which she is to be employed, that constitute the offense, and draw after it the penalty of forfeiture."[14] The Supreme Court ruled that even though there was no direct evidence that the ship was used to carry slaves, only circumstantial evidence that it was *likely* to have been used in the slave trade, the ship could still be confiscated. Two key points emerge from this ruling that apply today.

The first point rests on the remarkable fact that this judgment was handed down when the government had not enforced the ban on slave trading for decades, and that if the ruling were generally enforced, many otherwise legitimate businesses would be hit hard. Today a similar situation exists. There has been no enforcement of the prohibitions on profiting from slavery by American corporations for decades, and if the government suddenly began to enforce the existing laws, many companies would suffer.

The second point rests on the nature of the businesses linked to slavery. The Supreme Court referred to "the trader, who engages in a commerce, which, although not unlawful is necessarily suspicious from its theatre and circumstances."[15] Today a number of "traders" (companies) could be identified that are engaged in legitimate commerce but whose businesses are "necessarily suspicious." The most obvious companies are those that might directly exploit slave labor within the United States—agricultural labor contractors, operators of exotic dance clubs, escort services, and restaurants—all businesses where slavery has been found. Such violations can already be prosecuted under existing labor laws,[16] but the importance of this ruling is to extend responsibility to those companies that profit from slavery that occurs *outside* the national borders. On the one hand, this points to transportation as it did in the original *Slave Trade Cases*, the ships, aircraft, and vehicles used to carry victims of human trafficking. On the other hand, it also points to companies that are trading in the goods produced by slaves. What is the difference between a ship used to carry a trafficked person (thus providing a service to the slaveholder) and a shop that sells goods made by slaves (thus providing another supportive service to the slaveholder)? Without the ships, planes, and trucks, human trafficking would grind to a halt. Without the ability to sell and profit from slave-made goods, slavery in many places would cease to exist. Wolff explains, "The Court concluded that these supporting institutions, in feeding the slave trade and enabling it to function, formed an inextricable and culpable component of the larger practice."[17] At the same time, Wolff says that the argument is weaker when a U.S. company "is knowingly making use of the fruits of a slave system that it had no role in creating."

The regulation of foreign trade is the responsibility of the legislative and executive branches, but regulation of slave-made products sold *within* the United States is another matter. Remember that there is already a federal law that prohibits the importation of any goods made with child or slave labor. Individual states also have the right to determine which goods will be legally defined as *prohibited articles* or *controlled substances*. Both federal and state governments prohibit the possession or trade in such substances or goods, which can be anything from cocaine to eagle feathers to pirated software. States are allowed to decide whether and how alcohol will be sold. It is also common, in an interesting parallel to the *Slave Trade Cases* of 1864, that planes, boats, or cars used to transport a controlled substance like cocaine are regularly confiscated by state or federal law enforcement.

What this legal history boils down to is this: if the trade in slave-made goods is supporting slavery, and if U.S. companies are knowingly profiting from this trade, then the *Slave Trade Cases* should apply. What's more, the Supreme Court ruled that strong circumstantial evidence is good enough. As Wolff put it, "the leap from such circumstantial evidence to a finding that a particular merchant sought to aid and promote the slave trade was a substantial one."[18] In the *Slave Trade Cases*, the Court said that circumstantial evidence was enough to show that the shipbuilders were supporting slavery. To see how that ruling applies today, have a look at the modern business of importing and selling hand-knotted carpets.

There may be no better-documented slave-made product than the carpets woven by enslaved children in India, Nepal, and Pakistan. We have films, photos, and the testimony of dozens of survivors, as well as the eyewitness accounts of people who free children from the looms, like the raid described at the beginning of chapter 3. An estimated 100,000 enslaved children are thought to make a significant proportion of all hand-woven carpets that flow to U.S. markets.[19] Fortunately, a method exists for determining that a carpet was not made with slave labor. This method is the RugMark system, an inspection and labeling procedure that certifies that a rug came from a loom free of child and slave labor. Although proving that any particular rug without the RugMark label *has* been made by slave labor is normally impossible, strong *circumstantial* evidence exists given the large number of enslaved workers. At the same time, since RugMark and other antislavery organizations have been extremely active in publicizing the facts of child slavery in carpet weaving, few retailers, including large department stores, could be ignorant of the strong possibility that they are dealing in slave-made goods.

Given these facts, the chain of evidence is strong, if circumstantial: (1) handmade carpets from South Asia are easily identified as such; (2) a significant proportion of these carpets are made by slaves; (3) U.S. wholesalers often buy directly from large family businesses in South Asia known to exploit slaves; (4) U.S. retailers buy these rugs from the wholesalers with the knowledge that a significant proportion may be made by slaves; (5) these slave-made carpets (though obviously not advertised as such) are then sold in the United States in shops that are regulated by state and federal laws; (6) therefore, these businesses create and exploit a market for slave-made carpets and thus support slavery. (Although not immediately relevant to this chain of evidence, but important for businesses, an alternative supply exists in the form of slave-free carpets through the RugMark system.) This chain of evidence touches all of us, because while we don't normally think of the slave-made goods in our homes as contraband or illegal products, the law does. The Thirteenth Amendment would support the passage of state laws, for example, prohibiting slave-made goods from being sold and allowing the seizure of such goods. Under existing law, even a city government could pass ordinances that would treat slave-made goods in the same way as it does a controlled substance and could confiscate vehicles, shops, and any other means of transporting and distributing the prohibited items. The *Slave Trade Cases* combined with existing federal law are a sound foundation for a national and local legal response to slavery in the products we consume. If we really wanted to get tough on slavery, the law is there, waiting for us to pick it up and use it.

I know it sounds radical to talk about passing state and local laws that would allow the seizure of shops. But remember that the Supreme Court's original *Slave Trade* ruling requires a business owner to "keep his operations so clear and so distinct in their character, as to repel the imputation of prohibited purpose," and allows confiscation if they don't. If the ruling applied to businesses that supplied tools to the slave trade, it is difficult to imagine that it would not apply to companies knowingly selling slave-made goods to consumers. To keep people in slavery requires both the tools needed to control and exploit slaves and a means of marketing and profiting from their labor. Both the tools to control slaves and the shops that sell their produce are, in Wolff's words, "feeding the slave trade and enabling it to function."[20] The Supreme Court ruling was aimed at choking off companies that supported slavery, wherever and whenever that support occurred. With prohibitions based squarely on the Constitution and supported by the Supreme Court, how could federal, state, and even local governments *not* prohibit the sale of slave-made goods?

Still, state and local laws would serve the public best if they aimed first at education and regulation and went for prosecution only as a last resort. For example, a fixed period could be allowed to dispose of suspected slave-made goods that are currently on the market and in the inventory of businesses, along with time to discover either a slave-free version of the same product or an alternative. Such laws would also motivate businesses to investigate their product chains and consider how they might keep slave-made goods out of their shops or services, that is, how they could avoid even the "imputation of prohibited purpose." Additionally, a mechanism for the control of goods produced using exploitative labor exists. Known as the "hot goods" law, this mechanism could easily be extended to slave-made goods without any distortion of the underlying legal basis.

The "hot goods" law allows any U.S. labor inspector to seize goods, foodstuffs, or commodities, including goods that have "any part or ingredient thereof" tainted by illegal labor exploitation and even goods whose wrapping or packaging was made with slavery or child labor. The rule that a good can be seized if "any part or ingredient thereof" is made with slave labor means that a shipment of packaged apple pies can be seized if the apples were originally picked by slave labor. The law covers the goods all the way along their path of distribution but stops just before the final consumer. So the shipment of pies can be seized at any time from the orchard to factory to distribution center to local shop, but no one can confiscate the pie in your refrigerator. If the same rule were extended to apply to slave-made goods from overseas, then chocolate with slave-made cocoa or shirts with slave-made cotton could be seized.

Today federal officials can legally seize "hot goods" because workers are unpaid and exploited *inside* the United States. There is also precedent for the seizure of goods, ships, or vehicles used to support slavery *outside* the United States. I suspect that the "hot goods" law will soon apply to all slave-made goods in the United States no matter where they come from. Given the Supreme Court rulings and the existing labor law, only one court case, or one amendment to federal law, will be needed to extend the tool we use to protect slaves exploited in America to slaves everywhere. However, this case hasn't happened yet, and we are waiting for the lawmaker or lawyer ready to bring some uniformity to our legal commitment to end slavery.

Like the existing case law that supports seizure of goods or tools that support slavery anywhere in the world, the "hot goods" law should be used as a carrot first and as a stick later. The prohibition of importation, sale, or use of slave-made goods is embedded in our legal system, though it is rarely enforced. If we are going to end slavery, we have to bring out these laws, dust them off, and put them to use. Their application would be powerful, because it would bring the force of our common will as expressed in law to all businesses equally, motivating them to look carefully at their supply chains. Of course, a company would not be *required* to keep an eye on the commodities it uses, but then it would run the risk of having its products declared "hot goods." I understand that such provisions could be interpreted to violate World Trade Organization rules about nondiscrimination or the treatment of particular nations, but that is something we will have to deal with. Given that the prohibition of slavery has *jus cogens* status, overriding all commercial considerations, any test that confirmed that slavery law trumps trade law in the context of WTO rules would be welcome. In any event, the WTO does allow exclusion when production actually harms people. I cannot imagine any country, company, or individual arguing that slavery doesn't harm people.

THE END OF EATING, WEARING, AND DRIVING SLAVERY

Getting slave-made products out of our stores, homes, and lives means that businesses, consumers, and government have to work together. It is going to be a big job, but I think we all agree it is a job worth doing. We should also remember that we have some things on our side when it comes to cleaning slavery out of what we buy. The first is that in America our laws are clear: slave-made goods are illegal in the United States of America no matter how they got here, where they came from, or who is buying or selling them. We can start from a rock-solid place in getting these slave-made goods out of our lives.

We also need to remember that there are proven ways to build the cooperation that makes supply chain management possible without hurting poor people or businesses around the world. This is important, because if America suddenly and rigidly enforced its existing laws and the door slammed on imports of every country with slavery, the resulting economic havoc would likely increase slavery, at least in the short-run, and it would certainly harm many farmers, workers, and businesses in other countries who have nothing to do with slavery and hate it as much as we do. The logical way forward is to work and organize by economic sector, bringing together the companies that use pig iron or sugar or cotton or whatever product we know is marked with slavery. In the modern global market, most companies will be buying from many of the same sources and can trace their product chains to the same regions, mines, and even specific factories. The cost of investigating a product chain can be expensive for a single company but affordable if the expense is spread across a number of companies. When governments come into the partnership, incentives for cleaning up the product chain become possible. The U.S. government already has a law on the books that says anything it buys must be free of slave labor, but little investigation and enforcement back up this law. A significant increase in enforcement would occur if the U.S. government (and this could be enacted by all governments) bought first from suppliers that demonstrated that they police their supply chains. Likewise, governments could help companies make the transition to slave-free supplies by allowing tax credits, grants, or tax breaks against the cost of their product chain investigations. If such incentives were offered for only a few years, they would spur companies to make the transition to long-term systematic accountability for product chains sooner rather than later. In this way businesses are helped to clean up and governments have fewer arrests to make and fewer shipments to seize. Incentives could also apply to funds spent to free and rehabilitate slaves and to set up the mechanisms for monitoring and certifying commodities and products. Again, they should be available for only a limited time, since both businesses and consumers need to understand that the law against slave-made goods applies to everyone, and everyone needs to support it, even if that means paying a little more to enforce monitoring, to buy from a clean wholesaler, or to buy slave-free goods in the shops.

The federal government can play another role, one that is inexpensive but very effective. Remember that it was Senator Harkin and Congressman Engel who brought the chocolate companies together and spurred them to action. Using their good offices and the potential of an amendment that would have created a tough hurdle for the companies, these legislators were able to cut through the companies' normal defensiveness and get these competitive businesses working together. The result has been successful, but having the occasional senator or congressional representative muster the companies is not an organized or efficient way to accomplish this end. Given what we know about the fundamental basis of antislavery law in the United States, and the absolute and legally mandated necessity for businesses to avoid even the imputation of profiting from slavery, then a small unit, possibly within the corporate social responsibility section of the State Department, or the Justice Department, should be set up and empowered to bring businesses together. In the meeting room with the door closed and the chance to speak freely, officials could make clear the legal responsibilities of each company and then pose a choice: either the businesses could collectively decide to engage in a protocol-type agreement to monitor and clean up their product chains or they could let the government investigate their products and risk seizure and forfeiture. The carrot of cooperation is so clearly preferable to the stick of seizure that few businesses would choose to go it alone and risk sanction. The cost of the office, including its oversight role, would be more than offset by the savings on the enforcement side and the legal costs of seizure. Such an office could learn something from Brazil as well and list on its Web site those companies that choose to cooperate with one another and allow government to investigate their supply chains, as well as those that have not yet developed a plan to ensure that their supply chain is clean. This listing isn't exactly "naming and shaming"; it's really just giving consumers more information as they make their purchasing decisions.

Every day that passes brings more information to consumers about slavery in their shopping baskets. It took a while for shoppers to understand and ask for dolphin-friendly tuna and other green products. It will take a while for consumers to fully comprehend the slavery in the goods they buy, but when they get it, watch out. They will be asking, as many are asking today, why there are not Cocoa Protocol–type agreements in other industries, such as those using cotton, sugar, coffee, or pig iron. Consumers will be asking their elected representatives why the Customs Service and other law enforcement agencies don't have the resources to enforce the laws that ban slave-made goods. Baby boomers are going to want their retirement funds invested in industries that check their product chains for slavery. Consumer movements are slow to start, but once going they almost never quit. Smart businesses are already getting ahead of the slavery curve.

In the villages of northern India, slaves had to come to a conscious collective decision that they were going to reject slavery and face danger and risk in the push for freedom. In the great urban villages of North America and Europe, consumers have to do the same. The risk we take is so slight as to be nonexistent (literally a nickel here and a dime there), but it does require thought and commitment. The power of the consumer is great, and so is the power of our decision to bring slavery to an end. But to make that happen in our economy, we need three things: an understanding of the right changes needed in business for each slave-produced commodity (since each commodity has unique problems and challenges); an understanding of ways we can foster those changes as consumers through our purchasing decisions; and leadership. Scholars Susan Aaronson and Jamie Zimmerman recently studied whether policy makers think about the human rights implications of their trade policy decisions and whether they try to ensure that they promote human rights at home or abroad as they seek to expand trade. In talking to government officials, they found that "interestingly, in every country we visited, policymakers consistently stated that human rights and trade, and more specifically the national policies that govern them, exist in separate spheres. Yet . . . policymakers often have indeed responded to issues at the intersection of trade and human rights, though typically in an *ad hoc* manner."[21] In a word, the officials were not providing the consistent leadership that made it clear that human rights should play a part in their decision making on trade.

To end slavery we have to bridge that gap between human rights objectives (like ending slavery) and business objectives (like making a profit). How do we build a positive business case for ending slavery, as opposed to a risk-based case? In other words, how do we find a way for

WHAT CONSUMERS, BUSINESSES, AND THE GOVERNMENT CAN DO
TO FREE MORE SLAVES

*This chapter is about the potential of consumers and businesses to liberate slaves
and to help them achieve lives with dignity. Commerce touches our lives every
day, and we can have an enormous immediate impact if we choose to use our
consumer power and to unleash the creativity and resources of our businesses.
Government plays a role in commerce because of existing laws that regulate
trade, especially those that forbid the importation of slave-made goods. Here are
six things we can do as consumers, businesses, and citizens to end slavery:*

1. Consumers: Everywhere you shop, tell the store manager that you do not
    want to buy slave-made goods, and ask what the business is doing to fight
    slavery. Applaud and support companies that take responsibility for their
    product chains.

2. Investors: Ask of your mutual funds and savings and retirement funds, how
    is the investment of my money screened to exclude any profit from slavery?
    The investment industry should develop the screens and practices neces-
    sary to offer opportunities to invest without participating in slavery. For
    the latest information on the development of such screens, see www
    .slaveryscreen.org.

3. Employees: Encourage the business you work for to become an antislavery
    leader (see number 4). Ask that your employer donate money or in-kind
    services to antislavery organizations, both local and international, and ask
    that the business match employees' contributions to antislavery organiza-
    tions. Both types of contributions will get the business a tax deduction and
    build goodwill while also helping to end slavery.

4. Business leaders: Become one of the first antislavery business leaders.
    Explore your supply chain, and if you find slavery, approach antislavery
    experts to help you evaluate how best to eradicate it at its source. Enter into
    public-private partnerships in good faith and follow through on your commit-
    ments. Support good governance in the countries where you do business.

5. Businesses and governments: Form and support public-private partnerships
    to investigate product chains and find ways to rid them of slavery. Industries
    can form such groups through their trade associations, or the government
    can act as a facilitator. Antislavery organizations, child labor groups, trade
    unions, consumer groups, and international development organizations
    should join in the partnerships as they focus on specific commodities and
    products.

6. National governments: Authorize a task force of sufficient size and reach
    to effectively interdict importation of slave-made goods and goods with
    components that are tainted with slavery. Both national laws and inter-
    national conventions make it clear that importation of these goods is illegal.
    Such interdiction would include a mechanism for the seizure of "hot goods."

the end of slavery to be positive for businesses, rather than just portraying slavery in their supply chains as a risk and a threat? That sounds like a tall order, but we can do it if we take a collective decision as consumers *and* producers that we want to end slavery. As consumers we face similar questions every day, even if we respond to them in an impromptu manner. Every time we walk into a shop, we vote with our dollars (or pounds or euros) in the marketplace, and we are usually voting for or against slavery whether we know it or not. Americans have already decided to build a strict legal mandate that absolutely forbids slave-made products from entering our country. Somehow, perhaps because of that gap between human rights and trade in the minds of our officials, we have allowed those laws to lie in a disorganized heap like old tools in a shed. It is time to get them out, sharpen them up, and work as a team to use those tools as they were intended to be used. When we have done that, we'll stop eating and wearing and driving slavery.

8

Ending Poverty to End Slavery
to End Poverty to End Slavery

Twelve little boys from a village called Bochi in northeast India were lured into slavery. It wasn't that hard to do. The traffickers gave their parents an offer that was difficult to pass up, promising a way out of starvation and disease for each child. But the price of this miracle was the child himself, a soul-destroying choice that no parent should ever have to make. The parents looked at their little boys and imagined their future in this remote village. They saw hunger and desperation, sickness and despair. They saw their children ground down by landlords and corrupt officials, and their own lives of misery repeated in the lives of their sons. Anything, they thought, anything but this. And they gave their children away on the slender hope that somewhere, somehow, life would be better.[1]

Of course, the promised food and work did not exist, and the boys were locked in little dark rooms, where they knotted wool, making carpets till their fingers bled. Their story is an old one, of parents tricked and children trapped, little hands making money for slaveholders, and a village that every year gives up its children because it is too poor, too broken, and too cowed to know better. Many of the men of the village had already left, looking for work. With the boys gone, the women and small children were left to fend for themselves, always teetering on the edge of hunger, always raising another boy who might be enslaved by the traffickers. How can this cycle be stopped?

Such crushing poverty is the target of development agencies, whether they are government groups, U.N. agencies, or one of the many private development and antipoverty charities like Save the Children or Oxfam. A normal development model for this village might call for income-generating projects for the families or dam construction that would tame the annual flooding that makes their lives a misery or new agricultural techniques, but would any of these standard models address the abuse of power that underpins slavery and human trafficking? As it turns out, the twelve boys from Bochi, twelve slaves come to freedom, were the ones who showed the way out for everyone.

Rescued from slavery, the boys were taken to the Bal Vikas Ashram (described in chapter 3) and given the medical care, rest, food, and security they needed to begin their recovery. In this safe place, their minds became clear and their bodies strengthened, and they began the second stage of recovery, which prepares them to move forward and build new lives. They learn something that is practically unknown in their village: confidence and clarity about their own worth. This confidence is the fundamental tool that allows so many other accomplishments; it is the difference between acquiescence and action. From it grew the determination in the boys that no child would ever be stolen from Bochi again.

Ashaf was one of the first boys to return to the village. Coming home was intense for these children, some of whom had been taken as young as eight and been gone for as long as four or five years. After a six-month stay at the ashram, where their lives had order, cleanliness, inquiry, nutrition, and growth, they returned to a place of hunger, illness, unsafe water, and resignation. They returned to a village where the trafficking of children is so normal it is rarely talked about. Clearly, the rescued children had to go back to their parents, but ashram staff felt deeply troubled about sending them back into such dire conditions, where the children might return to a cycle of destitution, vulnerability, and reenslavement. It is a pattern repeated again and again around the world, and ashram staff were determined this would not happen in Bochi. The boys were now confident and strong, but their newly recovered strength might not stand being tested too severely. As it turned out, the ashram staff needn't have worried, because Ashaf and the other boys had the amazing resilience shown by so many ex-slaves. Together they began the work of slave-proofing their village, a job that was as much about economic development as it was about crime prevention and human rights.

Shortly after he reached the village, Ashaf set himself a job. He knew that children were especially vulnerable to being grabbed by traffickers as they walked to and from school, as a "nice man" offering sweets had tricked many children. Ashaf explained his self-appointed job: "I make sure all the children go to school. I take them from their homes at 8 A.M. each morning, and I accompany them home after school. If they don't go, I catch them and take them. I also teach them not to go out of the village with anyone."[2] Watching Ashaf and talking to him about what he was doing, villagers began to see the importance of watchfulness. They formed a Community Vigilance Committee to end child trafficking, and everyone demanded that Ashaf join the committee.

The committee became a nucleus around which development work grew. Staff from the Bal Vikas Ashram explained that as ex-slaves, Ashaf and the other boys had the right to certain benefits under Indian law. The benefits came in two ways: first, a lump sum of 20,000 rupees (about $450) was designed to help ex-slaves to get on their feet and have the basic necessities, and, second, a monthly payment of 200 rupees (about $4.50) was provided for children to help them stay in school. In Bochi these were significant amounts. At the ashram the freed boys had learned the power of cooperation and collective decision making. After careful thought, each of the twelve boys and his family used the first installment of the lump sum to buy a cow. Suddenly a village that had previously been without any real assets had a small herd producing milk for food and sale. A few months later, the boys' families set up a milk cooperative, selling their surplus in bulk to a wholesaler, plowing the profits back into improving life in the village, and buying more cows. Ginny Baumann, the partnership director for Free the Slaves, told me that it was getting hard to move around the village for all the cows strolling around the village like big sleepy pets. The cows are treated with extreme courtesy by all the villagers, which is not surprising when you see the new clothes, tools, roofs, and increased food supplies that result from the cows' milk production.

The success of the milk cooperative opened the eyes of the villagers to more possibilities, specifically two things that for years had oppressed the village like a curse and prevented any sort of decent life. One was the corruption of local officials. In the annual floods, the government provides food relief, but none of this food was reaching Bochi. Some villagers believed that district officials simply kept it for their own families and friends or sold it on the open market. The second curse was the lack of a dependable road out of the village. When the floods came, Bochi was cut off, a soggy island without access to medical care, supplies, work, or a place to sell its produce.

Although the Community Vigilance Committee was formed to prevent child trafficking, the members soon realized that isolation and corruption were making the work of human traffickers easy. Encouraged by the confidence of Ashaf and the other boys and coming to understand their rights as citizens, they began to ask things of the bureaucracy. They decided to visit the officials before the floods came to make sure there was a system in place for delivery of supplies. That way the officials would know that the people of Bochi were watching them, and they would think twice before making off with the emergency supplies. In the offices of other bureaucrats, they pushed for a new road, offering to contribute labor. Two important ideas about how to do successful development work come from their demands. First, the goals and projects they set themselves were the ones they knew would most benefit their lives and their village. No expert or agency told them what was best for them; this was a community-led antislavery program. Second, the key investment, the main input from outside the village that supported these transforming projects was not bags of rice or new agricultural techniques—it was ideas. The power of collective action and decision making learned from twelve ex-slave boys was a crucial idea that they could transfer to meet other needs. True, about $5,400 was injected into the village when the boys received their slave rehabilitation grants, and each boy's $4.50 a month helped put food on the table, but this is no financial sinkhole eating up outside funds year after year. That capital injection is still there as a productive asset in the form of livestock, which are paying dividends in milk and appreciating through the birth of calves.

After the American Civil War, freed slaves also knew what it would take to build a decent life in freedom. Their work experience told them that forty acres and a mule could feed a family and grow enough of a cash crop to make a life and get the children to school. American slaves never got their forty acres and a mule. In contrast, the $450 that went to each of the twelve boys from Bochi, combined with the education they got at the ashram, was the key to their transformation. Their transformation has pulled the whole village up and set it on a path to self-sufficiency and safety from both slavery and hunger. These twelve boys show that basic economic development can grow from antislavery measures and that a powerful antislavery strategy can bring economic development. Around the world thousands of people are working and millions of dollars are being spent on the critical pursuits of ending slavery on the one hand, and ending poverty and hunger on the other. Why haven't these two campaigns been pulled together to reinforce each other? Running on parallel tracks, antislavery work and antipoverty work have been relatively successful, but new evidence and new experience suggest that by joining together, their impact can be a powerful combination.

UTOPIAN AND NOT ASHAMED TO SAY IT

As I began to think through how we could bring an end to slavery, some people said that such an idea was just an impossible dream. When I said that in many cases we would have to attack the underlying poverty and corruption that supports slavery, I was accused of being naive and unrealistic. (I did notice that people saying this tended to come from countries like the United States that have been generally corrupt and poor in the past but have overcome many of those challenges.) One commentator insisted that it was acceptable to deal with the crime of slavery but crazy to try to do anything about the poverty and oppression. This makes as much sense to me as saying, "We'll cut out lungs that develop cancer, but we have no business getting people to stop smoking." No one has a problem with vaccinating children against smallpox or polio. Is slavery any less crippling? Is it any less life destroying? We have a way of vaccinating against slavery: helping families build lives that are economically secure, lives that have a sense of autonomy and rights.

With slavery festering in the mix of poverty and corruption, and freedom growing with education and economic autonomy, it makes sense to pull together the work that is attacking poverty with the movement that will end slavery. The largest numbers of slaves are in the developing world, which is where billions are already being spent to reduce poverty, improve health and education, and increase the quality of life. Slavery has been with us for some five thousand years and poverty at least that long. Aside from factors like international debt repayment and unfair trade subsidies that suck resources out of poor countries, economic development has been pouring money into the developing world for decades; if we have not made great human or economic progress in much of the developing world over the past fifty years, does adding slavery to the mix just mean that we are doubling our load of unsolvable problems? I don't think so. As it turns out, new research suggests that one of the reasons economic development is taking so long is precisely *because* we have not taken on slavery. Ending slavery may be one of the best things we can do to make a serious dent in poverty.

THE SHEET ANCHOR OF SLAVERY

Robert Smith is an economic and social statistician who wrote one of the bibles of social research and statistics. He has begun to explore why some poor countries have been making more progress than others in developing the quality of life and opportunities for their citizens. Appreciating that it was not fair to compare the richest countries with the poorest, stacking up Sweden against Senegal for example, he divided 138 countries into regional groups. To measure development he used a special scale designed by the U.N. called the Human Development Index (HDI). HDI is a measure of how nations are helping their people achieve a better quality of life; it measures what makes life good, not just whether a country is making money. The index combines life expectancy, literacy and education levels, and the purchasing power of citizens. Canada, the Scandinavian countries, and Australia all score near the top since their citizens *uniformly* have the highest levels of education, life expectancy, and standard of living. The United States and most of the European countries come next on the list, because even though their national incomes are high, they also tend to have pockets of real poverty marked by low education levels and shorter life spans. At the bottom of the list are the countries of sub-Saharan Africa and South Asia, where literacy is low, lives are short, grinding poverty is the rule, and slavery is common. Smith wondered why, particularly among countries in the same region, there could be large differences in development. Why, for example, do countries like Ghana and Gabon fare so much better than some of their neighbors like Mali and Niger, countries that are at the very bottom of the global HDI rankings?

As he built up a database of different economic and social measures for each country, Smith included measures of slavery and human trafficking. This is the first time that slavery has ever been included in a large-scale study of modern development. I was intrigued and guessed that slavery might turn out to have some small measurable impact on how countries develop. A rich literature from economists and historians already exists that analyzes the role of pre–Civil War slavery as either a drag or a boost to the U.S. economy. Now it might be possible to learn something about how slavery is related to the economies of modern countries. When the results came through, I was astounded.

Smith includes in his study a number of possible factors, in addition to slavery, that are already thought to increase or diminish human and economic development: corruption, the level of democracy, the amount of internal conflict, the amount of the national debt, as well as the regional groupings of countries, sometimes linked to culture. He notes, for example, that countries in Latin America, Africa, and Asia have fewer links to international nongovernmental organizations than countries in Europe and North America, and the difference has grown since 1960.[3] The analysis is complex and precise, using statistical controls to make sure that countries are being compared fairly.

The results are eye-opening: in a number of statistical trials, it is the amount of slavery that best explains differences in human development between countries. Other factors also play a role, but in predicting human development the amount of slavery was more important than the level of democracy, national debt, civil conflict, or corruption. The analysis shows that in the poorest parts of the world one of the greatest enemies to growth and to the chance to live a decent life is slavery, not just for slaves but for everyone. Obviously, slavery ruins the lives of slaves, but this research indicates that slavery is a major cause of depressed economies, low literacy levels, and shorter lifespans for *all* citizens in poor countries.

TURNING IT ON ITS HEAD

If slavery is so detrimental to human and economic development, why has it taken until now to figure this out? It may be because slavery is often hidden, so that development specialists simply didn't see it, or see enough of it. It may be because slaveholders are likely to avoid contact with officials and groups that are working with the poor. It may be because slavery is usually spread thinly across large areas, with the pockets of intense exploitation being the ones that are best concealed. And it may be that since this is a criminal activity, it simply wasn't included in the list of factors that development workers felt they could change. It may be that this was seen as a job for the police, not a development specialist. For whatever reason, most development projects, whether for groups as small as a few families or for entire countries, have been designed without taking slavery into account.

As it turns out, not only does combating poverty help to end slavery, but combating slavery helps to end poverty. Maybe this should have been clear to us from other evidence. The long history, both before and long after 1865, of low education levels, shorter life spans, doubtful democracy, and poor economic development in the states of the American Deep South certainly reflects the legacy of slavery. While the economic impact of the Civil War was devastating, other equally war-torn countries recovered much more quickly. I suspect that when the Deep South held on to the vestiges of slavery through peonage, share-cropping, and Jim Crow, it prolonged slavery's damaging effects and denied a better life to generations of people, both black and white. Smith's research is just one study, but if slavery really does have such a broad negative impact on human development, then we need to test this idea on the ground right away. Many have been in real despair over the lack of progress in economic and human development in the poorest countries of the world. Is antislavery work a secret ingredient that must be included in the mix for real change to come about? We won't know till we try, and the time to try is now. Inserting the elimination of slavery into the development process may seem a radical change to some and a distraction to others, but there is a model from the recent past we might follow. International development may profit from the discovery of slavery in the same way that it dramatically benefited from its "discovery" of women.

WOMEN HOLD UP HALF THE SKY (THE HEAVY HALF)

Development and the antislavery movement might fit together in ways similar to what happened when those in the field of human and economic development discovered a group of people who had been there all along—women. The story of this discovery begins when all of Africa and most of Asia came under European colonial control, and the "development" of their indigenous economies was highly exploitative at best and at worst, as in the Congo, simply amounted to slavery and genocide. In the 1950s, as these colonies broke free, new ideas emerged about how they might be successfully integrated into the world economy. Many well-meaning approaches were tried, with some benefiting the local people and others making conditions worse. In the 1960s the watchword was modernization, marked by the introduction of modern seeds, agricultural techniques, and machinery that were supposed to achieve in a few years the centuries-long process of industrialization and mechanization that had transformed Europe and North America. Reflecting common ideas of the time about the role of women, most modernization projects ignored or excluded women, and they often failed.

At the same time, the women's movement was gaining strength in the developed countries, prompting a rethinking of the role of women in local economies. A turning point came in 1970 when a Danish U.N.

worker, Ester Boserup, published the book *Woman's Role in Economic Development*.[4] Living and working in India, Senegal, and other parts of Asia and seeing male-centered development projects and the subsequent exclusion of women, she writes: "The confinement of all or most of the female labor force to unskilled routine jobs or low productivity work with primitive equipment is a wasteful use of labor, which helps to slow down the rate of economic development." In her careful and measured assessment of the modernization process pushed by the governments and agencies of the developed countries, she challenges the dominant idea that when men were the key recipients of aid and training, the benefits would somehow trickle down to women. Boserup's work, little known outside development circles, opened the door to new ideas of how development should be done. It prompted other women to explore the issue, and a new field began to emerge, the study of women in development. When the U.N. Decade for Women was launched in 1975, its theme was "Equality, Development, and Peace."

As time passed and this issue gained traction, international development agencies began to examine their projects and plans through a gender lens. The idea was not to exclude men or to address only the needs of women but simply to ask how development work affected the lives of women. With this lens in place, two things began to happen right away. First, projects that literally harmed women, by excluding them from the opportunities offered to men, were changed or stopped. Second, some new projects, designed using the gender lens and aimed at increasing women's access to economic development, began to show remarkable results. It turned out that women were often better than men at making the most of development aid. A small experiment giving tiny loans to women in Bangladesh grew to be a significant new approach in combating poverty. This microfinance helped women set up small businesses that did everything from growing herbs and sewing and selling clothes to setting up small workshops and factories. Remarkably, recent research by the U.N. suggests that 40 percent of all poverty reduction in Bangladesh can be attributed to microfinance aimed chiefly at women. What's more, these microcredit loan programs turned out to have a significant ripple effect. Even when they didn't take part, the neighbors of project participants also benefited. Microfinance also seemed to be linked to falling birth rates. In an intensely overcrowded and overstretched country like Bangladesh, the fall from an average of six or seven children per woman to three is a change with profound benefits for both mothers and their babies.

LOOKING THROUGH THE SLAVERY LENS

The significance here of the gender lens in economic development and how it brought enormous positive results is that it suggests that a slavery lens can work in the same way. Most international development charities have long thought that development is not just about economics but that it may, in fact, be more about equity and justice. Nelson Mandela tied development, slavery, and justice together when he said, "Like slavery and apartheid, poverty is not natural. It is man-made and it can be overcome and eradicated by the actions of human beings. And overcoming poverty is not an act of charity. It is an act of justice."[5] Most development agencies argue that while poor families may lack the tools to help themselves, or natural disasters might intervene to disrupt their lives, more often their poverty occurs because they are denied access to the things that make for a decent life, things like land to grow crops, available clean water, access to credit at a fair rate, or even the freedom to run their own lives and earn their own living.

The resources that these charities bring to bear are significant. World Vision is the largest, spending some $800 million a year on its projects. Save the Children spends $360 million; Oxfam, about $410 million; and CARE, about $450 million. Even some of the lesser-known groups have budgets far beyond that of any antislavery organization: Trócaire, the Irish relief charity, puts about $80 million into overseas projects. Heifer International is an Arkansas-based group that fosters development by providing livestock, a crucial addition to productive assets for many poor families. The organization distributes chickens, bees, fish, goats, pigs, llamas, cattle, ducks, geese, rabbits—whatever works best for the individuals needing help—and requires that once the animal reproduces, one of the female offspring should be given to a neighbor. Heifer spends some $58 million a year on its work, citing "justice" as one of its cornerstones. Some of these organizations have begun to take on slavery. World Vision has established projects to meet the needs of human trafficking victims. Oxfam and Trócaire have both addressed the causes of debt-bondage slavery in South Asia. In the field, some aid and development workers see the ravages of slavery, but ending slavery, as a key to human development, is not normally a part of the overall strategic aims of these organizations.

Of course, these organizations have to be rigorous and careful in their work, because there is never enough money to meet all the needs of the poor, and every penny must be well spent. Occasionally, especially in times of disaster or war, they need to take gambles, but to be good stewards of their resources, development charities tend to be somewhat risk averse. These organizations already face many challenges: war and conflict, environmental depletion and disasters, and the devastation and orphaning of whole communities by the AIDS epidemic. And while the majority of projects are successful, development experts will admit to the challenges that arise when projects don't succeed as they should. Development organizations have a lot on their plates; can forming alliances with the antislavery movement really be an effective strategy for them?

I think the answer is yes. The more I have watched and worked with grassroots antislavery organizations in India, Nepal, Haiti, and Ghana, the more I have come to believe that organizing communities to break out of slavery or to drive out human traffickers or slaveholders is a powerful inoculation against many of the toughest problems faced in community and economic development. I say that despite my normal skepticism about cure-all solutions. But in observing, visiting, questioning, and challenging the efforts of these small antislavery movements in several countries, I have been left reaching for one of the most underused and almost embarrassing words in my vocabulary—*panacea*.

Of course, if this is a panacea, it is a messy one, with no lack of daily setbacks and dilemmas. But if you peer through the fog of this antislavery war, you see that many of the blockages to real human development would be removed by this approach. When you set out to end slavery, changes occur that seem to have much wider and more profound significance.

First and foremost, development that is tied to ending slavery does not run the risk of further entrenching and hardening the existing disparities of power. When the aim is to help people who live under threats of violence to escape slavery, or to best protect children who are vulnerable to being snatched away, you rarely need to carry out surveys to make sure you are achieving your goals. When people in slavery are coming to freedom, you have a pretty sure indicator that you've reached the people most in need. Rescuing and bringing back enslaved children also turns out to be a highly successful way to engender trust with communities that have until then had no reason to trust outsiders. This was the case with the twelve little boys from Bochi village, a community that had previously gotten nothing from outsiders except graft, corruption, trickery, lies, and the enslavement of their children. For the ashram workers, these rescued slaves were like a homing device, leading them to the poorest villages. Once back, the rescued slaves made manifest for the villagers the genuine, practical care that the workers had devoted to these boys. The workers gained tremendous credibility, and they were welcomed into the community and were able to get to work on the destitution that under-pinned slavery. What's more, good antislavery work nearly always brings benefits to other people who are at risk. If the returning child slave needs access to a decent school and the teacher is not in attendance or midday meals are not being served, improving the school for that child benefits all the other children as well.

If you're determined that people should not fall back into slavery, you will soon be in a discussion with them about what it will take for them to survive and be independent. With a relentless antislavery focus, you run less risk of funder-led solutions and cookie-cutter development pro-grams. The answers you get from ex-slaves about what they need are complicated and sometimes neither quick nor cheap. In recent projects I've heard ex-slaves say they need things as various as income-generating skills for those best placed to save their families from slavery (often women), local improvements and access to natural resources (forests, water, sustainable farming methods, land), help to form groups that can access loans (microfinance), schools that work, and teachers who teach. Ex-slaves have also asked for things that can be achieved only by upset-ting the status quo—access to the underutilized land of absentee landowners, the firing of corrupt officials, or the collective and public denunciation of human traffickers. Ex-slave communities also tend to teach us something we probably should have known already, that all three of the powerful entities blocking development (landowners, cor-rupt officials, human traffickers) are usually known to one another, may be connected by generations of collusion, and may even be the same people. Focusing on slavery can bring contention and conflict into what have been relatively stable structures of exploitation. But when ex-slaves are organized around their collective demands, they learn things about their countries, their laws, their rights, and themselves—things they will never forget and that can never be taken away from them.

Such a deep engagement with poor communities helps achieve a key goal held by development organizations: making sure that local people "own the process." When ex-slaves feel ownership of change and devel-opment, new groups emerge, groups ranging from milk cooperatives to social movements. Such groups may be tiny and informal, but they are likely to reach out to others. They instinctively look for allies, people and groups that will protect them when slaveholders fight back or corrupt officials deny justice. When one of the first outcomes of a development project is freedom, you can bet the participants have a strong vested interest in holding on to it. Human development is also essential to maintain freedom. In practically every case of someone falling back into slavery that I have seen, the key cause is the lack of the economic and food security that is the aim of most development work.

Development workers tend to talk only among themselves about those projects that seem to remain unchanged down through the decades. Among these might be the organization that goes on digging wells and more wells, or the group that started with immunization and can still be found years later immunizing the same villages. Providing wells and immunizations are good, but near those projects you sometimes see children who are still hungry and dazed, women who are still beaten, or families who are still in the chains of illegal debt. At best, these projects alleviate but do not eliminate suffering. At worst, as the Sankalp organization realized about its own work (causing it to change its focus), such projects can actually subsidize the corrupt officials and slaveholders who get free health care for the people they exploit. Arrive on the scene with a slavery lens and the possible ways forward multiply, and the development process takes off. Growth and change that result may be difficult to manage at first, but they are the hallmarks of freedom, the true and underlying goals of all development.

Most of the big development agencies (and many of the small ones) have someone who is clued in to slavery—someone who is both familiar with modern slavery and already knows the workings of the organization. One way forward would be to ask that person to audit the organization's ongoing projects with a slavery lens. This is important because slavery can be hard to see if you are not used to looking for it. Certainly not every community is beset with slavery, but many are, if only in a minority of the population. The lens needs to be pointed at every project around the world, no matter how rich the country. In Long Island, south Florida, and San Francisco, immigrant assistance projects have run head-on into slavery. The same has happened in cities in Western Europe and East Asia. For these projects, first we need to uncover the slavery and then we need to pry loose the slaves and launch them into free, productive, and decent lives.

Groups like World Vision, Oxfam, Save the Children, Heifer International, and others are brilliant, carefully and relentlessly focusing on the poorest, most disadvantaged groups.[6] They've been determined to give a voice and strength to those most disempowered. By helping the poorest and most vulnerable, they have often ended up addressing slavery. This work takes on different shapes in different places—fighting sex trafficking in some places, debt-bondage slavery in others—but I believe it is time for both those agencies and the antislavery movement to take a conscious look across all their work to determine how they can work together to address slavery as a global phenomenon.

MAKING THIS HAPPEN

When it comes to poverty, slaves are the poorest of the poor. They own nothing, not their labor, not even their own children. Their past, present, and future belong to someone else. They have no choice in this poverty; it is bounded by violence and pain. Slaves may risk everything for a chance at destitution in freedom, but that is not good enough. We do not have to end global poverty to end slavery, but we do have to end the poverty of slaves to secure their freedom. And it turns out that ending slavery can have a significant impact on poverty, not just for the slaves but also for the rest of their community, both slave and free. A great deal of thought, theory, and practice focuses on ending poverty, rather less on ending slavery. What is becoming clear is that these two goals should be harnessed together; their combined strength is greater than the sum of the parts.

How these two goals can be brought together is something that we need to talk about, negotiate, and test, but a few points are clear: we need to expand projects that take this approach to really put it to the test. I have seen this method achieve amazing things in India, Nepal, and Ghana, but we have to try it in other situations and places. We also need more research like Robert Smith's, work that includes slavery in the global analysis of contemporary poverty and development. Smith's work seems to be a breakthrough, and now it is time to replicate and extend the research in new ways, such as examining not just whole countries but slavery and development within counties or provinces within a country.

We know that when aid and development workers started to examine problems through a gender lens, good things began to happen. The experience of the antislavery movement is that a slavery lens can help in fighting poverty. Both poverty and slavery are all about power and justice. I would argue that slavery is the darkest hole of poverty and injustice, and for that reason perhaps it is one of the best places to start. Agencies like Oxfam, World Vision, Save the Children, and the Heifer Project are doing an amazing job, using their money wisely, thinking hard about every move, focusing on solving the problems they face, and treating the causes, not just the symptoms. These agencies and others know more about ending poverty on the ground than anyone else, and they are the ones that will take the slavery lens and turn it into a powerful tool for liberation and human dignity.

MONEY SHOUTS

I remember earning my first few dollars, not the allowance my parents gave me but money I earned with my own labor. I remember the sense of accomplishment it gave me, and the sense that I was free to spend that money, or not, just as I pleased. I wasn't even ten years old, but I liked that feeling. Salma mint Saloum also remembers the first time she got paid because she burst into tears. A slave in Mauritania, she escaped and made her way to the United States. In 2001, not long after she arrived, she told me about her life:

I worked when I got here, braiding hair. That was the first time I had been paid for work I had done. To be paid for my work, that was really liberty. To work for someone and be paid, I can't even explain it. I had never believed in that. Even here, in New York, I believed that I would be treated like I was in Mauritania. The first time I was paid here, I cried that day. That really helped me. I didn't know that. I had never seen a person paid for her work before in my life. It was a very, very good surprise. Now I am used to that. It has really made me happy.

How we can help more slaves like Salma hold that first paycheck? When you can earn, you can feed your children and make sure they are safe and warm. If you have never had one, a paycheck can seem like a miracle of enormous power. We call paid work "earning a *living*" for a reason. I have seen slavery, and I know that it is no life. There are some truths about the world that are so basic that they can be the foundation for deep despair or fervent hope. One of these truths is that there really is enough to go around, enough food and enough money. We know that this world can easily afford an education for every child. Finding ways to move resources to make sure everyone gets enough to eat and every child goes to school is a tall order, but whatever the cost of food and school, it is nowhere near what is spent on weapons each year. The amount needed to end slavery is much less than that, but it could translate into such powerful changes—the chance for women in Nepal to make their own choices and end the violence they suffer, a childhood for the little boys and girls in Ghana enslaved and working sixteen hours a day in the waters of Lake Volta, literacy for a slave child in Haiti, and the new life that can bring, away from physical and sexual abuse. When we make sure development is for everyone, slaves included, then the opportunity for freedom opens and can lead to a secure and healthy life for all.

WHAT DEVELOPMENT ORGANIZATIONS, CHARITIES, AND WE AS SUPPORTERS OF OVERSEAS DEVELOPMENT CAN DO TO FREE MORE SLAVES

This chapter is about the potential of bringing a slavery lens to the work of international development. Because of the link between antipoverty work and antislavery work, these two efforts can be mutually reinforcing. Whether individually or through our faith communities, businesses, or labor unions, many of us support organizations that fight poverty and hunger. Here are four things we can do to end slavery by working through the development organizations we support:

1. Individuals can support both antislavery groups that are liberating slaves and the development agencies that are attacking the causes of slavery. Donations do not have to be large, but it is crucial that this support is committed and long lasting. Reducing the factors that support slavery and helping slaves to freedom and then autonomy and citizenship take time. One of the greatest needs for the antislavery movement today is reliable, committed funding.

2. Development organizations, as well as government agencies doing development work, should assign staff to examine projects and organizational strategy through a slavery lens. The staff might find small adjustments to existing excellent projects that will have a dramatic impact in reducing slavery.

3. More research and analysis must be done to explore the relationship of development and slavery eradication. A university could establish a center for such inquiry that would also serve as a repository for the information that exists.

4. Antislavery groups and development groups should meet together to explore how they can make their work more mutually reinforcing. In South Asia especially such coordination could result in many more slaves being liberated and achieving lives of dignity.

Conclusion
The Beginning of the End of Slavery

The day they told me that I was going to be free, a bird came and told me at the window. I was very sad that day, and the bird came. With his little beak, he knocked on the window, and I knew I was going to have some good news . . . I have a lot of people around me who have been supporting me in different ways. They don't know me, they just hear about me, but they believe in me. Their support means a lot to me. I will keep that forever. I'm sitting here today because of all those people. I owe my freedom to them all.

MARIA, ENSLAVED AT AGE FIFTEEN IN THE UNITED STATES, SPEAKING IN 2005

People ask me how I can bear the work I do. They read about the hell of slavery and ask how I can look into it every day and keep going. It's a fair question, and I will admit there have been times when the horrors I have seen have consumed my heart and mind and left me despairing, sickened, and useless. Getting to know the tortured lives of teenage girls raped again and again in the brothels of Thailand filled my sleep with nightmares and my days with visions of their helpless pain. Yet every day my job gets easier, not because my heart is getting harder but because my pain and anxiety are balanced by the joy I see and feel as more and more slaves come to freedom. I watch as every day brings us closer to freedom for all slaves.

In the liberation of one slave, we can see the liberation of all slaves. In every newly freed voice, I hear the harmonies of a world without slaves. The little boys on the cover of this book were once locked in dirty sheds, beaten, starved, and exploited. Today they laugh and play, as children should. They eat with gusto and stretch their minds in the classroom. Some of these boys are still dazzled by the world they find themselves in, still watchful. They carry the scars of their enslavement, but they are looking ahead. And in their eyes and their smiles I see the future for all slaves—as long as we can reach them in time.

The road to the end of slavery has been long. For most of human history, only a very few people dared to think that slavery should end. When one voice would cry freedom, thousands of greedy mouths would shout it down, and millions would continue to be silenced in chains. The toll has been terrible; the thirteen million lives harvested and destroyed in the transatlantic slave trade are just a fraction of all the slaves who have been sacrificed to greed and indifference. For centuries, only the slaves themselves truly resisted, quietly or forcefully, and were tortured and killed for their efforts. Yet, somehow, over the past two hundred years, a great change has come about. First the great minds, then all of the rest of us, came to see slaves for exactly who they are—people just like us. Listen to the words of a twenty-three-year-old Mozart, in his powerful antislavery opera of 1779, *Zaide*, an opera that no one dared produce in his lifetime:

> You powerful ones are unconcerned about your slaves; because of your position you lose touch with your brothers.

Listen to the young college graduate Thomas Clarkson, reflecting in 1786 on his senior thesis on the morality of slavery:

> A thought came into my head, if the contents of the Essay were true, it was time some person should see these calamities to their end.

Clarkson spent the rest of his life working to end slavery. Listen to an escaped slave, Frederick Douglass, in 1847:

> I know that victory is certain. I go . . . back, for the sake of my brethren. I go to suffer with them; to toil with them; to endure insult with them; to undergo outrage with them; to lift up my voice in their behalf; to speak and write in their vindication; and struggle in their ranks for the emancipation which shall yet be achieved.

And hear the words of Salma mint Saloum, who escaped from slavery in the late 1990s:

> *The first time I tried to escape . . . they bound my wrists and ankles and tied me to a date tree in the middle of the family compound and left me there for a week. He cut my wrists with a razor, so that I bled terribly. I still have scars on my arms.*

The ugliness of slavery has not really changed in thousands of years, but the light of freedom grows stronger. Listen to Salma today:

> *To work, and to learn things, to go to school, . . . to talk with people I choose to talk to: these things are liberty to me. To have the liberty to discuss with*

people, to be free to go where I want, to eat what I want, to sleep where I want. Before, I didn't have that. Really, seriously, before, I didn't have that.

After centuries of frozen indifference, the past two hundred years have brought an avalanche of change, from the slave revolution in Haiti to the American Emancipation Proclamation of 1863, from the U.N. conventions to the freed children in the Bal Vikas Ashram. Thousands of lives have been sacrificed to end slavery, and all to bring us to this day, the day that slavery truly begins to end because, together, we have decided to end it.

The job before us will not be easy, but it is far from impossible. We face two great obstacles before we can end slavery, but we have two tools within reach that we can use to overcome those obstacles. The obstacles are culture and criminality; the tools are awareness and resources. In a world where most people loath slavery, awakening their awareness will unleash great power. When we come to know that we are living in a world with slaves, that their stolen labor feeds into our shops and homes, the urge to act becomes irrepressible. When that urge, that desire that all should be free, sweeps across our world, the end of slavery will be near. From that desire will flow the resources needed to get the job done and the liberators needed to help more and more slaves to walk free. Though they may have no sense of it, many slaves are standing on the edge of freedom. Around the world are millions of slaves whose liberation will be challenging and difficult but eminently possible. With a will and a way, freedom is theirs.

But when these have been freed, millions whose liberation will be grueling, complex, and dangerous will remain. These are the slaves whose chains are tightened by culture and locked by criminals. The greatest obstacles we face in ending slavery are not poverty and violence; they are the toxicity of some cultures and the perversion of organized crime. Many countries exhibit either a wholesale indifference to slavery or a pervasive acceptance. The greatest obstacle to freedom in Thailand, Italy, and Japan is the ready assumption by men of their own superiority. When this assumption combines with the false belief of racial or ethnic supremacy, as in Sudan, Burma, or Serbia, the chains that must be broken first are those that bind the minds of the population. Cultural change takes time, often generations, but if we dream of a world without slavery, we must work for a world without the poison of racism and prejudice as well.

At the end of our task will be the criminals who will not want to give up their bloody profits. When the grip of small-scale slaveholders in rural India is broken, they usually find it difficult to find new slaves. But for the sophisticated, transnational criminal, new avenues of exploitation are always opening. Organized crime, hidden, vicious, and cunning, will be the last holdout of slavery. Smashing its hold on lives and economies will require great integrity and effort.

And beyond these great challenges lies one more, harder perhaps but also gracious and splendid. If the lives of ex-slaves and their children, and the lives of all of us who have profited in large and small ways from their slavery, will ever be truly free of the stain of slavery, then our last task is reconciliation. Forgiveness will be hard—for many it may be impossible—but is there full freedom without forgiveness? If the slaves of today carry their pain and recrimination into liberation, bitterness will flow down through the generations. We will have to let freed slaves lead us; let them say how they can best ease their anger and pain. The children of slaves and the children of slaveholders will have to find a way to share the world without anger. Even as we seek to destroy the evil of slavery forever, we must help build the reconciliation that silences slavery's echo of hatred.

None of these tasks are beyond us. Human beings have shown they can overcome cruelty, hatred, and greed. At the birth of the American republic, few people anticipated, or even desired, the abolition of legal slavery in the United States. But less than a hundred years later, after decades of abolitionist protest, slavery *was* made illegal. We can do great things: cure diseases that once cut like a scythe through whole cities, put people on the moon, and unravel our own genome. We can also end slavery. Slavery is big and old, but it is ready to topple. The question is not, can slavery end? The question is, when? The answer is, as soon as we choose to end it. How long will it take? Martin Luther King answered this question when he said, "How long? Not long, because the arc of the moral universe is long, but it bends toward justice."

For all of our human failings and challenges, we have before us a gift of incomprehensible worth. Here is the end of suffering for millions. Here is the end of the common ugly sin we have carried for centuries. Here is the end of guilt and the damage we suffer when we pretend we have no guilt. Yet the best part of this gift is the part we cannot know. It is the new knowledge of our own power and the ability to dream as never before. It is the new world that will be created when slavery is no more.

We can be the generation that says: enough! We've had five thousand years of slavery, and now we're bringing it to an end. Ending slavery will be humanity's watershed, separating the time of the truth that we are one people from the millennia of the great lie that some people are subhuman. Ending slavery will free each of us.

What YOU Can Do to End Slavery

Two key obstacles stand in our way on the road to ending slavery: lack of awareness and lack of resources. If every citizen decided to do one or two small things, those two obstacles would fall, and fall quickly.

MARSHALLING THE RESOURCES

In 2006 a student at the University of Tennessee asked her professor, what was the best thing she could do to help end slavery? After talking it over, the student and professor realized that there were a number of possibilities, but they didn't know which was the best and most effective action she could take. Recognizing a teachable moment, the professor gave her student the assignment to carefully compare the alternatives and determine the most effective thing a person could do to end slavery. The student spent weeks in research and analysis, exploring alternatives such as volunteering with human rights groups, organizing film shows or letter-writing campaigns, and raising funds through everything from dance-a-thons to pizza parties. For every possible activity, she calculated how much money and resources would actually flow to where it was needed most—to the antislavery groups that are freeing slaves. Her ultimate measure of effectiveness was the likelihood that any action would help slaves gain their freedom.

When the student told me about her research, she was almost apologetic. She explained that when people learn about modern slavery, they want to do something dramatic and forceful. Other students talked about volunteering to go to a country like India and taking part in the raids that free slave children. She calculated, however, that for these students this was an ineffective use of time and money in terms of freeing slaves. After all, the cost of flying one college student to India would pay a full-time antislavery worker's salary for a year in that country. At the end of her analysis, one action stood head and shoulders above the others. According to her research, the most effective thing the average person can do to end slavery is this: *Join an antislavery organization like Free the Slaves, and send it $10 a month.* I appreciate that her recommendation is not terribly dramatic, but it is logical. Slave families can come to freedom and be helped to build new lives in rural India at a cost of about $700 (their illegal debts are never paid off; this is the cost of running the program and schools that help them get free and on their feet). The cost of returning child slaves in Ghana to their families and stabilizing their freedom is about $800 a child.[1] The local groups that rescue or free slaves are extremely cost effective. For the most part, however, it is not possible to donate directly to a small local group in Ghana or India or most other countries in the developing world, nor do they have the necessary infrastructure to manage international donations. A global organization like Free the Slaves (or Anti-Slavery International in Europe) acts as a conduit that carries our commitment to end slavery to the people who are actually helping slaves to freedom. This simple action also overcomes one of the greatest challenges that antislavery organizations face—the unpredictability of funding.

We all understand how important a regular paycheck is when we have children to feed or rent to pay. The same applies to supporting slaves in their journey into freedom and beyond. Antislavery workers have enough to worry about (like violent slaveholders and corrupt cops) without uncertainty about funds for salaries and projects. They need funds that they can count on year in and year out. Although large donations are certainly welcome, what the antislavery movement needs more than anything is for every person who wants slavery to end to make a small *regular* donation. When that happens, there will be the stable income needed to build the long-term projects that will roll back slavery around the world.

GETTING THE WORD OUT

Awareness of modern slavery is growing every day, but there are still plenty of people who think slavery doesn't exist and who have no idea of the extent of their own involvement in global slavery. You have gained awareness by reading this book. If you want to help others see the reality of global slavery, please share this book widely. You might want to donate a copy to your local library, school or university, or church. Send a note to your mayor and local council members, your state legislators, and your congressional representative, with a copy of this book to get them started. Let them know that you are expecting great things, that you want real leadership from them in ending slavery.

To raise awareness in other people is actually very easy. Today there are some great books, films, Web sites, and blogs that are ready to introduce people to slavery. One of the most moving and yet easiest to share is a ten-minute film called *Modern Slavery*. This film can be watched directly on the Internet at www.freetheslaves.net. In the film you will see the teenagers who were enslaved on the cocoa farm that you read about in chapter 7, as well as the young women enslaved in Washington, D.C., and children rescued from carpet looms in India. An e-mail sent to a friend can link to this film and dramatically raise awareness of slavery in a short time. If watching the film on the Web isn't convenient, you can order it on video tape or DVD, by phone or mail, from Free the Slaves (1012 14th Street, NW, suite 600, Washington DC, 20005; (202) 638-1865).

On the same Web site (or by phone or mail) you will find a number of other powerful new films about modern slavery. *Dreams Die Hard* explores slavery in America today. In *The Silent Revolution*, a village of slaves in India fights for and achieves their freedom. *Freedom and Beyond* takes you into the Bal Vikas Ashram and lets you meet the boys liberated from slavery in the carpet looms and follow them home to their families. Books geared for different audiences are also available from the Free the Slaves Web site and from bookstores and online booksellers. *Global Slavery Today* (Groundwood Books, 2007) is aimed at teenagers and young people and is a brief but deep introduction to modern slavery. My book *Disposable People: New Slavery in the Global Economy* (University of California Press, revised ed., 2005) is considered the basic work on modern slavery; the book has been printed in ten languages and is used by many book clubs and university classes.

A *Teaching Pack on Modern Slavery* can be downloaded from the Web site and is appropriate for grades four and up. When students use this pack, they catch fire and bring their parents into the antislavery movement. *Slavery Still Exists: And It Could Be in Your Backyard* is a community member's guide to fighting human trafficking and slavery. This booklet, which can also be downloaded or ordered, explains modern slavery and what individual citizens can do about it. Copies of this guide are often handed out in churches and community groups. When you combine these with a showing of one of the short films, the impact is clear and powerful.

WE'LL ALL GO TOGETHER!

Fannie Lou Hamer said it years ago, and it is just as true today: we can end slavery forever if we all go together. If you would like to see the end of slavery, if you would like to make the gift of freedom to the world and your children, then decide now to do something to make that happen. It may be that reading this book is part of a growing calling in you to fight slavery. That is wonderful, because there are great things that only *you* can do. Movements need leaders, but they also need people like Rosa Parks, people who in their workplace or school or on the bus going home, will say: "No more, slavery ends now." In your job, church, school, or family are perfect opportunities to share the truth about slavery and help others join our movement. We stand at a moment in human history when our economies, governments, understanding, moral beliefs, and our hearts are aligned in a constellation that can bring slavery to an end. Spurred by our imaginations, and guided by a common dream, we will achieve a world without slavery.

Measuring the Effectiveness of Antislavery Work

If we are going to make real progress against global slavery, we need to design programs and policies that will be powerful and lead to permanent freedom. To design such programs we must first have a way to evaluate the programs and policies that are currently in place. Then we must learn and improve as we go, always aiming for three basic goals: freedom for slaves, rehabilitation of slaves leading to full citizenship with dignity, and the replication and extension of our projects and policies until all slaves are free. I offer ideas that focus on these goals in the hope that they might be helpful to others working for the end of slavery.

I. MEASURING PROGRESS ACHIEVED THROUGH LOCAL/REGIONAL MOVEMENTS AGAINST SLAVERY

Measuring absolute progress made by local and regional organizations against slavery in a quantitative way is difficult. For example, an increase in the number of prosecutions could indicate many things (an increase in prevalence of the crime, better government counting of prosecutions, or a higher proportion of cases being prosecuted).

A better way to measure progress against slavery is to construct indicators based on our evolving knowledge of the factors and processes that create an adverse environment for slavery to thrive. If antislavery movements are successfully creating a combination of those adverse conditions, we can have reasonable confidence that progress is being made against slavery.

Following are two key changes that need to occur in order to create those adverse conditions—and a range of measurable indicators relevant to local or regional programs that show whether those changes are occurring.

KEY CHANGES

A. COMMUNITIES ARE RESISTANT TO TRAFFICKING AND SLAVERY (ADDRESSING SUPPLY FACTORS)

Indicators of outcomes, and key contributors:

1. Communities (especially those sections of communities worst affected) have made conscious decisions about the negative effects of slavery; they have created action plans against slavery and trafficking; and they have access to continuous, dedicated expertise to help them implement those plans. They are prepared to face down the traffickers and slaveholders in a united way.
2. Communities have economic protections in place (e.g., flood relief, food distributions) and economic interventions (microenterprise, land rights) targeted at the most vulnerable.
3. Communities hold government accountable for provision of key services known to protect against slavery (e.g., heath care).
4. Women especially are organized against violence of all kinds and know what to do when confronted with violence and threats against women and children.
5. Schools are functioning and available to all children, of all economic and social groupings in the community.
6. Communities have monitoring systems that show that women and children are not leaving against their will or in conditions that are unsafe.
7. Communities are making progress toward a sustainable local economy. Local environmental resources (water, forestry, land) are being used and enhanced for shared benefit.

B. DETERRENCE AGAINST SLAVERY IS REAL (ADDRESSING DEMAND FACTORS)

Indicators of outcomes, and key contributors:

1. Communities know how to use the law as a tool against slaveholders and traffickers, and evidence shows they are doing this in ways that work for them.
2. Police in the area are competent in taking up cases as they arise and are focused on the human rights of victims.
3. At least some punitive sentences are being imposed and are being publicized.
4. Systems are in place for community members to safely report cases as well as to apply community pressure to deter slavery.
5. State-mandated sentences are significant and proportional.
6. Prosecutions result in convictions often enough to show that the criminal justice system is not corrupt.

In order to eliminate slavery, these are some of the processes we believe need to be in place. Local or regional movements can set these processes in motion.

II. MEASURING ELEMENTS OF SAFE AND SUSTAINABLE PROGRAMS FOR RECOVERY

In addition to creating climates adverse to slavery, those currently in slavery must be rescued or in some other way remove themselves from exploitation. Social protections for these survivors need to be addressed as a priority. Although pressure is increasing on countries to impose significant sanctions against the perpetrators, insufficient emphasis has been placed on creating safe conditions for recovery for victims and on providing adequate compensation.

A. KEY ELEMENTS OF SAFE AND SUSTAINABLE RECOVERY

1. Knowledge on the part of survivors that their human rights have been violated and conscious decisions that they will no longer be exploited. Ideally, such decisions are a precursor to emergence from slavery (with support from community organizers working with groups of those in slavery), but often due to the isolated conditions of people in slavery, this decision can occur only after rescue has taken place. Any service provision or victim care that sidesteps this internalizing of human rights is likely to result in fragile rehabilitation and continued vulnerability.

2. Steps toward economic independence and emphasis on viable livelihoods begun soon after freedom.

3. Replacement of "dependence" on slaveholders for survival with viable systems of mutual dependence at the local level—within strengthened families or ongoing self-help groups with capacity to build up economic and social protections (often in the form of savings). Freed slaves also need to fully exercise their social rights (e.g., to welfare benefits, free education, housing rights).

4. School enrollment for children and market-relevant skills enhancement for adults and youth.

5. Financial compensation for victims. Ensure such compensation does not get directly passed to present or future creditors but is invested in income-enhancing resources.

6. Legal aid and attainment of restorative justice.

B. OVERALL CHARACTERISTICS OF SUCCESSFUL PROGRAMS:

1. Flexibility to adapt to local contexts, with programs that change from year to year as organizations learn from those most affected.
2. Evidence of leadership and problem-solving ability within those programs by workers at the front lines (those who are with the target group every day).
3. A range of local, independent programs that are rooted in the affected communities. Such programs are more likely to achieve genuine progress than large multiregional programs that make grand claims about the number of areas benefited—unless those programs consist of genuine alliances with locally rooted NGOs.
4. Programs with a secure financial base—multiple funders and multiyear funding (even if that funding is not large) and funders who are willing to stay the course and cope with short-term setbacks.

III. THE POLICY ENVIRONMENT

The way to create capacity for such programs and movements is to work together to change the overall environment, including shared critical analysis, improvement of the policy context, and creation of new laws. Such networks must maintain their connectedness with those on the front lines, and they must prioritize development of the skills and leadership of frontline workers—rather than simply taking existing leadership away from the field to be in meetings elsewhere.

When these processes are in hand, and the two key changes are taking place, we will see these antislavery movements playing their part in making progress toward the following tipping points in eradicating global slavery:

A. Many parts of the world have antislavery movements with the capacity to
   1. Multiply their numbers and foster new movements
   2. Identify problems in regions and start to work on them together
B. Every major international development organization (IDA) is prioritizing slavery and understands that good development work requires working actively and specifically against slavery (just as now many IDAs understand that it is imperative to adopt a gender lens in order to do effective development work).

C. In a region or country, it is generally impossible to continue as a law enforcement professional without being adequately trained in trafficking, slavery, and victims' rights.

D. The U.N. has adequate mechanisms for policing the behavior of national governments regarding slavery and trafficking and for facilitating the improvement of governments' responses.

E. Transnational corporations are required to make their supply chains transparent.

F. Businesses that sell slave-made goods face a challenge in finding buyers.

G. Adequate laws are in place for every national and state or provincial government.

H. International financial institutions are sensitive to the impact of loan conditions that would either expand or reduce slavery and design their conditions with a focus on antislavery measures.

I. Funding for antislavery work at all levels and from a wide variety of sources increases massively.

Notes

1. THE CHALLENGE: UNDERSTANDING THE WORLD OF NEW SLAVERY

1. Quotations from Rose were gathered in interviews for the film *Slavery: A Global Investigation*, TrueVision Productions, London, 2001.

2. "Sally" didn't want her real name to be used. I have changed the names of all the people, enslaved or freed, whom I interviewed for this book, with the exception of those people whose stories have already been publicized, activists and abolitionists with public roles, and public officials. The safety of some anti-slavery workers and freed slaves depends on their anonymity. Those still enslaved are under enough threat without my adding to it.

3. The information on the outcomes of the trials was gathered in interviews for the film *Dreams Die Hard*, Free the Slaves, Washington, D.C., 2005.

4. The U.S. Department of State estimates that around 17,500 people are trafficked into the United States each year. We know from work done by Free the Slaves and the Human Rights Center, University of California, Berkeley, that the average period that trafficking victims are enslaved in the United States is between three and five years. For more on slavery in the United States, see Free the Slaves and Human Rights Center, University of California, Berkeley, *Hidden Slaves: Forced Labor in the United States*, 2004, available at http://freetheslaves.net/files/Hidden_Slaves.pdf; or at "Hidden Slaves: Forced Labor in the United States," *Berkeley Journal of International Law* 23, no. 1 (2005): 47–111.

5. For an explanation of the estimate that there are about twenty-seven million slaves in the world, see Kevin Bales, *Disposable People: New Slavery in the Global Economy* (Berkeley: University of California Press, 1999); or "International Labor Standards: Quality of Information and Measures of Progress in Combating Forced Labor," *Comparative Labor Law and Policy* 24, no. 2 (Winter 2004).

6. A slave in India costs less than 1 percent of the price of a productive field, or about 10–15 percent of the annual wages of a farm laborer (one of the lowest-paid workers in India), and around 17 percent of the price of an ox. In the

Ivory Coast today, a slave costs just under 4 percent of the annual wages of a poor farm worker. Antislavery field workers in India collected the prices of land, oxen, agricultural ages, and slaves in 2005 and 2006.

7. These categories, of course, cannot portray the realities of poverty around the world and are used as guidelines. There is justified criticism of this structure ($1 a day equals abject poverty, and $1 to $2 equals moderate poverty) because it may be much harder to live on $2 a day in a shantytown than it is to live on less than $1 in a place where people grow their own food. The suffering that accompanies poverty may not be diminished just because someone has crossed from $1 to $2 a day. As we will see, vulnerability to slavery often has more to do with lack of access to productive assets than it has to do with income.

8. Table 1 shows the relationship between poverty and slavery in the world today. The table groups 193 countries according to poverty as measured by their Gross Domestic Product (GDP) and shows the amount of slavery that occurs for each group of countries. The relationship between these two measures is statistically significant at greater than the .001 level (Chi-square = 76.44, df = 16), and the Spearman's correlation is –.496, also significant at greater than the .001 level.

TABLE 1. LEVELS OF POVERTY AND LEVELS OF SLAVERY FOR 193 COUNTRIES

	Level of Slavery in Country (%)					
	No slavery	Rare or very little slavery	Persistent low level of slavery	Regular slavery in a few sectors	Slavery in many sectors	Total % (nations)
Extreme poverty	0	3.2	48.4	32.3	16.1	100 (31)
Moderate poverty	13.8	17.2	24.1	17.2	27.6	100 (29)
Low income	21.2	33.3	39.4	1.5	4.5	100 (66)
Middle income	30.0	55.0	10.0	5.0	0	100 (47)
Rich nations	20.2	30.1	30.1	10.9	8.8	100 (20)

9. For a further discussion of debt overhang see Jeffrey Sachs, *The End of Poverty* (New York: Penguin, 2005).

10. Table 2 shows the link between international debt and slavery for 204 countries. The relationship between these two measures is statistically significant at greater than the .001 level (Chi-square = 42.62, df = 4), and the Spearman's correlation is .433, also significant at greater than the .001 level.

TABLE 2. LEVELS OF DEBT AND LEVELS OF SLAVERY FOR 204 COUNTRIES

	Level of Slavery in Country (%)					
Countries	No slavery	Rare or very little slavery	Persistent low level of slavery	Regular slavery in a few sectors	Slavery in many sectors	Total % (nations)
High-debt	2.6	5.3	42.1	26.3	23.7	100 (38)
All other	25.3	36.1	25.9	7.8	4.8	100 (166)

11. Table 3 shows the link between slavery and government corruption for 177 counties. An annual report by the organization Transparency International scores most of the countries in the world on their level of corruption. I have grouped these countries into those with high, medium, and low levels of corruption. The relationship between these two measures is statistically significant at greater than the .001 level (Chi-square = 66.68, df = 8), and the Spearman's correlation is .589, also significant at greater than the .001 level.

TABLE 3. LEVELS OF CORRUPTION AND LEVELS OF SLAVERY FOR 177 COUNTRIES

			Level of Slavery in Country (%)			
Countries	No slavery	Rare or very little slavery	Persistent low level of slavery	Regular slavery in a few sectors	Slavery in many sectors	Total % (nations)
Low corruption	48.3	53.7	0	0	0	100 (29)
Medium corruption	32.8	34.4	21.9	6.3	4.7	100 (64)
High corruption	3.6	19.0	44.0	19.0	14.3	100 (84)

12. I once owned part of a business in Moscow, and another businessman there explained to me in detail the nature of the corruption he faced.

13. Human Rights Commission of Pakistan, *State of Human Rights in 2006* (Lahore, Pakistan, 2007), pp. 239 and 251.

14. The eight Millennium Development Goals (MDGs)—which range from halving extreme poverty to halting the spread of HIV/AIDS to providing universal primary education, all by the target date of 2015—form a blueprint agreed to by all the world's countries and all the world's leading development institutions. The MDGs have galvanized unprecedented efforts to meet the needs of the world's poorest. However, it has to be said that at the beginning of 2007, the world was already falling behind on the timetable to achieve these goals. The plan to end extreme poverty by 2025 is explained in Jeffrey Sachs, *The End of Poverty*.

2. BUILDING THE PLAN

1. Quoted in Henry Mayer, *All on Fire: William Lloyd Garrison and the Abolition of Slavery* (New York: St. Martin's Griffin, 1998), p. 120.

2. "Raj" is not this boy's real name. I interviewed him in the Mukti Ashram in 2000, and a colleague interviewed him in 2001. Further reports came to me from ashram staff of his progress in 2002 and 2003. He has now returned to his family and is rebuilding his life. Because he was a minor at the time of our interview and because he has had enough attention, I feel it is best to protect his identity.

3. Amy O'Neill Richard, *International Trafficking in Women to the United States: A Contemporary Manifestation of Slavery and Organized Crime*, DCI Exceptional Intelligence Analyst Program, an Intelligence Monograph (Washington, D.C.: Center for the Study of Intelligence, Central Intelligence Agency, November, 1999).

4. A coup d'état in 2006, followed in 2007 by elections widely thought to be fair, point to the potential for positive change in Mauritania. The antislavery movement is watching the situation there carefully.

5. See chapter 6, "India: The Ploughman's Lunch" in my book *Disposable People: New Slavery in the Global Economy* (Berkeley: University of California Press, 1999), p. 195.

3. RESCUING SLAVES TODAY

1. The raid in Nai Basti took place on April 5, 2005. I have assembled this report from the accounts of people who took part in it and from other antislavery workers who have taken part in these raids. Especially helpful was the Free the Slaves South Asia director, Supriya Awasthi. Although I would like to provide a firsthand report, nothing is more likely to alert slaveholders and stop a rescue dead in its tracks than the arrival of a tall, pale European.

2. I would like to tell more about the remarkable individuals who take part in raids to free slave children, but their lives are often threatened, and many have suffered violence or arrest on false charges by corrupt police. If I were to highlight one of them it would simply increase the chance that he or she would be harmed. Like conductors on the Underground Railway, we will honor these heroes in person and in their true identity when their job is finally done. For now I will refer to the leader of this rescue as the "ashram coordinator."

3. Freed child slave interviewed at Bal Vikas Ashram by Free the Slaves communications director Peggy Callahan, 2005.

4. These interviews were part of the Emmy and Peabody Award–winning film *Slavery: A Global Investigation*, TrueVision Films, 2001. This film is available in DVD format at http://freetheslaves.net/store/slavery-a-global-investigation/.

5. Interview at Bal Vikas Ashram for the film *Freedom and Beyond*, Free the Slaves, 2006. This film is available to view online or to purchase in DVD format at http://freetheslaves.net/store/freedom-and-beyond/.

6. Interview at Bal Vikas Ashram for the film *Freedom and Beyond*, Free the Slaves, 2006.

7. Several of the organizations that work against child slavery and child labor in carpet weaving suggest that more than 300,000 children are exploited in this way. However I have not seen any strong research that underpins this estimate. Given the size of the global carpet market and the size of the carpet belt that stretches across Pakistan, India, and Nepal, I would suggest a more conservative estimate of 100,000, but I will admit that my figure is also a guesstimate.

8. See Free the Slaves, *Recovering Childhoods: Combating Child Trafficking in Northern India* (Washington, D.C.: Free the Slaves, 2005), p. 21, available at http://freetheslaves.net/files/Free-the-Slaves_Recovering-Childhoods_India.pdf.

9. Quoted in Monika Parikh, "Slavery in the Yeji Fishing Area" (internal research report, Free the Slaves, 2004).

10. Over the past several years, APPLE has been rescuing children from slavery in the fishing industry at Lake Volta, Ghana. As well as ensuring that fishermen give up the use of children in slavery, it educates parents in home communities about the risks of sending children to work in distant locations. Its locally

based, trained community coordinators work closely with parents and teachers once children have returned home to prevent retrafficking. APPLE provides skills training and microenterprise start-up funds to enable these poor families to increase their incomes. And the organization gets children enrolled in local schools and monitors their attendance and progress.

11. Cassandra Vinograd, "Empty-Eyed Children Escape Slavery in Ghana," *Mail and Guardian Online*, September 8, 2005, http://www.mg.co.za/articlePage .aspx?articleid=250367&area=/breaking_news/breaking_news__africa/, accessed February 8, 2007.

12. Quotations from the officer involved in the Tecum case are from an interview conducted by Steven Lize of Free the Slaves as part of a larger study of human trafficking in the United States for the National Institute of Justice.

13. The costs of rehabilitation will double that sum, at least. A fifty-day stay at the government shelter in Ghana costs $260, in addition to costs to send the child to school and to get parents economically strengthened.

4. HOME-GROWN FREEDOM

1. Quotations from Sonebarsa are from interviews conducted by Peggy Callahan, Free the Slaves director of communications. Many of these filmed interviews were used in the film *Silent Revolution: Sankalp and the Quarry Slaves* (Washington, D.C.: Free the Slaves, 2005).

2. See Free the Slaves and Human Rights Center, University of California, Berkeley, *Hidden Slaves*.

3. Anabel Hernandez Garcia, "Children Forced into Prostitution in San Diego Agricultural Camps," trans. Chuck Goolsby, *El Universal*, January 9, 2003, http://www.captivedaughters.org/sandiego-english.htm.

4. The details of Reina's story come from Marisa Ugarte; Garcia, "Children Forced into Prostitution"; and interviews with a number of service providers and others in San Diego.

5. Quoted in Garcia, "Children Forced into Prostitution."

6. Details on this case were provided by Austin Choi-Fitzpatrick of Free the Slaves, who was working with the antitrafficking coalition in San Diego at the time.

7. Interview with ICI staff, fall 2006.

8. In the original collection of narratives by Works Progress Administration (WPA) workers, the stories were often recorded in a way that reflected the accents and dialect of the speaker. Although the use of dialect may have been well-intentioned at the time, I feel strongly that it demeans the voice of any English speaker. For that reason I have restored the voice of Delia Garlie to speaking the same English that she shared with other citizens.

9. Adam Hochschild, "Against All Odds," *Mother Jones*, January/February, 2004. Hochschild has written a riveting and definitive history of the world's first antislavery movement in *Bury the Chains: Prophets and Rebels in the Fight to Free an Empire's Slaves* (New York: Houghton Mifflin, 2005). The book contains important lessons for the antislavery movement of today.

10. Although American and European students are keen to work against slavery on the ground, it is not easy for local antislavery groups in the developing world to send Western volunteers into the field, even if they are well trained in issues of slavery. What these projects really need are people who can serve as intermediaries between the frontline workers and the outside world—ideally people who speak the language of the region as well as one of the international languages. Such individuals could come to understand the issues of slavery in the local context but also in the context of international development agencies and the general public in richer countries. They would serve as vital communicators, helping antislavery projects get funding and publicity and protection.

11. Related by Ginny Baumann, Free the Slaves director of partnerships, 2006.

5. GOVERNMENTS: CARRYING THE BIGGEST STICK

1. Alexis de Tocqueville, *Democracy in America* (1835/40; repr., New York: Harper Perennial Modern Classics, 2006).

2. Pratyoush Onta, "Government Chided for Plight of Kamaiyas," *Kathmandu Post*, July 14, 2000.

3. Hemlate Rai "Kamaiya Situation—Free to Suffer" *Nepal Times*, July 24, 2000.

4. Hemlate Rai, investigating in September 2000 for the Danish Organization for International Cooperation/MS Nepal.

5. Shiva Sharma and Ram K. Sharma, *Sustainable Elimination of Bonded Labour in Nepal: Impact Assessment* (Geneva: International Labor Organization, 2006).

6. David McNeil, "Smart and Sexy, One Sector That Won't Be Left Behind, Japan's Massive Sex Industry," *Japan, Inc.*, September 2003.

7. Organization of American States, "OAS Rapid Assessment Report: Trafficking in Persons from the Latin American and Caribbean (LAC) Region to Japan," November 2005, p. 34.

8. Based on an interview with Sri conducted by House for Women, SAALAA Shelter staff, Japan, 2003; published in International Labor Organization, *Human Trafficking for Sexual Exploitation in Japan* (Geneva: International Labour Office, 2005).

9. U.S. Department of State, Office to Monitor and Combat Trafficking in Persons, *2006 Trafficking in Persons Report*, "Japan," May 2006.

10. The annual *Trafficking in Persons Reports* are available from the Office to Monitor and Combat Human Trafficking in the State Department; the 2004 report may be downloaded at http://www.state.gov/g/tip/rls/tiprpt/2004/.

11. Suzanne Miers, *Slavery in the Twentieth Century: The Evolution of a Global Problem* (New York: Altamira, 2003).

12. Ministry of Foreign Affairs of Japan, "The Recent Actions Japan Has Taken to Combat Trafficking in Persons," http://www.mofa.go.jp/policy/i_crime/people/action0508.html, accessed May 15, 2007.

13. David T. Johnson, "Above the Law? Police Integrity in Japan," *Social Science Japan Journal* 6 (2003): 19–37.

14. Organization of American States, "OAS Rapid Assessment Report," p. 28.

15. United Nations Distr. General, "Report of the Special Rapporteur on Violence against Women, Its Causes and Consequences," February 7, 1996, http://www.comfort-women.org/coomaras.htm.

16. Yayori Matsui, "The Sex Tourist's Yen," *New Internationalist*, July 1993.

17. Lana Cristina, "Lula Blames Slavery for Brazil's 'Social Abyss,'" *Brazzil Magazine*, July 1, 2005.

18. Allesandra Bastos, "18,000 Slave Workers Rescued in Brazil, but No One Went to Jail," *Brazzil Magazine*, February 9, 2006.

19. Some readers may wonder why I continue to refer to this country as *Burma* when it has changed its name to *Myanmar*. Traveling in Burma, and speaking to people, I came to the conclusion that the majority of the population did not support the military dictatorship in its decision to rename the country. In the limited freedom of their own homes, people still call their country Burma and look forward to when it can regain its former name.

20. United Nations Office on Drugs and Crime, *Anti-corruption Toolkit*, 3rd ed. (Vienna: United Nations Office on Drugs and Crime, 2004), p. 5.

21. To learn more about this group, GMFP (Rural Womens' Innovative Society), see http://freetheslaves.net/about/partners/gmsp/.

22. Free the Slaves, *A Legislative Agenda for Ending Slavery* (Washington, D.C.: Free the Slaves). Copies are available from Free the Slaves, 1012 14th St., NW, Washington, D.C. 20005, or from the Web site: www.freetheslaves.net.

6. GLODAL PRODLEM, GLODAL REACH

1. For appointed governors, enslaving their subjects was something like a retirement plan, as Suzanne Miers explains: "A good governor might keep some control . . . but when he left, having no security of office, he and his followers plundered the local people, seizing livestock and possessions and carrying off men, women, and children as slaves, to insure against their own uncertain future." Miers, *Slavery in the Twentieth Century*, p. 146.

2. League of Nations, *Slavery Convention of 1926*, 60 LNTS 253, Article 1(1).

3. Miers, *Slavery in the Twentieth Century*, p. 130.

4. I attended this session of the working group and was simply astounded by this refusal to endorse the report of the ILO on Burma. Like a number of other human rights workers who attended, I left the meetings discouraged but keen for the U.N. to find other ways to address slavery, which is after all a central part of its mandate.

5. I hope that I do not embarrass the following U.N., ILO, and World Bank workers who have been real leaders in the understanding and eradication of slavery. Their stories could form another chapter of struggles and successes. Although I try to raise constructively critical ideas about the U.N., World Bank, and WTO in this chapter, I also want to salute the following people: Andrea Rossi and others at the UNICEF Child Protection Section; key workers, including Elaine Pearson and John Frederick, in the ILO-IPEC TICSA program; Burkhard Dammann of the U.N. Office on Drugs and Crime; Richard Danzinger, Patrick Belser, and Patrick Daru at the ILO; and Maurizia Tovo and Anne Kielland at the World Bank.

6. Convention 182 on the Worst Forms of Child Labour, adopted June 1999, came into force November 2000. Note that the ILO and U.N. definition of *child* is a person under the age of eighteen.

7. International Labour Office, *The End of Child Labour: Within Reach*, International Labour Conference, 95th Session, Report I (B) (Geneva, 2006).

8. International Labour Office, *A Global Alliance against Forced Labour*, International Labour Conference, 93rd Session, Report I (B) (Geneva, 2005).

9. If I could have written an entire book about the U.N. and its response to slavery, I would have included much more about other agencies that have both done good work on slavery and have great potential for doing more. If I have not described them in more detail it is because I have concentrated on those agencies that have labor rights, slavery, or trafficking in their mandate, or ones that I thought would be illustrative to a general audience of the broad capabilities within the U.N. Please do not take my selections and economy of writing to deny the importance of the Food and Agriculture Organization; the U.N. Development Programme; the U.N. Development Fund for Women; the U.N. Population Fund; the U.N. High Commissioner for Refugees; and the U.N. Commission on Human Rights, or any other U.N. agency.

10. The countries are Iraq, Israel, China, Yemen, Libya, and Qatar.

11. There are numerous reports documenting U.S. pressure on countries to stop the formation of the ICC. See, for example: "U.S. Punishes Latvia in Campaign against the ICC," *Human Rights Watch*, August 6, 2003; or Kenneth Roth, "Human Rights, American Wrongs," *Financial Times*, July 1, 2003.

12. International Law Commission, "Report of the International Law Commission to the General Assembly," U.N. Doc.A / CN.4 / Ser.A/Add.1 (1963).

13. The type and nature of the sanctions were hotly debated at the time. The key question was how to craft sanctions that discouraged Hussein's dictatorial regime without increasing the suffering of the average Iraqi. This question has never been resolved, and we know that Hussein was willing to shift the impact of the sanctions from his own government and elite directly onto the backs of the people, and especially onto the backs of ethnic groups such as the Kurds that he wished to destroy.

14. Office to Monitor and Combat Trafficking in Persons, U.S. Department of State, *Trafficking in Persons Report* (2005); U.S. Department of Justice, *Assessment of U.S. Government Activities to Combat Trafficking in Persons, Fiscal Year 2003* (2004).

15. Jeffrey Boutwell and Michael T. Klare, "A Scourge of Small Arms," *Scientific American* 6, August 2000, pp. 30–35.

16. United Nations Department of Peacekeeping Operations, "Factsheet," DPI/2429/Rev.1 (September 2006), http://www.un.org/Depts/dpko/factsheet.pdf.

17. See, for example, Colum Lynch, "U.N. Faces More Accusations of Sexual Misconduct: Officials Acknowledge 'Swamp' of Problems and Pledge Fixes amid New Allegations in Africa, Haiti," *Washington Post*, March 13, 2005, A22.

18. Colum Lynch, "U.N. Halted Probe of Officers' Alleged Role in Sex Trafficking," *Washington Post*, December 27, 2001.

19. United Nations, "U.N. to Hold High-Level Meeting Aimed at Eliminating Sexual Exploitation and Abuse," news release, November 30, 2006.

20. For example, using Google Earth, some knowledge I gained doing research there, and a bit of luck, I was able to locate a charcoal camp in Mato Grosso do Sul, Brazil. The beehive-shaped domes of the low ovens used to burn the forests into charcoal for use in the steel industry are lined up on each side of a dirt road. Smoke is rising from the ovens, and the ground is blackened near the road where charcoal has been spilled. To the east of the camp, you can see where the forest has been clear-cut to feed the ovens. Looking at satellite images, I cannot tell if the workers in this camp are free or enslaved, but I do know exactly where the camp is. If you would like to see this camp, the GPS coordinates are 19°52'14.22" S, 53°03'30.84" W.

21. World Bank Operations Policy and Country Services, *Review of World Bank Conditionality: 2005 Conditionality Survey*; Executive Summary and Detailed Survey Results (May 2005), siteresources.worldbank.org/PROJECTS/Resources/40940-1114615847489/ConditionalitySurveytablesincl.pdf.

22. It is true that smaller developing country farmers don't produce for export, suffer from poor transport to get the commodities to market, or can't comply with industrialized country food safety standards, and these factors also restrict their access to the global market.

23. Oxfam International, "Milking the CAP: How Europe's Dairy Regime Is Devastating Livelihoods in the Developing World," Oxfam Briefing Paper no. 34, 2005. This paper uses the OECD Producer Support Estimate, which is an indicator of the annual monetary value of gross transfers from consumers, as well as taxpayers, to agricultural producers, measured at the farmgate level, that support agriculture.

24. In the aftermath of apartheid, debate continues as to the role played by sanctions and divestment in the end of that regime. Not wishing to get embroiled in that debate, I will simply quote Archbishop Desmond Tutu: "The end of apartheid stands as one of the crowning accomplishments of the past century, but we would not have succeeded without the help of international pressure—in particular the divestment movement of the 1980s." *New Internationalist*, January/February 2003.

25. Andrew T. Guzman, "Trade, Labor, Legitimacy," *California Law Review* 91, no. 3 (May 2003), p. 885.

26. Sara Ann Dillon, "A Deep Structure Connection: Child Labor and The World Trade Organization," *ILSA Journal of International & Comparative Law* 9, no. 2 (Spring 2003): 443–56.

7. ENDING THE (PRODUCT) CHAIN

1. *Slavery: A Global Investigation* (London: TrueVision Productions, 2001), film.

2. Interview with Abdul Makho in *Slavery: A Global Investigation*.

3. As an unpaid technical adviser on this research, I have to take some responsibility for not trying hard enough to get the right questions asked and answered.

4. Michael Smith and David Voreacos, "The Secret World of Modern Slavery" *Bloomberg Markets*, December 2006, p. 48. This article also includes some remarkable photographs taken by Claudio Perez.

5. Quoted in Smith and Voreacos, "The Secret World of Modern Slavery," p. 50.

6. One such charcoal camp is in Mato Grosso do Sul, Brazil. If you would like to see this camp using Google Earth, the GPS coordinates are 19°52'14.22" S, 53°03'30.84" W.

7. A good example is the pernambuco tree (*Caesalpinia echinata*) of Brazil. This species is currently endangered because of severe losses due to clear-cutting and logging. This tree provides the wood used for nearly all of the high-quality bows used to play violins, cellos, and other stringed instruments. Burning a tree like this to make charcoal, or clear-cutting it in order to make pasture for cattle, is a terrible loss, and thoughtful assessment of the existing trees and their management is desperately needed.

8. Tobias Barrington Wolff, "The Thirteenth Amendment and Slavery in the Global Economy," *Columbia Law Review* 102 (2002).

9. *Slaughter-House Cases*, 83 U.S. 36 (1872); *Clyatt v. United States*, 197 U.S. 207 (1904).

10. These cases were handed down as companion decisions and include: The Slavers (*Kate*), 69 U.S. 350 (1864); The Slavers (*Sarah*), 69 U.S. 366 (1864); The Slavers (*Weathergage*), 69 U.S. 375 (1864); The Slavers (*Reindeer*), 69 U.S. 383 (1864).

11. See *Pollock v. Williams*, 322 U.S. 4 (1944), holding that it was unconstitutional under the Thirteenth Amendment for a state to require specific performance on labor paid for, but not completed; *Slaughter-House Cases*, 83 U.S. 36 (1872).

12. Note, for example, the origin of the word *slave*: extensive slave-raiding and taking in areas of what is now Eastern Europe by groups in what is now Germany fed hundreds of thousands of victims into the slave markets of ancient Rome. So extensive was this trans-European trade that the word *slav*, meaning the Slavic people captured into slavery, became synonymous with and then acquired wholly the meaning *slave*.

13. The context reads "It does not seem unreasonable, since it is the paramount interest of humanity that the traffic in men be, at all events, arrested, to require of the trader, who engages in a commerce, which, although not unlawful, is necessarily suspicious from its theatre and circumstances, that he keep his operations so clear and so distinct in their character, as to repel the imputation of prohibited purpose." The Slavers (*Kate*), 69 U.S. 350, 364 (1864).

14. The Slavers (*Weathergage*) 69 U.S. 375, 380 (1864).

15. The Slavers (*Kate*) 69 U.S. 350, 364 (1864).

16. 18 U.S.C. §§ 1581–1594. See, e.g., United States v. Bibbs, 564 F.2d 1165 (involuntary servitude in agriculture); *United States v. Bradley and O'Dell*, 390 F.3d 145 (involuntary servitude in tree removal service).

17. Wolff, "The Thirteenth Amendment," 1020n61.

18. Ibid.

19. Estimates of how many children are working the carpet industry range up to 500,000. The methodology of many of these estimates is unreported, so based on the known size of carpets exports and the few studies that attempted more representative research, I feel that a conservative estimate of 100,000 is reason-

able. For more information, see Pharis Harvey and Lauren Riggin, *Trading Away the Future: Child Labor in India's Export Industries* (International Labor Rights Education and Research Fund, May 1994); S. Vijayagopalan, *Child Labor in the Carpet Industry: A Status Report* (New Delhi: National Council of Applied Economic Research [NCAER], February 1993).

20. Ibid.

21. Susan Aaronson and Jamie Zimmerman, *Righting Trade: Public Policies at the Intersection of Trade and Human Rights* (New York: Cambridge University Press, 2007), p. 39.

8. ENDING POVERTY TO END SLAVERY TO END POVERTY TO END SLAVERY

1. The story of Bochi and the boys who returned was provided to me by Supriya Awasthi and Ginny Baumann of Free the Slaves.

2. Interviews are by Ginny Baumann, partnership director for Free the Slaves, Bihar, India, 2006.

3. Robert B. Smith, "Global Human Development: Explaining Its Regional Variations," unpublished paper, September 11, 2006, p. 10; another version of this paper is Robert Smith, "Why Human Development Varies by Region: Exploring Correlates and Causes," paper presented at the annual meeting of the American Political Science Association, at http://www.allacademic.com/meta/p62810_index.html.

4. Ester Boserup, *Woman's Role in Economic Development* (London: Earthscan Publications, 1995).

5. Nelson Mandela, Speech launching the Campaign to Make Poverty History, London, February 3, 2005.

6. I mention these agencies primarily because I have personal experience of their work. I am also aware of the hundreds of other development and antipoverty groups, large and small, which are so important. Please think of the agencies mentioned simply as examples standing in for all of those dedicated antipoverty groups.

CODA: WHAT YOU CAN DO TO END SLAVERY

1. It is important to remember that these costs are not fixed; they rise and fall depending on the context, the type of slavery, and the challenges encountered. Think of these as guideline figures.

Index

Text: 10/13 Sabon
Display: Akzidenz Grotesk
Compositor: BookMatters, Berkeley
Indexer: Gerald VanderSwaay
Printer and binder: Maple-Vail Book Manufacturing Group